Andrew Blick
Democratic Turbulence in the United Kingdom

Democracy in Times of Upheaval

Series Editor
Matt Qvortrup, Coventry University

Volume 6

Andrew Blick

Democratic Turbulence in the United Kingdom

—

DE GRUYTER

ISBN 978-3-11-073935-0
e-ISBN (PDF) 978-3-11-073592-5
e-ISBN (EPUB) 978-3-11-073594-9
ISSN 2701-147X
e-ISSN 2701-1488

Library of Congress Control Number: 2023943429

Bibliographic information published by the Deutsche Nationalbibliothek
The Deutsche Nationalbibliothek lists this publication in the Deutsche Nationalbibliografie;
detailed bibliographic data are available on the internet at http://dnb.dnb.de.

Acknowledgements

I would like to thank the following people and organisations: my colleagues at the Department of Political Economy, King's College London; Nat le Roux, Dr. Dexter Govan, Alex Walker, and other associates – past and present – of the Constitution Society; Prof. Peter Hennessy; Prof. Matt Qvortrup; Tony Mason; Michaela Göbels; and Alex Miller.

My family make everything possible: Karen, Robin and Katharine Blick; and most of all Frederick, George and Nicola Blick.

Andrew Blick
Acton, London
June 2023

https://doi.org/10.1515/9783110735925-202

Contents

Terms of Reference

To assess literature dealing with problems in democracy internationally since 2016.

To consider themes arising from this review in the context of the UK during the same period; In doing so, to draw on: secondary materials; and on primary sources including media reports; official publications; campaign materials; and accounts produced by participants in events.

To present analysis in the form of literature reviews; explanatory tables; contemporary historical research; an illustrative chronology of events; a critical self-review of the work; a reform tract; an essay written under exam conditions; and analysis of speeches by incoming, ongoing, and outgoing speeches by prime ministers during the period.

https://doi.org/10.1515/9783110735925-204

About the Author and the Series Editor

About the Author

Andrew Blick is Professor of Politics and Contemporary History and Head of Department of Political Economy, King's College London. The author of numerous book and articles, he uses history to provide fresh perspectives on contemporary political issues. Areas of interest include constitutional and democratic development in the UK and internationally. Andrew has previously worked in the UK Parliament and at No.10 Downing Street.

About the Series Editor

Matt Qvortrup is Professor of Political Science at Coventry University. A political scientist, his research centers on the tension between political actors being driven by emotion and driven by rational argument. Author of many books on referendums and democracy, the new edition of Qvortrup's *Death by a Thousand Cuts* (DeGruyter 2023) pioneers interdisciplinary research in Neuropolitics and shows how political debates can be analysed using insights from fMRI-scans, history, and philosophy. Matt is also editor of *European Political Science Review*.

https://doi.org/10.1515/9783110735925-205

Chapter One
Democratic Malaise Since 2016: An Overview of Literature

The period since 2016 has seen numerous analysts raise concerns about the international prospects for democracy. They have presented a phenomenon spread across different countries and continents (including Europe and North America). The developments depicted can appear as less the immediate supplanting of one system within another, and more a process of incremental debilitation. For instance, in a work first published in 2018, two US academics, Steven Levitsky and Daniel Ziblatt, remark that:

> American politicians now treat their rivals as enemies, intimidate the free press, and threaten to reject the results of elections. They try to weaken the institutional buffers of our democracy, including the courts, the intelligence services, and ethics offices. America may not be alone. Scholars are increasingly concerned that democracy may be under threat world-wide – even in places where its existence has long been taken for granted. Populist governments have assaulted democratic institutions in Hungary, Turkey, and Poland. Extremist forces have made dramatic electoral gains in Austria, France, Germany, the Netherlands, and elsewhere in Europe. And in the United States, for the first time in history, a man with no experience in public office, little observable commitment to constitutional rights, and clear authoritarian tendencies was elected president.[1]

As the allusion at the end of this passage showed, alongside broad international tendencies, particular individuals – in this instance, Donald Trump, the Republican US President from 2017–2021 – were judged important.[2] Probing the pattern they identified further, Levitsky and Ziblatt analyse the post-Cold War period, and note that breakdowns in democracy have become less likely to involve sudden lurches into full authoritarianism through such events as coups; and are more likely to be implemented gradually by elected governments. Such administrations might even depict themselves as engaged in 'efforts to *improve* democracy – making the judiciary more efficient, combating corruption, or cleaning up the electoral process.' Beyond the immediate realm of government, in the media, '[n]ewspapers still publish but are bought off or bullied into self-censorship'.[3]

---

1 Steven Levitsky and Daniel Ziblatt, *How Democracies Die: What History Reveals About Our Future* (London: Penguin, 2019), 2.
2 See also, e.g.: David Runciman, *How Democracy Ends* (London: Profile, 2018), e-book loc. 35.
3 Levitsky and Ziblatt, *How Democracies Die: What History Reveals About Our Future* (London: Penguin, 2019), 5–6.

https://doi.org/10.1515/9783110735925-001

Along similar lines, in their 2021 work, *Backsliding: Democratic Regress in the Contemporary World*, Stephan Haggard and Robert Kaufman analyse the phenomenon of 'backsliding', which they define as: 'incremental erosion of democratic institutions, rules and norms that results from the actions of duly elected governments, typically driven by an autocratic leader.'[4] Backsliding does not entail an extra-democratic power seizure, and often does not lead to 'outright authoritarian rule', though it might do. It could affect countries in which democracy was less well established, along side those previously regarded as more stable, including – with the election of Trump – the US. Haggard and Kaufman refer to the Brexit experience in the UK as relevant in this regard.[5] The authors identify a number of key themes connected to backsliding: a polarising incident that impacts upon political parties internally and in their relations with each other, the bringing to office of leaders hostile to democracy; and – referring to the separation of powers[6] – the undermining of mechanisms by which the executive is overseen, including legislatures, the judiciary and bodies responsible for upholding ethical standards. They draw attention to the impact of international trends, of developments in communications technology, and of episodes such as the pandemic. Haggard and Kaufman stress the piecemeal nature of backsliding, occurring through a series of discrete interventions rather than more sweeping change. Key tendencies they subject to analysis include the erosion of electoral standards, the undermining of civil and political rights, and the compromising of media freedom, combined with the dissemination of misleading information.

Another significant entry in this field comes from Natasha Lindstaedt, whose *Democratic Decay and Authoritarian Resurgence*, published in 2021, states that: '[a]fter decades of progress, democracy around the world has hit a snag. From Hungary to India, Venezuela to Turkey, Brazil to the Czech Republic, the quality of democracy is faltering.'[7] Lindstaedt discusses a variety of related themes. They include the importance of public opinion and the way in which it can come to give support for political leaders who are hostile to democracy, enabling them to take power by constitutionally proper means. Lindstaedt considers the importance of international trends, of digital communications, of socio-economic in-

---

4 Stephan Haggard and Robert Kaufman, *Backsliding: Democratic Regress in the Contemporary World* (Cambridge: Cambridge University Press, 2021), 1.

5 Stephan Haggard and Robert Kaufman, *Backsliding: Democratic Regress in the Contemporary World* (Cambridge: Cambridge University Press, 2021), 1.

6 Stephan Haggard and Robert Kaufman, *Backsliding: Democratic Regress in the Contemporary World* (Cambridge: Cambridge University Press, 2021), 3.

7 Natasha Lindstaedt, *Democratic Decay and Authoritarian Resurgence* (Bristol: Bristol University Press, 2021), 1.

equality and of popular perceptions of migration. Depicting an incremental pro-cess of democratic deterioration, Lindstaedt refers to such factors as corruption, the compromising of a free media, the undermining of institutions, and the ma-nipulation of elections. Individual leaders, often of a populist disposition, are – in Lindstaedt's account – central to such processes (see below for discussion of populism).

The journalist Anne Applebaum covers similar themes, and depicts the UK as part of a wider pattern of deterioration. Applebaum argues that the sources of this tendency can be found on the different parts of the political spectrum; but that it is the political Right that deserves the most attention, because it is groups of this ori-entation that have been the most significant. Applebaum identifies '[a]n authoritar-ian sensibility' on the 'far-left' internationally, referring among other examples to 'the intellectuals turned spin doctors of the British Labour Party who prevented any challenge to Jeremy Corbyn's leadership, even as it became clear that Corbyn's far-left agenda would be rejected by the country.' Applebaum notes further that this quality 'was present among the Labour activists who first denied and then downplayed the anti-Semitism that spread within the party'. Yet, Applebaum goes on, it was movements of authoritarian leanings associated with the Right that had 'attained real *political* power in Western democracies . . . operating inside govern-ments, participating in ruling coalitions, guiding important political parties'. They were, however, 'a specific kind of right, one that has little in common with most of the political movements that have been so described since the Second World War'. This: 'new right does not want to conserve or to preserve what exists at all.' For instance, in the US and in the UK it had 'broken with the old-fashioned, Burkean small "c" conservatism that is suspicious of rapid change in all its forms. Although they hate the phrase, the new right is more Bolshevik than Burkean: these are men and women who want to overthrow, bypass, or undermine existing institutions, to destroy what exists.'[8]

Some observers have focused on more specific issues. There was interest in the idea of the manipulation of perception, for instance by a political movement that presented itself as promoting democracy while pursuing other ends.[9] In a 2019 work that made this observation, Peter Pomerantsev refers to the those who suc-cessfully advocated a 'leave' result in the 2016 EU referendum in the UK and their 'great catchphrase "Take Back Control"' that was 'so utterly spongy it could mean anything to anyone, with the EU framed as the enemy conspiring to undermine

---

8 Anne Applebaum, *Twilight of Democracy: the failure of politics and the parting of friends* (Lon-don: Penguin, 2021), 18–20.
9 Peter Pomerantsev, *This Is Not Propaganda: Adventures in the War Against Reality* (London: Faber and Faber, 2019), locs 758–766.

whichever cause it was you cared for.'[10] Pomerantsev identifies a tendency towards 'reconfiguring identity around a notion of "the people".' It was present, he feels, in the 2016 referendum campaign, and also in the approach that the UK Labour Party took towards the 2017 General Election, for which '[i]ts slogan became "For the many, not the few" . . . "The people" had been reconfigured into "the many", the "enemies of the people" into "the few".'[11] Pomerantsev describes an international pattern of 'pop-up populism, where each social and political movement redefines "the many" and "the people", where we are always reconsidering who counts as an "insider" or an "outsider", where what it means to belong is never certain, where bubbles of identity burst, crack and are then reformed as something else.'[12]

A further force Pomerantsev holds to be at work is that of Russian interference in the political systems of other countries through covert propaganda.[13] He takes particular interest in online communications, and notes the practice of microtargeting – that is, delivering messages tailored to specific recipients according to their personal characteristics, using social media.[14] Another author with an interest in such practices is Martin Moore, who holds that they have brought about a

> fundamental transformation of our communications environment. The revolution in digital communications – the collapse of news media and the rise of dominant tech platforms like Google, Facebook and Twitter – is buffeting our elections, capsizing conventional candidates and drowning centrist parties. More than that, it is restructuring our politics, undermining existing institutions and remaking the role of the citizen. It is creating openings for those who previously had none, space in which to sidestep norms, rules and established practices, and opportunities for gaming and distortion.[15]

The reference Pomerantsev makes to 'populism' engages with a significant strand of recent literature. In a 2017 work, Cas Mudde and Cristobal Kaltwasser identify a series of possible definitions of this term. The 'popular agency'[16] model envisages it

---

10 Peter Pomerantsev, *This Is Not Propaganda: Adventures in the War Against Reality* (London: Faber and Faber, 2019), loc. 2939.

11 Peter Pomerantsev, *This Is Not Propaganda: Adventures in the War Against Reality* (London: Faber and Faber, 2019), locs 2953–2957.

12 Peter Pomerantsev, *This Is Not Propaganda: Adventures in the War Against Reality* (London: Faber and Faber, 2019), locs 2957–2960.

13 Peter Pomerantsev, *This Is Not Propaganda: Adventures in the War Against Reality* (London: Faber and Faber, 2019), Part 3.

14 Peter Pomerantsev, *This Is Not Propaganda: Adventures in the War Against Reality* (London: Faber and Faber, 2019), loc. 2930.

15 Martin Moore, *Democracy Hacked: Political Turmoil and Information Warfare in the Digital Age* (London: Oneworld, 2018), 5–6.

16 Cas Mudde and Cristobal Kaltwasser, *Populism: A Very Short Introduction* (Oxford: Oxford University Press, 2017), 3.

in a positive, democratic sense, entailing wider public engagement in political processes. Another approach depicts it (again favourably) as a means whereby marginalised groups can challenge liberal democracy. An economic version of populism portrays it 'primarily as a type of irresponsible economic policy, characterized by a first period of massive spending financed by foreign debt and followed by a second period marked by hyperinflation and the implementation of harsh economic adjustments.'[17] A further interpretation depicts it as 'a political strategy employed by a specific type of leader who seeks to govern based on a direct and unmediated support from their followers.' Such a version of populism stresses 'the emergence of a strong and charismatic figure, who concentrates power and maintains a direct connection with the masses. Seen from this perspective, populism cannot persist over time, as the leader sooner or later will die and a conflict-ridden process for his replacement is inevitable.'[18]

Lastly, Mudde and Kaltwasser explain, there is a model of populism involving 'amateurish and unprofessional political behaviour that aims to maximise media attention and popular support. By disrespecting the dress code and language manners, populist actors are able to present themselves not only as different and novel, but also as courageous leaders who stand with "the people" in opposition to "the elite."'[19] This concept of 'some kind of appeal to "the people" and a denunciation of "the elite"'[20] lies at the core of the Mudde and Kaltwasser definition of populism as a 'thin' outlook that can attach itself to a diverse range of different ideologies. Populism therefore counterposes 'the pure people' with 'the corrupt elite', with its exponents advocating what they depict as the 'general will' of those 'people'.[21] The authors note that, in the EU, 'many populist parties accuse the political elite of putting the interests of the EU over those of the country.'[22] Furthermore, 'combining populism and anti-Semitism, some populists believe the national political elites are part of the age-old anti-Semitic conspiracy, accusing them of being "agents of Zion-

---

17 Cass Mudde and Cristobal Kaltwasser, *Populism: A Very Short Introduction* (Oxford: Oxford University Press, 2017), 4.

18 Cass Mudde and Cristobal Kaltwasser, *Populism: A Very Short Introduction* (Oxford: Oxford University Press, 2017), 4.

19 Cass Mudde and Cristobal Kaltwasser, *Populism: A Very Short Introduction* (Oxford: Oxford University Press, 2017), 4.

20 Cass Mudde and Cristobal Kaltwasser, *Populism: A Very Short Introduction* (Oxford: Oxford University Press, 2017), 5.

21 Cass Mudde and Cristobal Kaltwasser, *Populism: A Very Short Introduction* (Oxford: Oxford University Press, 2017), 6.

22 Cass Mudde and Cristobal Kaltwasser, *Populism: A Very Short Introduction* (Oxford: Oxford University Press, 2017), 13.

ism."[23] Mudde and Kaltwasser go on, 'xenophobic populists in Europe often define the people in ethnic terms, excluding "aliens" (i.e., immigrants and minorities)' and claiming 'that elite favours *the interests* of the immigrants over those of the native people.'[24] Populism can entail hostility towards representative forms of government and support for direct democracy, for instance through referendums.[25]

Another analyst of populism, Jan-Werner Muller, categorises its adherents as those who present themselves as the only true representatives of the people, who are in turn defined in a way that does not include the whole population of a territory. In this account, therefore, populism seeks to deny legitimacy both to rival political groups and to the claims of those it regards as not belonging to the public for whom it purports to be the sole vehicle. Often a particular leader is presented as the means by which the popular will is expressed. Muller depicts various forms of activity that are characteristic of populism, such as:

- cultivating a voter base through the offering of material inducements;
- employing referendums not so much as a genuine means of discerning the views of voters, but of endorsing predetermined courses of action;
- a tendency to attribute problems to elite groups, even after the populists have taken office;
- efforts, when in power, to restrict public opposition;
- the undermining of judicial independence;
- corrupt practices, carried out often in a relatively open way, but which do not necessarily impact negatively upon the appeal of the populists, perhaps because such methods are integral to their approach;
- incremental erosion of aspects of democracy that stop short of more drastic usurpation, through such means as changes to election laws, and the intimidation of media outlets; and
- hostility towards constitutional limitations, procedures and institutions, which might protect minority groups and restrain arbitrary conduct, on the grounds that they are obstacles to the immediate relationship between leader and people.[26]

23 Cass Mudde and Cristobal Kaltwasser, *Populism: A Very Short Introduction* (Oxford: Oxford University Press, 2017), 14.
24 Cass Mudde and Cristobal Kaltwasser, *Populism: A Very Short Introduction* (Oxford: Oxford University Press, 2017), 14.
25 Cass Mudde and Cristobal Kaltwasser, *Populism: A Very Short Introduction* (Oxford: Oxford University Press, 2017), 14.
26 Jan-Werner Muller, *What is Populism?* (London: Penguin, 2017).

Further exploration of the populism concept comes from Pippa Norris and Ronald Inglehart in *Cultural Backlash: Trump, Brexit and Authoritarian Populism*. They define it as 'a style of rhetoric reflecting first-order principles about who should rule, claiming that legitimate power rests with "the people" not "the elites". It remains silent about second-order principles, concerning what should be done, what policies should be followed, what decisions should be made.' Populism can, they hold, 'adapt flexibly to a variety of substantive ideological values and principles, such a socialist or conservative populism, authoritarian or progressive populism, and so on'. Populism, they observe, 'challenges the legitimate authority of the "establishment."' Among its '[f]avourite targets' are: 'the mainstream media . . . elections . . . politicians . . . political parties . . . public-sector bureaucrats . . . judges . . . protests . . . the intelligence services . . . lobbyists . . . intellectuals . . . scientists . . . interest groups . . . the constitution . . . international organizations like the European Union'. Those who lead such movements 'claim that the only legitimate source of political and moral authority in a democracy rests with the "people."'[27]

Norris and Inglehart also explore the related concept of 'authoritarianism'. They describe it as 'a cluster of values prioritizing collective security for the group at the expense of liberal autonomy for the individual.' Characteristics include criticism of the supposed impact of the arrival of people from other countries; promotion of adherence to what are claimed to be traditional internal values; and subservience to anointed political leaders.[28] The authors hold the UK Independence Party (UKIP) to be an example of an authoritarian populist entity which, despite little success at UK parliamentary elections, successfully promoted 'rabid anti-European and anti-immigration sentiment, pressuring the Conservatives to call the Brexit referendum, with massive consequences.'[29] Norris and Inglehart stress the importance of 'generational birth cohorts' to the support bases of such parties, which tend to mobilise: 'the Interwar generation, non-college graduates, the working class, white Europeans, the more religious, men, and residents of rural communities'[30] Socio-economic factors were also significant. In the UK, 'support . . . to Leave the EU was concentrated in northern England and the Midlands. Leave votes were disproportionately in "left-behind" areas characterised by low income, high unemployment,

27 Pippa Norris and Ronald Inglehart, *Cultural Backlash: Trump, Brexit and Authoritarian Populism* (Cambridge: Cambridge University Press, 2019), 4–5.

28 Pippa Norris and Ronald Inglehart, *Cultural Backlash: Trump, Brexit and Authoritarian Populism* (Cambridge: Cambridge University Press, Cambridge, 2019), 7.

29 Pippa Norris and Ronald Inglehart, *Cultural Backlash: Trump, Brexit and Authoritarian Populism* (Cambridge University Press, 2019), 12.

30 Pippa Norris and Ronald Inglehart, *Cultural Backlash: Trump, Brexit and Authoritarian Populism* (Cambridge: Cambridge University Press, 2019), 15–16.

and historic dependence on manufacturing industry.'[31] Yet, 'in predicting Leave votes, libertarian-authoritarian values and populist attitudes were far stronger factors than social class and experience of unemployment.'[32]

Further analysis of such tendencies and their impact in the UK context came from a politician who had first-hand experience of the subject matter. In a discussion of 'populism',[33] the Labour MP and Shadow Cabinet member under Starmer, Lisa Nandy, describes how '[a]cross the world, in just a few years – on both left and right' it 'leapt from fringe protest to shaping mainstream political debate.' Nandy lists movements including 'the Tea Party and Occupy Wall Street in the USA, to Marine Le Pen's National Rally in France, the Alternative for Germany (AFD), Syriza in Greece and the Indignados and Podemos in Spain', which 'shook the foundations of traditional party systems'. Nandy also refers to 'populist strongman leaders – Modi, Trump and Bolsonaro' who secured office 'in some of the most powerful countries in the world.' In parallel to this pattern, 'mainstream political leaders in the UK' came 'routinely [to] frame themselves as for the people, against the elites. This framing, pitting MPs, journalists, civil servants and the judiciary against the people, continued to unfold in Britain even after the assassination of the young MP Jo Cox by a far-right activist in the street. Verbal attacks against civil servants became the norm, the BBC became a regular target, and the front page of one national newspaper labelled the judiciary "the enemies of the people".'[34]

As the analysis Nandy offers suggests, there is a case for exploring in greater detail the possible manifestation within the UK of the themes that have been identified. The chapters that follow will perform this task, first in relation to Brexit and second to wider tendencies. In doing so they engage with themes contained in the literature discussed above, and further UK-specific literature. The latter output includes various analyses of the relationship between Brexit and populism that appeared shortly after the 2016 referendum.[35] It focuses on matters including issues arising during the campaign, such as hostility towards the concept of expertise. Much has transpired since that needs to be incorporated into any such analysis. An important assessment of the applicability of international trends in the UK context

---

31 Pippa Norris and Ronald Inglehart, *Cultural Backlash: Trump, Brexit and Authoritarian Populism* (Cambridge: Cambridge University Press, 2019), 17.

32 Pippa Norris and Ronald Inglehart, *Cultural Backlash: Trump, Brexit and Authoritarian Populism* (Cambridge: Cambridge University Press, 2019), 22.

33 Lisa Nandy, *All In: How We Build a Country That Works* (Manchester: HarperNorth, 2022), 49.

34 Lisa Nandy, *All In: How We Build a Country That Works* (Manchester: HarperNorth, 2022), 50.

35 See e.g.: John Clarke and Janet Newman, 'People in this country have had enough of experts: Brexit and the paradoxes of populism', *Critical Policy Studies* 11, no. 1 (2017), 101–116.; Michael Freeden, 'After the Brexit referendum: revisiting populism as an ideology', *Journal of Political Ideologies* 22, no. 1 (2017), 1–11.

has come from Alison Young, who published 'Populism and the UK Constitution' in 2018. Young cautioned against an assumption that the UK political culture and constitution were exceptionally resistant to populism. The pragmatic and flexible aspects of the UK system, Young held, might make it particularly vulnerable to such a tendency, which it might even serve to encourage.[36] Further evidence in this regard, linked to Brexit and other matters, can be identified in the years since 2018. Some analysts, such as Maria Sobolewska and Robert Ford, have focused on patterns of public opinion connected to Brexit.[37] This work considers such research and what it reveals, and connects it to wider political and constitutional developments. In *The Conservative Party After Brexit*, a 2023 volume, Tim Bale depicts the party in question as leaning in a populist direction during the period covered in the present work. Bale makes some useful observations, including that there is a need to regard sections of the media and various think tanks as forming part of the Conservatives, broadly conceived.[38] It is possible to expand some of these ideas beyond the Conservatives, to other parties and to different aspects of the political system.

There are also UK-based academics, such as Matthew Goodwin, who display sympathy for ideas relied on by populist leaders about the existence of a social elite pursuing internationalist, liberal goals which serve to alienate large sections of the population.[39] The present work does not endorse such notions (while acknowledging that those who are more favourable towards such interpretations may regard many academics – perhaps including the author of the present volume – as part of the problem). Difficulties with this approach include the degree of ineptitude it implies on the part of a supposedly dominant group. How can it be that an internationalist, hegemonic UK elite allowed the holding of a referendum on EU membership; failed to secure the outcome it wanted in the vote that followed; and permitted the implementation of the legally non-binding leave result on terms including exclusion from the Single Market and Customs Union? Furthermore, it might be asked, how can the idea of dominance by this group be reconciled in the period since 2016 with a succession of prime ministers and governments em-

---

36 Alison L. Young, 'Populism and the UK Constitution', *Current Legal Problems* 71, no. 1 (2018), 17–52.
37 Maria Sobolewska and Robert Ford, *Brexitland* (Cambridge: Cambridge University Press, 2020), 323–324.
38 Tim Bale, *The Conservative Party After Brexit: Turmoil and Transformation* (Cambridge: Polity, 2023).
39 Matthew Goodwin, *Values, Voice and Virtue: The New British Politics* (London: Penguin, 2023), see e.g.: p. 20.

ploying populist rhetoric and pursuing programmes to match; while the main opposition party has also displayed, in some respects, populist characteristics?

In this book and generally, the present author is reluctant to suggest that there are substantially sized groups of people sharing in and successfully enforcing certain values and objectives in the way that analyses such as that advanced by Goodwin might suggest. These reservations apply to elites as depicted in populist-inclined scenarios. They also lead to a reluctance in accepting certain theories that might be attractive to those who regard themselves as opposed to populism and democratic backsliding. For instance, this author is wary of attributing excessive importance to supposedly sinister think tanks, receiving funding from outside the UK and operating in concerted fashions to further dubious agendas, though such bodies should be and are considered here. However, this book recognises that certain dispositions and alignments can attach more to some within society than others. Such divergences of outlook can take on pronounced political significance. For instance, the way in which certain groups voted in particular places in the 2016 EU referendum and in the 2019 General Election had a substantial impact on the political system. So too did the attitudes that polling suggested they held on wider issues. Moreover, this work treats the study of the political positions and activities of people at elite level as also of importance. As such, they should be considered in their complexity and diversity, with descriptive over-generalisation avoided. For instance, it should be recognised that the possession of qualities such as populism is often a matter of degree, and that they can co-exist with other tendencies.

This work adds value through applying accounts of democratic malaise – including backsliding, populism and associated tendencies – more fully to the UK. While the literature discussed in this chapter often makes references to the UK, and in particular Brexit, it leaves scope and suggests a need for a fuller examination of this particular country in this context, and one that takes in but is not confined to the subject of departure from the EU. Building on earlier contributions by the author, in particular a study of the Johnson period written with Peter Hennessy,[40] this work considers the whole period from 2016 onwards. It therefore encompasses not only the entirety of the Johnson premiership but also that of his predecessors from 2016 and successors. It considers a wide range of elements, such as different parties, leaders, popular attitudes, and constitutional developments. Key ideas it addresses are: a polarising incident, in the form of the 2016 EU referendum; populism as variously defined in the literature; the role of leaders and their conduct; parties and their motivations; ideological patterns; the erosion of rights; the

---

40 Andrew Blick and Peter Hennessy, *The Bonfire of the Decencies: Repairing and Restoring the British Constitution* (London: Haus, 2022).

undermining of standards, institutions, and constitutional principles; the weakening of limitations on the executive; the position, nature and behaviour of the media; the promulgation of misleading information; and the relationship to wider tendencies beyond the UK. The book presents an exploration of these themes using a series of formats: a literature review (Chapter One); contemporary history assessments (chapters Three and Four); a review of the book itself (Chapter Six); a polemical tract (Chapter Seven); excerpts from prime ministerial speeches with commentary (throughout the book); tables of terms with definitions and commentary (Chapter Two); a timeline of events in a single year, 2022 (Chapter Five); and an answer to an essay question on the period that might be set for a student (Chapter Six).

Part of the rationale for the use of these varied stylistic approaches is that they enable the treatment of a complex and rapidly unfolding contemporary phenomenon from a variety of perspectives, thereby making possible a wider understanding than might otherwise be available. They also assist in addressing the issue that complete neutrality is never possible, while objectivity can and should be aspired to. Most academics investigating such tendencies as populism and democratic backsliding seem to regard them as regrettable; and are interested in the means by which they might be reversed. This book seeks to make more explicit that the author shares such an outlook. It does so by, first, attempting a somewhat dispassionate assessment of events and trends (especially in chapters Three and Four); after which, second, the author presents (particularly in Chapter Seven) an account of their own personal perspective, including criticism of participants and proposals for corrective action. Chapters Six and Seven also as serve as conclusions, but offer responses more than finality. It is probably impossible entirely to exclude the personal perspectives of authors from their work. They help determine the questions they ask and how they go about answering them. Indeed, it might not be desirable to make such a separation, since it is values which invest worth in activities such as scholarship. However, it is also important to recognise and remain aware that these endeavours are shaped by personal predilections. Rather than suppress the outlooks that inform it, this work is open about them, while at the same time seeking to ground itself factually. Such an approach, beneficial in itself, has the additional value of preempting possible charges of hidden agendas and manipulation.

The analysis contained in this book rests on the techniques of the historian, applying them to contemporary events. It seeks to assess the causes, meaning and consequences of particular episodes; the nature of change; and the motivations and impact of individuals and groups, and the way in which they presented themselves. The primary sources it draws on include diaries and memoirs; assorted other writings by politicians; campaign outputs such as leaflets and manifestos; reports from think tanks and pressure groups; parliamentary and government publications; opinion research and analysis; texts of speeches; media reports; and online materials. First-hand, insider accounts – though they must be approached cautiously – can provide insight into previously unpublicised events, and into the agendas and viewpoints of participants at elite level. In their observations regarding colleagues and rivals, their authors can be astute, though perhaps less so in their self-evaluations. Works produced by politicians such as articles, novels and histories, can help provide clues regarding their motivations and perspectives. Leaflets and manifestos can be revealing regarding the objectives of different groups, and how they sought to present themselves, and persuade the public. They can be used by politicians as a means of legitimising subsequent actions, since it can be claimed by a winning side in a contest that its proposals now have democratic force behind them. Yet they can also be controversial for their tone or content; and be a basis for criticism on the grounds that the pledges they set out were misleading or have not been properly implemented. Publications from organisations such as think tanks and pressure groups can contain useful analysis; and also be indicative of particular political positions and agendas. The status and objectives of such entities is itself a significant topic.

Official texts contain informative factual content and can help us to understand the relationship between the turbulence of the party-political environment and more formal governmental activities. They include parliamentary debates. The texts of these proceedings are important because they often comprise arguments about legislative proposals and other government programmes. Contributions made in the UK legislature are different from other forms of speech. They are immune from legal proceedings that would apply outside Parliament; but at the same time subject (in theory at least) to rules regarding standards of discourse and factual accuracy. If politicians fail to meet such standards, then this tendency is significant in itself, and it can have consequences. Another form of official publication given attention is that of documents setting out constitutional principles and standards of conduct, such as the *Ministerial Code* issued by UK prime ministers. These texts provide a means by which we might assess adherence to norms. The way in which they are enforced is a further subject of significance in its own right.

Polling is important both because it contributes to an awareness of public opinion with respect to democratic issues; and because it can itself influence the behaviour of politicians seeking to achieve electoral success. Speeches, in what they contain and what they omit, are significant for a number of reasons. They help to reveal the objectives and personal styles of leaders; tell us something about how they wished to be perceived; and because words are so important to democracy and any challenges it faces. Media content also has a variety of uses. It can establish the details of certain occurrences. But it is also part of the processes it ostensibly seeks to describe. It suggests which tendencies and interpretations were receiving public attention at a given time. Furthermore, it helps to reveal agendas being pursued at given times. The alignment and conduct of different sections of the media have themselves been subjects of controversy, and require examination. Online materials – such as those contained in social media – are important to the development of political debate and perceptions. Allowing rapid communication and response, they provide means by which discourse is conducted, and also arguably have consequences for its quality. They are both a platform for debate and have themselves come under critical scrutiny. As these remarks suggest, all sources have value, and all have limitations. It is important both to consult them and look behind them. We must compare them with one-another, in order that we might construct a fuller – but necessarily never complete – picture of events. They all contain truths of some kind, whether lying at the surface, or to some extent concealed.

The book produces material that might form part of the ongoing debate about democracy in the world, and specifically in the UK. It discusses the impact of a specific polarising force, which in the UK context is that arising from the 2016 EU referendum and Brexit. This work also discusses other factors, some of which were closely connected to Brexit, others of which had more of their own momentum. Again following Young to some extent, it shows how tendencies such as backsliding and populism played out within and were shaped by the particular characteristics of the UK constitutional and political system. It depicts the interplay between leaders, institutions and public opinion (or at least perceptions of the latter); and discusses the relationship with international tendencies. The work seeks to convey some of the dynamics that drive backsliding and populism, and the form they can take, in a state commonly regarded and perceiving itself as a mature, stable, democracy. It makes specific value judgements and recommendations about how to address difficulties. All of these contributions are of potential interest from the perspective of the UK and beyond.

When it refers to democracy, this book means a form of social governance which derives its legitimacy from the public; which at the same time is supposed to operate according to consistent, impartial rules and limitations (for instance, judicially enforceable rights), which are provided by a constitution though which in the UK is not codified. Within this general definition, the UK – like other contemporary equivalents – is broadly a representative democracy, in which decision-making authority is vested in elite groups accountable by various means to the population they serve, and which has the opportunity to replace them, at elections, with others. The author of this work – who supports this form of governance, and wishes to see it maintained and strengthened – avowedly sets out to identify weaknesses manifested in this system in the UK since 2016. At the same time, he acknowledges that other perspectives: describing strengths in the UK model, and taking a longer term historical context, are possible. They might enable a weighing of the problems faced since 2016. However, it is necessary, before proceeding to such an exercise, to uncover problems encountered in the UK:

the task performed here. There is a preliminary assessment of this broader context, with some illustrative examples, in Chapter Six. The author will return to these matters in a forthcoming work.

Rishi Sunak's first speech as Prime Minister, 25 October 2022[41]
Excerpts with commentary

Excerpts

I have just been to Buckingham Palace and accepted His Majesty The King's invitation to form a government in his name.

It is only right to explain why I am standing here as your new Prime Minister.

Right now our country is facing a profound economic crisis.

The aftermath of Covid still lingers.

Putin's war in Ukraine has destabilised energy markets and supply chains the world over.

I want to pay tribute to my predecessor Liz Truss, she was not wrong to want to improve growth in this country, it is a noble aim.

And I admired her restlessness to create change.

But some mistakes were made.

Not borne of ill will or bad intentions. Quite the opposite, in fact. But mistakes nonetheless.

And I have been elected as leader of my party, and your Prime Minister, in part, to fix them.

And that work begins immediately.

I will place economic stability and confidence at the heart of this government's agenda.

This will mean difficult decisions to come.

But you saw me during Covid, doing everything I could, to protect people and businesses, with schemes like furlough.

. . .

This government will have integrity, professionalism and accountability at every level.

Trust is earned. And I will earn yours.

I will always be grateful to Boris Johnson for his incredible achievements as Prime Minister, and I treasure his warmth and generosity of spirit.

And I know he would agree that the mandate my party earned in 2019 is not the sole property of any one individual, it is a mandate that belongs to and unites all of us.

And the heart of that mandate is our manifesto.

I will deliver on its promise.

A stronger NHS.

Better schools.

Safer streets.

Control of our borders.

Protecting our environment.

Supporting our armed forces.

---

41 Rishi Sunak, 'Rishi Sunak's first speech as Prime Minister: 25 October 2022', accessed 7 May 2023, https://www.gov.uk/government/speeches/prime-minister-rishi-sunaks-statement-25-october-2022.

(continued)

Levelling up and building an economy that embraces the opportunities of Brexit, where businesses invest, innovate, and create jobs.

I understand how difficult this moment is.

After the billions of pounds it cost us to combat Covid, after all the dislocation that caused in the midst of a terrible war that must be seen successfully to its conclusions I fully appreciate how hard things are.

And I understand too that I have work to do to restore trust after all that has happened.

Commentary

In this speech, the new Prime Minister offers to explain how he came to be in this role, but does little to do so. He refers to 'some mistakes . . . made' during the tenure of his immediate predecessor, Liz Truss, without specifying what they were. Sunak leans heavily on Covid and the Ukraine conflict, rather than Brexit, as a source of problems. He claims a strong record during the pandemic, without noting that he personally broke the law by attending a gathering in the Cabinet room. The Prime Minister refers to the need to 'restore trust' and ensure 'integrity, professionalism and accountability' within government. How effective he would be at doing so would prove to be open to question. Sunak – who was, earlier the same year, instrumental in the removal of Boris Johnson as Prime Minister, in direct response to behaviour that fell short of standards of acceptability – nonetheless praises Johnson. However, Sunak also seeks to dispel the idea that Johnson had secured a personal mandate through the 2019 General Election, stressing that it belongs to the Conservatives in government as a whole. His policy pledges seemed aimed at maintaining the coalition of support that the Conservatives achieved in 2019.

Chapter Two
Democratic Deterioration in the United Kingdom: Perspectives

When seeking a fuller appreciation of the subject matter of this book, it is useful to view the UK political system from a number of different perspectives. What follows is an examination of some key features of UK politics, and an assessment of their significance.

Feature	Doctrine of parliamentary sovereignty
Description	The concept has deep historical roots, stretching into medieval times. The late nineteenth and early twentieth century legal academic, Albert Venn Dicey, popularised the term, defining it as meaning that Parliament had 'the right to make or unmake any law whatever; and further that no person or body is recognised by the law of England [sic] as having a right to override or set aside the legislation of Parliament.'[1] It means that an Act of Parliament is the ultimate source of legal authority. Where two Acts of Parliament come into conflict, normally the more recent prevails over the earlier.
Significance to present discussion	There has been some debate about the desirability and viability of this doctrine. But whatever its merits or otherwise, it is recognised as being a key tenet of the UK constitution. It means that a government that can carry Parliament with it is able to legislate in ways that have immense democratic implications, without being subject to formal external limitations. Changes, such as those pertaining to the timing of elections, can be effected through standard law-making procedures. In other polities, measures of this kind might require the fulfilling of more demanding processes, for instance support from supermajorities in legislatures or from referendums. Once it has been passed, prevailing orthodoxy is that an Act of Parliament cannot be struck down by a court, even if it appears to infringe important constitutional principles. The possibility of being able to change the rules through standard law-making practices, and not being subject to possible judicial blockage, can be assumed to encourage policymakers to consider options that they might otherwise be less likely to. For instance, critics of the nature of human rights protection in the UK have advocated legal changes in this area that might be harder in other territories to bring about.

---

1 Albert Venn Dicey, *Introduction to the Study of the Law of the Constitution* (London: Macmillan, 1915), 3–4.

https://doi.org/10.1515/9783110735925-002

Feature	The 'unwritten' or 'uncodified' constitution
Description	The concept of the uncodified constitution is linked to that of parliamentary sovereignty. It means that there is no single text specifically labelled The Constitution, setting out the fundamental rules of the system. Such provisions, in as far as they exist, are scattered across a variety of sources, including Acts of Parliament, judicial decisions, the rules of the UK, Welsh, Scottish and Northern Ireland legislatures, codes that may lack a statutory basis, and implicit assumptions. Some of the most important tenets of UK democracy lack clear, formal, definition. For instance, the principle that the head of the UK government – the Prime Minister – must be a member of the House of Commons (MP), has far from firm official existence; as does the concept of a Prime Minister or government needing to possess what is known as the confidence of the Commons. A codified constitution would generally create special amendment procedures that must be met if key components of the system are to be changed; and would be likely to allow for the judiciary to uphold constitutional principles and nullify actions and laws that conflicted with them.
Significance to present discussion	To ask what precise difference the lack of a 'written' or 'codified' constitution has made to the UK is to pose the wrong question. To seek to construct an alternate model in which the same past events are filtered through a different system is a difficult exercise. Speculations about the difference a 'written' or 'codified' constitution would make in future are perhaps of more value. In the area of devolution, for instance, it might be that a full constitutional text would provide hard legal enforcement for principles about the need for devolved consent to certain types of UK legislation. It might require a formal vote to confirm or approve the appointment of a Prime Minister before it took place. Such a text could entrench the independence of certain public office holders and oversight bodies, and introduce new regulations governing the appointment of members of the House of Lords. It might place constraints on the introduction of measures intended to restrict the scope of the judiciary, and limits on the vesting of delegated power in ministers. While some of these changes might be brought about by other means, including them in a 'written' or 'codified' constitution might protect them from future interference and make them fully judicially enforceable. Indeed, it might make clear that it was proper for the judiciary to adjudicate on constitutional matters, even if of a politically controversial nature.

Feature	Self-regulation by holders of high office
Description	The effective functioning of democracy relies upon good behaviour. People in positions of authority must be willing to some extent to act in ways that support wider interests, rather than simply pursuing their own narrow political or personal gain. At times, such compliance has to be voluntary, since hard enforcement mechanisms might not exist or might not be effective in every area.
Significance to present discussion	This principle applies across different countries and types of system. Perhaps the lack of a 'written' or 'codified' constitution in the UK heightens the relative importance of self-regulation. Again, it is hard definitively to establish this point. But certainly the need for people holding high office to adhere to and promote compliance with standards, even if they do not strictly have to, is a prominent component of the UK system. Documents such as the *Ministerial Code*, which has no basis in statute, and lacks wholly independent enforcement mechanisms, set out various important rules and practices. When the assumption of good conduct is not met, disruption can follow. For instance, in recent times, the tendency for the UK government to communicate in a misleading way has arguably undermined the principle of its being accountable to Parliament and public.

Feature	The law and the judiciary
Description	The concept of the 'rule of law', one which is widely subscribed to in principle in the UK, is that everyone in society, including holders of high office, is subject to the law; and that the way the law is made and applied should be fair and in accordance with proper processes. The judiciary is crucial to the upholding of the rule of law, including through the process of Judicial Review whereby it assesses whether public authorities have acted lawfully or otherwise. Judges need to retain autonomy if law is to be a basis for genuinely impartial dispute resolution. They should be free from intimidation and there should be no selection or promotion on a party political basis.

(continued)

Feature	The law and the judiciary
Significance to present discussion	Threats to the rule of law include legislative measures that are excessively complex and difficult to understand, and that are irrational or arbitrary in nature. The use of delegated law-making authorities by ministers, especially so-called 'Henry VIII powers' under which secondary legislation can be used to amend or repeal Acts of Parliament, potentially poses a threat to the rule of law. These powers can mean excessive law-making power being vested in an executive able to act with little or no legislative oversight.
	Parliament sometimes passes laws containing 'ouster clauses', that seek to exclude the courts from reviewing the executive use of legal powers. Ultimately, in accordance with the doctrine of parliamentary sovereignty, the UK legislature can have the last word over the judiciary. Even if it violated fundamental principles such as those associated with the rule of law, for the courts to annul an Act of Parliament on grounds of being unconstitutional would be a break with established practice that is hard to contemplate happening.
	When UK ministers behave in ways that generate constitutional controversy, the judiciary can be drawn into the disputes that arise and asked to settle them. But, in the process, the courts can then become exposed to hostile scrutiny.
	Ministers – sometimes in parallel with sections of the media – can exert political pressure on the judiciary, seeking to intimidate it into becoming more amenable towards the executive's agendas.

Feature	Equality and human rights
Description	In the UK, individual rights are provided for variously by the common law, specific statutory provisions, and by the *Human Rights Act 1998*, which incorporates the European Convention on Human Rights (ECHR), first agreed in 1950, into UK law.
	The *Equality Act 2010* prohibits discrimination on a basis of eight 'protected characteristics' (age; disability; gender reassignment; marriage and civil partnership; race; religion or belief; sex; and sexual orientation).

(continued)

Feature	Equality and human rights
Significance to present discussion	Even with legal safeguards and other mechanisms in place, a government intent upon undermining rights in areas such as freedom to protest can impose significant restrictions.
	Moreover, the concept of legally enforceable human rights, particularly those derived from a European agreement, is controversial. In theory, the UK Parliament could amend (or even repeal) the Human Rights Act; and the UK could withdraw from the ECHR. Courses of action of this type have received some political support.
	The courts cannot strike down an Act of Parliament that they find contravenes the ECHR, and can only go as far as to find it incompatible with the Convention, leaving ministers and Parliament to resolve the matter.
	The Human Rights Act provides principally for civil and political rights. Economic and social rights do not receive the same type of protection in the UK. Socio-economic inequality is not addressed directly by the list of protected characteristics in the Equality Act.
	The legal prohibition of discrimination does not in itself necessarily prevent it from taking place.

Feature	International law and treaty obligations
Description	The UK is signatory to various agreements that require good practice in the way states conduct themselves externally; and in their internal governmental arrangements and treatment of individuals.
	Northern Ireland, its status and possible future as a territory, is itself the subject of international agreements.
	The UK leans towards a dualist model in its reception of treaties. That is, an international agreement cannot directly change domestic law in itself, and any such alterations it requires must be authorised by Parliament.
Significance to present discussion	It is difficult to reconcile adherence to international law and treaty commitments with a fetishisation of sovereignty, if defined as full freedom of action internally and externally for the political leadership of a given state.
	The dualist model can provide some degree of protection against the executive altering important internal arrangements without parliamentary consent. But, in accordance with the doctrine of parliamentary sovereignty, it is theoretically possible for the UK Parliament to legislate in ways that violate international law and treaty obligations, if it chooses to do so, though there may be repercussions.

Feature	The territorial state
Description	The UK – made up of Wales, Scotland, Northern Ireland and England – is characterised by pronounced internal territorial diversity. Cultural, linguistic, religious, legal and constitutional characteristics differ. Reflecting some of this variety, devolved systems including extensive primary law-making and tax-raising powers exist in Northern Ireland, Scotland and Wales.
Significance to present discussion	The status of the devolved systems is not always clear and firm, and is vulnerable to interference and imposition from UK level. Significant portions of the population, especially in Northern Ireland and Scotland (and seemingly to a lesser extent Wales), are supportive in principle of their particular territory ceasing to be part of the UK. The size of England – accounting for about 85 per cent of the population of the UK – can have a destabilising impact. It is difficult to reconcile such preponderance with the idea of a state in which each component part is accorded full consideration. Decisions taken at UK level can appear to amount to England imposing itself on others. For instance, both Northern Ireland and Scotland produced Remain majorities in the 2016 EU referendum, while in England and Wales there were Leave victories. The UK left, notwithstanding the differing outcomes in Scotland and Northern Ireland.

Feature	Parliamentary government
Description	UK governments are formed out of, and are accountable to, Parliament (similar principles apply at devolved level). They are not directly elected, and their ability to govern is derived via the legislature. By convention, ministers sit in one or other of the two Houses of Parliament: the Commons and the Lords. An administration or Prime Minister must possess the confidence of the elected chamber, the House of Commons. The executive is able to determine the appointment of members of the unelected chamber, the House of Lords.

(continued)

Feature	Parliamentary government
Significance to present discussion	This relationship implies countervailing tendencies. The executive can be in a relatively strong position relative to the legislature. The former has significant powers of patronage with respect to the latter, notably through the ability to appoint ministers. Governments dominate the parliamentary timetable. They can manipulate the extent of parliamentary oversight of legislative measures through the creation and use of delegated law-making powers. Normally, governments are formed by single parties with a majority in the Commons, which is therefore likely to support them most of the time. No one party has a majority in the Lords. However, the second chamber is limited by law and practice as to how much resistance it will offer to a government. Yet governments are also accountable to Parliament, and are scrutinised by it in a variety of ways, some of which can be a source of discomfort and inconvenience. It is possible for parliamentarians, especially those who belong to the governing party, in various ways to pressurise ministers to follow or abandon particular courses of action; and even deliberately to destabilise a government of which they are in theory supporters.

Feature	Political parties
Description	Parties are crucial to the operation of politics both within legislatures and executives at UK and devolved levels; and in the wider country. They provide an outlet for political activism; in practice they comprise the framework for electoral contests; and are the basis for the formation of the executive. Much debate within and outside legislatures relates to the competing agendas of parties. At UK level, since 1918, the Conservatives and Labour have dominated. Both have tended to be regarded as relatively politically moderate, at least until recently.

(continued)

Feature	Political parties
Significance to present discussion	The pursuit of party political advantage, particularly by those who hold high office – for instance, UK ministers – can have problematic implications for the maintenance of public standards and even for the upholding of democratic principles. Party members and activists can at times take on important roles in determining political outcomes. Yet they may not hold any elected office, and may be accountable to no-one. They are small in number relative to the population as a whole, and may well be unrepresentative in their support for certain policy positions. Divergences of outlook between party members as a whole and parliamentary cohorts can have destabilising consequences; for instance, if the former elect a leader towards whom there is significant opposition among the latter. There is potential for particular factions at different times to gain positions of elevated importance within parties, perhaps driving their parties in more extreme directions. In recent times, both the Conservative and Labour parties have been seen to lean towards populist-type positions.

Feature	Elections and representative democracy
Description	Politicians derive their legitimacy to hold office from public votes: either because they were directly elected to their posts, or because they answer to those who were. They do not need direct approval from voters for each decision they make and in this sense have a degree of discretion about how they operate. But they are subject to expectations surrounding pledges they have made to voters; and to various rules – formal and informal – and accountability mechanisms. At the end of their terms, if they wish to continue in their posts, they must seek approval through election again.

(continued)

Feature	Elections and representative democracy
Significance to present discussion	Politicians can claim both that they have mandates for particular courses of action as set out in their election programmes, and that they have a general authority to act, including in response to unforeseen circumstances. Such claims are an accepted part of democracy. But there must be limits to how far they should be stretched. UK and devolved governments are not directly elected, and rest upon legislatures. Moreover, is it reasonable to claim decisive popular endorsement for every item in a manifesto, particularly given that whether, how and when it will be implemented is likely to be subject to the discretion of ministers? There is a risk of the mandate concept being abused, and to avoid this outcome, it is important that those who govern are subject to, and willing to comply with, devices for limiting them and holding them to account. Furthermore, and crucially to the validity of the system, close attention needs to be given to maintaining the fairness and freedom of elections. Those who obtain office through elections, for instance, should not use the authority they obtain from this status to change the rules in ways which improperly favour their chances of retaining their positions in future contests. It is possible that (depending partly on the electoral system used) voters will support a party that takes a questionable approach towards democracy, in sufficient numbers for it to take office. They may do so either because they actively support that party's approach to democracy, or are willing to tolerate it because they are attracted to the party for other reasons.

Feature	Electoral systems
Description	The UK employs a number of different voting systems. They vary in their manner of operation and the extent to which the balance of candidates returned reflects votes cast. Elections to the House of Commons of the UK Parliament take place on a basis of 'First-Past-the-Post' or Single Member Plurality. This system has a tendency to reward a party that has won well under half of votes cast with more than half the seats available.

(continued)

Feature	Electoral systems
Significance to present discussion	Single Member Plurality can contribute to an adversarial, winner-takes-all culture in politics, rather than one of cooperation and consensus-seeking.
	Parties can form governments alone despite receiving less than half the votes cast. They also assert that policies or wider programmes have been endorsed, as though all those who voted for them were fully aware and supportive of the entire contents of their manifesto and platform. Single Member Plurality tends to favour dominance by two parties. They in turn become broad-based entities, incorporating a wide range of viewpoints and interests. For any given grouping, tendency, or faction within a party, the chances of electoral success in a new party on the outside will seem slim, encouraging them to remain where they are. But the presence of divergence within a party can lead to internal conflict. Such tensions are driven partly by Single Member Plurality, which at the same time magnifies their importance, since they take place within a party the electoral performance of which is potentially artificially inflated by that same electoral system. Extreme groupings can potentially achieve prominence within parties, and via the electoral system can become forces within government, perhaps out of proportion to the direct authority they would attain under another system.
	Single Member Plurality can cause the views of relatively small numbers of people to receive significant attention from political parties, because they reside in marginal constituencies that might change hands at the next General Election, and they are judged (or hoped to be) susceptible to persuasion to change their voting behaviour. Equally, larger numbers of people might be overlooked because they are not in locations of tactical importance, or their electoral preferences are perceived as being more fixed.
	Parties that are territorially specific, such as the Scottish National Party, can also prosper under Single Member Plurality, given their geographically concentrated support base.
	Parties that are more removed from the mainstream are disadvantaged by Single Member Plurality (SMP), but can potentially achieve a degree of electoral success under different electoral systems, such as that which was employed for elections to the European Parliament in the UK from 1999–2019. Moreover, while it is difficult for them to secure representation in the House of Commons, more extreme parties can influence the outcome in individual constituencies through attracting voters from one of the competing larger parties. In such a scenario, there is the potential for them to pressurise that larger party to adopt given policy agendas.

Feature	Referendums
Description	Referendums involve voters being asked to make a choice between options on a specific matter of public policy. They are an example of direct democracy. Their use contrasts with the representative model discussed above, whereby members of the public choose through elections governors who will implement broad programmes and make decisions on their behalf. Thirteen major referendums have been held in the UK from 1973 onwards (three of which were UK-wide, with ten territorially specific). Subjects addressed have included whether or not to introduce devolution in particular parts of the UK, whether a particular territory should remain within or leave the UK, continued participation in or withdrawal from the European integration project, the voting system for UK parliamentary elections, and the Northern Ireland peace process. Some referendums produce a result that has legal force, for instance the 2011 referendum on the voting system. Others, such as the 2016 EU referendum, do not – though they may achieve considerable political weight.
Significance to present discussion	There is a lack of clarity and of agreement regarding various important aspects of the use of referendums. These areas of uncertainty include what subjects it is and is not appropriate to hold referendums on, and the circumstances in which a referendum is required, how frequently they can be held, and the nature and extent of any mandate or obligation they might create. How far is it reasonable to claim that the people have a collective will that can be expressed through a choice between predetermined options, that might not even be well defined? What actions can the outcome of a popular vote be used to justify? How far should it be used to argue that a particular controversy is settled and should be excluded from the political agenda? These questions and others are difficult – perhaps impossible – to answer in an entirely satisfactory way. In the absence of their resolution, it remains open to those who wield power under the representative system to seek to deploy referendums and their outcomes in ways that serve their purposes – though they might not be successful in such endeavours.
	Referendums have managed to co-exist with representative democracy in the UK, as they have in other countries. At times they have arguably had a stabilising impact – for instance, through demonstrating support in Northern Ireland (and in the Republic) for the 1998 Belfast/Good Friday Agreement in the year it was reached. But the 2016 EU referendum and its aftermath shows that they can be polarising and a source of disturbance. Brexit uncovered and augmented pronounced party political, social, territorial and cultural divisions. It produced a result to which majorities in both Houses of Parliament were opposed. Implementing Brexit entailed significant constitutional disruption and challenges to prevailing norms. It elevated to positions of influence and responsibility individuals and groups whose conduct and agendas augmented these tendencies further.

Feature	Cabinet, ministers, and Prime Minister
Description	Within the UK executive, according to orthodox interpretations, ultimate decision-making authority generally rests with a committee of senior ministers, the Cabinet, rather than with an individual. It and its subcommittees deliberate as a group, in private, and having reached conclusions ministers are required publicly to unite behind them, whatever those conclusions may be. The members of Cabinet answer individually to Parliament for policies and activities falling within their particular portfolio. The most senior member of Cabinet is the Prime Minister. Prime ministers chair and set the agenda for Cabinet meetings, and have various other levers of influence at their disposal. But they do not have a direct personal electoral mandate, and can be removed from post without a General Election taking place.
Significance to present discussion	Irrespective of constitutional principles, prime ministers tend to be the key public focus for the governments of which they are heads. Their role is fairly loosely defined, but without doubt prime ministers perform important functions. The prime ministerial remit includes the appointment and removal of ministers, the promotion of standards within government, the management of the Civil Service, intelligence and security matters, the handling of relations with the monarch, and the request of dissolutions of Parliament leading to general elections. These powers are also considerable responsibilities. Much rests on the occupant of the office being a reliable individual. Doubts about their reliability or integrity are a serious matter. Prime ministerial power is variable. It can be extensive in circumstances that are politically favourable to the government; but it can also drain if fortunes alter. A premier whose political capital has declined can experience difficulties in managing ministers as a group and individually. In such circumstances, a premier might be removed from post by their own colleagues in government. If ministers do not see any need to abide by principles of collective responsibility, the cohesion of government can erode substantially. The effective operation of individual responsibility of ministers depends in part on their cooperation with Parliament, for instance through providing it with accurate information.

Feature	The Civil Service
Description	Ministers within the UK executive and at devolved level are supported by officials known as civil servants. Largely, they are employed on permanent contracts and are not appointed at the discretion of the party politicians who hold office at a given time. Permanent civil servants are required to be objective: that is, to bring relevant information to the attention of ministers, even if it is inconvenient. They are also subject to a political impartiality principle: they must loyally support their current political heads, while at the same time retaining the ability to offer the same assistance to future office holders, of the same or of a different political party. Ministers are required to give proper consideration to the views of civil servants, as well as taking into account other advice they might receive from elsewhere. Civil servants are required to act with integrity and honesty.
Significance to present discussion	Civil servants are potentially a valuable source of objective advice, helping to ensure that decision-making and policy is rational and evidence-based. They can also, through their counsel, help promote integrity and uphold constitutional principles. Career officials have the potential to provide a perspective that is longer-term and less coloured by party political considerations. They can contribute an awareness of relevant precedents and conventions. However, civil servants are not independent from the government and – while they can offer advice – ministers make final decisions. Some politicians tend to regard the permanent Civil Service as in some senses an obstacle to the attainment of their objectives, rather than a useful resource. There are various means by which ministers can pressurise the official machine into being more compliant, and less committed to objectivity and impartiality. They can also appoint (subject to approval from the Prime Minister) and heavily rely upon special advisers, who are not required to be objective or impartial (though whose formal powers within the system are restricted).

Feature	Constitutional monarchy
Description	The office of head of state in the UK is hereditary. There is a strong convention that, though monarchs have formal responsibility for a range of functions (such as those grouped under the 'Royal Prerogative', and others that have a basis in statute), in practice they should avoid being seen to pursue their own agendas. Though they can wield a certain amount of influence in private, most of their authorities are disposed of in accordance with advice provided by ministers. It is conceivable that – in extreme circumstances – decisions about whether or how to exercise some of their functions, such as responding to requests to dissolve Parliament and trigger a General Election, could require a degree of personal judgement on their part and that of their advisers. However, the expectation placed upon politicians is that they should seek to ensure that the monarch is protected from involvement in matters of a party political nature and any controversy that could arise from their being seen to take a position on a disputed matter.
Significance to present discussion	The principle that that the monarch should remain above party politics is important to the integrity of the democratic system. Certain royal functions, such as the appointment of members of the House of Lords and the calling, proroguing and dissolution of Parliament, are constitutionally highly sensitive. It is unsatisfactory for them to be employed in a way that challenges democratic principles (or is simply perceived as doing so), for instance by preventing (or assisting in) the removal of a Prime Minister or avoiding parliamentary oversight of the executive. Much rests, therefore, on senior office holders wishing to uphold this principle. Such discussions about the constitutionally impartial role of the monarchy emphasise the need for that impartiality to be protected. The idea that it might be an active defender of the integrity of the system does not receive serious consideration: understandably, since the hereditary nature of the office means that it lacks the democratic legitimacy it would need in order to make interventions. Indeed, were the UK head of state to become a more overt player in the political system, some observers would respond with concern about their behaving in a way that their status does not justify.

Feature	Media
Description	The term 'media' covers a wide variety of forms of communication that play an important part in democratic processes. They include more traditional newspapers and broadcast media, and the Internet, which has to some extent lowered barriers between pre-existing formats. The media provide information, promote particular opinions and political agendas, and enable campaigning. They are regulated in different ways and to different extents. Broadcasters are subject to strict impartiality rules, which the 'press' is not; while the UK government has for some time contemplated establishing a new regulatory framework for online platforms, and has brought forward a bill to achieve this end.
Significance to present discussion	Independent media are is essential in a democracy to properly inform the public and provide scrutiny of politicians and government. But the concept of independence is a complex one. Some outlets have agendas of their own, and particular players in the field, possibly with specific political objectives, can achieve concentration of ownership, distorting the overall balance of coverage. Media interests can develop troublingly close relationships with those they are supposed to be holding to account. The dissemination of false information, especially online, is recognised as a threat to the integrity of democracy. In addition to the agendas of commercial media operators, external forces hostile to democracy, whether state sponsored or otherwise, can pursue their objectives through a diverse range of media communications. Public service broadcasters can be placed under political pressure by government and others. Members of the public can take part in political activities through online media. While the Internet is democratising in the sense that it has reduced entry costs for participation, it has arguably also had destabilising implications.

Feature	The people
Description	In a democracy, the people are regarded as the ultimate source of political authority. People can express their political perspectives through various forms of participation. These include voting; being active in a party; sharing online content; taking part in protests; signing petitions; supporting charities or pressure groups; responding to opinion polls and taking part in focus groups. The UK is a diverse society, with a wide variety of identities, opinions and values. It is a relatively prosperous state, though with divergencies of wealth between groups and territories.
Significance to present discussion	People might not always be committed to democratic principles; discerning their precise views on these matters is a difficult task. The Brexit issue has exposed and exacerbated various divisions involving social profile and outlooks. The Conservative Party has seemingly sought to mobilise controversy around issues such as migration and trans rights as a political campaigning tool.

Liz Truss's final speech as Prime Minister, 25 October 2022[2]
Excerpts with commentary

Excerpts

It has been a huge honour to be Prime Minister of this great country.

. . .

In just a short period, this government has acted urgently and decisively on the side of hardworking families and businesses.

. . .

We are taking back our energy independence . . . so we are never again beholden to global market fluctuations or malign foreign powers . . .

We simply cannot afford to be a low growth country where the government takes up an increasing share of our national wealth . . . and where there are huge divides between different parts of our country.

We need to take advantage of our Brexit freedoms to do things differently.

This means delivering more freedom for our own citizens and restoring power in democratic institutions.

It means lower taxes, so people keep more of the money they earn.

. . .

Democracies must be able to deliver for their own people . . .

We must be able to outcompete autocratic regimes, where power lies in the hands of a few.

And now more than ever we must support Ukraine in their brave fight against Putin's aggression.

---

2 Liz Truss, 'Liz Truss's final speech as Prime Minister: 25 October 2022', gov.uk, accessed 7 May 2023 https://www.gov.uk/government/speeches/liz-trusss-final-speech-as-prime-minister-25-october-2022.

(continued)

Commentary

In her outgoing speech, Truss stresses that her policy agenda was driven by a desire to capitalise on Brexit. She emphasises the idea of democracy entailing a self-sufficient UK, and of being engaged in a struggle against autocratic forces in the world. There is no acknowledgement of the possibility that Russia may well have welcomed the UK decision to leave the EU, and possibly even tried to influence it.

Liz Truss's resignation statement, 20 October 2022[3]
Excerpts with commentary

Excerpts

I came into office at a time of great economic and international instability.
Families and businesses were worried about how to pay their bills.
Putin's illegal war in Ukraine threatens the security of our whole continent.
And our country had been held back for too long by low economic growth.
I was elected by the Conservative Party with a mandate to change this.
We delivered on energy bills and on cutting national insurance.
And we set out a vision for a low tax, high growth economy – that would take advantage of the freedoms of Brexit.
I recognise though, given the situation, I cannot deliver the mandate on which I was elected by the Conservative Party.
I have therefore spoken to His Majesty The King to notify him that I am resigning as Leader of the Conservative Party.
This morning I met the Chair of the 1922 Committee Sir Graham Brady.
We have agreed there will be a leadership election to be completed in the next week.
This will ensure we remain on a path to deliver our fiscal plans and maintain our country's economic stability and national security.
I will remain as Prime Minister until a successor has been chosen.

Commentary

In this speech, the Prime Minister stresses the idea that her mandate came from being elected by her party. She had won on a vote of members beyond Westminster; but her reference to the chair of the 1922 Committee shows the importance that the parliamentary party, of which the 1922 Committee is representative, can achieve. Truss stresses that her policy agenda is the product of a desire to realise the opportunities supposedly created by Brexit.

---

3 Liz Truss, 'https://www.gov.uk/government/speeches/prime-minister-liz-trusss-statement-in-down ing-street-20-october-2022', gov.uk, accessed 7 May 2023, https://www.gov.uk/government/speeches/ prime-minister-liz-trusss-statement-in-downing-street-20-october-2022.

Liz Truss's first statement in Downing Street as Prime Minister, 6 September 2022[4]
Excerpts with commentary

Excerpts

I have just accepted Her Majesty the Queen's kind invitation to form a new government.
Let me pay tribute to my predecessor.
Boris Johnson delivered Brexit, the Covid vaccine, and stood up to Russian aggression.
History will see him as a hugely consequential Prime Minister.
. . .
We now face severe global headwinds caused by Russia's appalling war in Ukraine and the aftermath of Covid.
Now is the time to tackle the issues that are holding Britain back.
. . .
United with our allies, we will stand up for freedom and democracy around the world – recognising that we can't have security at home without having security abroad.
As Prime Minister, I will pursue three early priorities.
Firstly, I will get Britain working again.
I have a bold plan to grow the economy through tax cuts and reform.
I will cut taxes to reward hard work and boost business-led growth and investment.

Commentary

The references the Prime Minister makes to Johnson avoid recognising the manner of his departure, following a series of irregular episodes and immense pressure from within his own parliamentary party. This circumspection probably reflects his persistent popularity in sections of the Conservative Party, by which Truss had been elected as leader. Truss emphasises working with 'allies' to defend freedom in the world. Truss does not mention that she had recently declined to state clearly that France was a friendly power rather than a foe. Truss sets out the policy agenda the pursuit of which would undo her premiership.

---

4 Liz Truss, 'https://www.gov.uk/government/speeches/prime-minister-liz-trusss-statement-6-september-2022', gov.uk, accessed 7 May 2023, https://www.gov.uk/government/speeches/prime-minister-liz-trusss-statement-6-september-2022.

Chapter Three
Brexit and Democracy

The literature review identified a series of concerns that observers internationally have raised since 2016 as being troubling from a democratic perspective. Chapters Three and Four assess developments in the UK over this same time period from the point of view of these concerns. In the discussion of possible democratic deterioration, Brexit appears as a focus, consequence and cause. The term, 'Brexit', which refers to the UK's departure from the European Union (EU), is used here to describe a political phenomenon that began with the referendum on membership of the EU which took place on 23 June 2016, and its expansive consequences, which continue to the present, and will in a sense persist unless and until the UK re-joins the EU, or a successor to it. It is relevant to possible democratic deterioration as considered in this work in a number of ways, set out below.

Citizenship Rights

Brexit entailed all the inhabitants of a country of approximately 65 million people being indefinitely deprived of European citizenship, on the basis of a proposition supported by about 17.4 million voters in a referendum. The UK population would no longer have access to a series of rights enjoyed by all those who lived within what was a 28- (before UK exit) member state organisation, wherever they were in that bloc. The post-EU form of citizenship available in the UK was less extensive both in its substance and in its geographical extent. A defining expression of the European citizenship that was lost is found in the Charter of Fundamental Rights of the European Union, which entered into force with the Treaty of Lisbon in December 2009. Applying to those areas in which the EU had responsibility, the Charter was markedly broad in scope, dividing into a series of categories:

– Dignity: including the right to life, and freedom from torture, slavery and forced labour
– Freedoms: including the right to liberty and security, respect for family and private life; the right to marry and to found a family; freedom of thought; the safeguarding of personal data; freedom of expression; academic freedom; freedom of association including participating in political parties and trade unions; freedom of assembly; the right to education; the right to choose an occupation and to engage in work; the right to operate a business; the right to property; and the rights of people being deported and claiming asylum

https://doi.org/10.1515/9783110735925-003

- Equality: including equal treatment before the law; the prohibition of discrimination on a wide range of grounds; the right to culture, language and religion; equality between women and men; the rights of children and of older people; and disability rights
- Solidarity: including the right to consultation and to information in the workplace; the right to collective action and collective bargaining; safeguards against unjustified dismissal; rights involving work, such as weekly hours, health and safety in the workplace, and leave allowances; protection of young people with respect to work; parental leave; social security; health care; safeguarding of the environment; and protection of consumers
- Citizens' rights: including the right to vote and to stand in local authority and European Parliament elections; the right to good administration; the right to access official information; the right to appeal against institutional maladministration; the right to petition the European Parliament; freedom of movement; and freedom of residence
- Justice: including the right to a fair trial and to effective remedy, with legal aid available to those who are unable to afford representation, and the right of an individual to defend themselves against a charge, and to be presumed innocent; the prohibition of retrospective punishment; the requirement for punishment to be in proportion to the gravity of crimes committed; and the prevention of individuals being tried or punished more than once for the same crime[1]

While the UK government sought to preserve general legal continuity at the point of departure from the EU, it chose not to attempt to replicate the Charter (or at least those elements of the Charter it would have been possible to retain). Exit from the EU – and the particular way in which it was implemented – meant the removal of the specific form of protection that the Charter had previously provided for members of the UK population as EU citizens. More broadly, it entailed a shift away from the model of a supranational order in which a wide range of freedoms – political, legal, socio-economic, cultural, environmental – were subject to judicial enforcement, even to the point of taking precedence over regular domestic law. In as far as it pertained to the implementation of European law, the legislation of EU member states – including Acts of the UK Parliament while the UK was an EU member – could be disapplied for failing to conform to the Charter.[2] Moving away from this system drew the UK closer to a more arbitrary arrangement in which the rights

---

1 See: 'Charter of Fundamental Rights of the European Union', EUR-Lex, accessed 17 March 2023, https://eur-lex.europa.eu/legal-content/EN/TXT/?uri=celex:12012P/TXT.
2 For a discussion of the Charter in the context of Brexit, see: House of Lords Select Committee on the Constitution, European Union (Withdrawal) Bill, 9th Report of Session 2017–2019 (House of

of individuals were ultimately subject to the UK Parliament,[3] an institution unrestrained by the higher law of a 'written' or 'codified' constitution, and within which the executive enjoyed a privileged position of influence. In a sense, the 'political constitution' was being enhanced at the expense of its juridical counterpart.[4]

Rights included in the Charter might be provided for by other means, for instance through judicial recognition, through laws dealing with specific subjects, or wider provisions such as the *Human Rights Act 1998*[5] and the *Equality Act 2010*. But the Charter, notable for its comprehensive nature[6] and special legal status, no longer applied in the UK. Matters that were previously in the remit of the EU, and therefore subject to the Charter, were now repatriated to the UK, and not subject to a direct equivalent to the Charter. The option of seeking to void or disapply an Act of Parliament on the grounds that it violated a fundamental principle would not be available. Up to a point this transformation was a reversion to the position prior to 1973, when the UK commenced participation in European integration, and no Act of Parliament could be disapplied. In another respect, the removal of these restraints upon Parliament could be seen as congruent with a general pattern of democratic deterioration. It might fit with a narrative according to which governments could pursue projects on behalf of the people, free from the obstructions of elite groups such as the courts and the EU. Moreover, in as far as it weakened protections, departure from the Charter potentially made the violation of norms easier to achieve than it might otherwise have been. More generally, it is possible to detect a further populist strand in Brexit. It entailed disavowing supranational citizenship for the UK population, both when inside the UK and when inside the EU; and denying its benefits to citizens of continuing EU member states when within the UK. In its place was a more exclusionary version of belonging.

As well as representing a turn away from one constitutional model and towards another, leaving the EU made the exercise of certain citizenship rights practically impossible, even had the UK government and Parliament wished to preserve or replicate them. Inhabitants of the UK, for instance, could no longer

---

Lords, London, 29 January 2018), HL 69, chap. 6, 32–26, accessed 18 March 2023, https://publications. parliament.uk/pa/ld201719/ldselect/ldconst/69/69.pdf.

3 Vernon Bogdanor, *Beyond Brexit: towards a British constitution* (London: I.B.Tauris, 2019), 266–267.

4 For a classic statement of the political constitution concept, see: J. A. G. Griffith, 'The political constitution', *The Modern Law Review* 42, no. 1 (1979), 1–21.

5 Incorporating another international agreement separate from the EU, the European Convention on Human Rights of the Council of Europe, of which the UK remained a member.

6 Alison Young, 'Four Reasons for Retaining the Charter Post Brexit: Part 1 – A Broader Protection of Rights', *Oxford Human Rights Hub*, 2 February 2018, accessed 18 March 2023, https://ohrh.law.ox. ac.uk/four-reasons-for-retaining-the-charter-post-brexit-part-1-a-broader-protection-of-rights.

vote in European elections, rendering a Charter right unrealisable. Yet – even after the cessation of membership – the processes participated in by the European Parliament would retain considerable significance to the UK. The laws and policies adopted by a vast, neighbouring political-economic bloc would always be important to its former Member State. No longer being able to participate in elections to the European Parliament was in this sense the removal of an important democratic entitlement. A further inevitable loss for members of the UK public was of the enjoyment of rights, such as freedom of movement, throughout the EU. Whatever freedoms members of the UK public might possess in future, they would not do so across the EU, as they had previously, for so long as the UK remained outside.

Polarisation and its Party Political Consequences

In a book based on his Reith Lectures given in 2019 and first published in the same year, the former Supreme Court justice Jonathan Sumption remarked that: 'Brexit is an issue on which people feel strongly, and on which Britain is divided, roughly down the middle. These divisions are problematic, not just in themselves, but because they roughly correspond to other divisions in our society: generational, social, economic, educational and regional.'[7] The difficulty arose, Sumption held, partly because of the nature of the device used to make the decision to the leave the EU: a referendum. In his assessment, the consequences were serious. As he put it:

> A referendum obstructs compromise, by producing a result in which 52 per cent of voters feel entitled to speak for the whole nation, and 48 per cent do not matter at all. This is, after all, the tacit assumption of every minister who declares that 'the British people' has approved this or that measure, as if only the majority were part of 'the British people'. It is the mentality which has created an unwarranted sense of entitlement among the sort of people who denounce those who disagree with them as 'enemies', 'traitors', 'saboteurs' or even 'Nazis'. This is the authentic language of totalitarianism. It is the lowest point to which a political community can sink short of actual violence.[8]

Brexit, in the account offered by Sumption, was connected to pathological polarisation. The origins of this perceived disorder, as he suggested, lay in the referendum, which condensed the complex matter of UK membership of the EU into a binary. It created two camps, remainers and leavers, crystallised around the deceptively simple wording: '[s]hould the United Kingdom remain a member of the

---

7 Jonathan Sumption, *Trials of the State:* (London: Profile, 2020), 29.
8 Jonathan Sumption, *Trials of the State:* (London: Profile, 2020), 31.

European Union or leave the European Union?'[9] In the years following the vote, the side people associated with became a key source of identity. Research conducted in mid-2018 and reported by John Curtice, for instance, found that Brexit affiliations were stronger among the public than attachments to parties: 44 percent of respondents said their Brexit identity was 'Very strong'; 33 percent 'Fairly strong'; 12 percent 'Not very strong'; and 11 percent that they had no Brexit identity. In contrast, only 9 percent had a 'Very strong' party identity; 28 percent 'Fairly strong'; 27 percent 'Not very strong'; and 36 percent 'None'.[10] There was evidence that this attachment was for many fundamental in nature. It was more than just an opinion on a particular issue that might readily change. When asked whether they would vote the same way in another referendum, the percentage saying that they would was in the mid-to high 90s for all who had a remain or leave identity, other than those with a 'Not very strong' 'Leaver' identity, 68 percent of whom said they would vote the same way.[11]

The Brexit effect, of which this research provided evidence, appeared divisive and destabilising. The cleavage it created around the question posed in the referendum was made up of a series of sub-fissures, some of which were already established though possibly intensified by Brexit, others of which were less well known or at least had not been politicised. It cut across more regular party divisions, both within the elite and among the public. For instance, at high political level, within the Conservative cabinet, Cameron found it necessary to introduce a suspension of collective responsibility, allowing ministers publicly to diverge from the government support for the remain side during the 2016 referendum campaign.[12] This decision created practical and political difficulties for the functioning of the executive. Civil servants providing support to a secretary of state who chose to oppose the official stance, for example, were placed in an awkward position.[13] Identifying another problem, Andrea Leadsom, a leaver within the government, recalls that 'David Cameron's experiment in relaxing collective Cabinet

9 European Union Referendum Act, 2015, c.36, s.1(4).

10 John Curtice, *Legacy of Brexit: how Britain has become a country of 'remainers' and 'leavers'* (London: National Centre for Social Research, 2018), 8, accessed 19 March 2023, https://whatukthinks.org/eu/wp-content/uploads/2018/10/WUKT-EU-Briefing-Paper-15-Oct-18-Emotional-legacy-paper-final.pdf.

11 John Curtice, *Legacy of Brexit: how Britain has become a country of 'remainers' and 'leavers'* (London: National Centre for Social Research, 2018), 10, accessed 19 March 2023, https://whatukthinks.org/eu/wp-content/uploads/2018/10/WUKT-EU-Briefing-Paper-15-Oct-18-Emotional-legacy-paper-final.pdf.

12 Michael Everett, *Collective responsibility* (London: House of Commons Library, 2016), 17–20, accessed 18 March 2023, https://researchbriefings.files.parliament.uk/documents/CBP-7755/CBP-7755.pdf.

13 Suzanne Heywood, *What Does Jeremy Think? Jeremy Heywood and the making of modern Britain* (London: William Collins, 2021), chap. 50.

responsibility . . . unleashed a beast, straining our unity to the extent that one of my clearest memories of the campaign is the outrage I felt at finding myself on the terrace of the House of Commons responding on social media to George Osborne telling elderly people their pensions would be destroyed and so would our NHS if they dared to vote Leave.'[14]

Leadsom's account also suggests that difficulties continued long after the referendum had taken place and collective responsibility had supposedly been restored. She writes that: '[t]aken together, Theresa's Cabinet ministers formed an interesting group. I was wary of some of the Remainers, who had been so overtly hostile during the referendum campaign. There was a constant sensation of a subtext, of things going on behind the scenes, that people weren't being frank about.'[15] A prominent minister who had been on the leave side displayed a willingness to depart from the principle that Cabinet members should maintain a united front in public. Alan Duncan was a Conservative MP who served as a Minister of State in the Foreign Office when Boris Johnson was Foreign Secretary. Duncan complained in his diary entry for 24 September 2017 about an article Johnson had written 'on his views – indeed his terms and conditions – for any deal' with the EU. Duncan regarded the act as 'a total challenge to the PM, and to the concept of collective responsibility.'[16]

At popular level, among those who supported the two main parties, Conservative voters were more inclined to leave, Labour voters to remain – though in both cases, significant minorities favoured the opposite side. Of those who voted Conservative at the 2015 General Election, the split was 58 percent for leave and 42 percent for remain. With Labour it was 63 percent for remain and 37 percent for leave.[17] Following the referendum result, the leave position became ascendant within the Conservative Party. Of the four prime ministers who succeeded David Cameron in little over six years following his resignation, two – Theresa May (2016–2019) and Liz Truss (2022) – were remainers in 2016 who subsequently affirmed conversion to the Brexit cause. When campaigning for the leadership in July 2016, May famously said: 'Brexit means Brexit and we're going to make a success of it.'[18] Six years later, with another such

---

14 Andrea Leadsom, *Snakes and Ladders: navigating the ups and downs of politics* (London: Biteback, 2022), 68.

15 Andrea Leadsom, *Snakes and Ladders: navigating the ups and downs of politics* (London: Biteback, 2022), 127.

16 Alan Duncan, *In The Thick Of It: the private diaries of a minister* (London: William Collins, 2021), diary entry for 24 September 2017, 227.

17 For analysis of this issue see: John Curtice and Victoria Ratti, *Culture Wars: keeping the Brexit divide alive?* (London: National Centre for Social Research, 2022), 25, accessed 19 March 2023, https://www.bsa.natcen.ac.uk/media/39478/bsa39_culture-wars.pdf.

18 'Theresa May vows to put Conservatives "at service" of working people', *BBC News*, 11 July 2016, accessed 18 March 2023, https://www.bbc.co.uk/news/uk-36760953.

contest taking place, the Conservative MP Steve Baker discussed in a media interview why he was endorsing Truss. Baker, who was a senior figure in the European Research Group (ERG), an assertive pro-Brexit faction within the Conservative parliamentary party, said that 'Liz has completed the journey that the whole nation needs to go on.'[19] The two other post-Cameron premiers to date – Boris Johnson (2019–2022) and Sunak (2022–) had publicly supported the campaign to leave.

The Brexit division manifested itself in a hardening of the Conservative position, notably after Johnson became leader on 24 July 2019. An expression of this tendency came on 3 September, when 21 Conservative MPs – including former Cabinet members – were expelled from the party for voting against the government line and in favour of a plan to preclude the UK from leaving the EU without a deal (ten of them subsequently had the whip restored).[20] A General Election always turns on more than a single question. However, Brexit was certainly a defining feature of the 2019 contest. The ongoing political struggle over the issue generated the context in which the election took place, and was the very reason for its occurrence, sought by Johnson to resolve deadlock.[21] Moreover, Brexit shaped the outcome. As one analysis puts it: '[t]here was . . . a clear relationship between how a constituency voted on Brexit in 2016 and how the parties fared in the 2019 election'.[22] Opinion research suggested that Brexit was the third most important issuing in determining how people voted overall; and it came first among those who voted Conservative.[23] At the 2019 General Election, the Conservatives managed to make themselves the beneficiaries of the Brexit fissure – while Labour suffered from it.

---

19 LBC (@LBC), 'Liz has completed the journey that the whole nation needs to go on', Twitter, 20 July 2022, accessed 18 March 2023, https://twitter.com/LBC/status/1549805838189166592.

20 Andrew Woodcock, 'Churchill's grandson among 10 Tories to have whip restored after rebelling against no-deal Brexit', *Independent*, 29 October 2019, accessed 18 March 2023, https://www.independent.co.uk/news/uk/politics/boris-johnson-tory-whip-brexit-no-deal-conservative-mps-churchill-general-election-a9176741.html.

21 John Curtice, Stephen Fisher and Patrick English, 'The Geography of a Brexit Election: How Constituency Context and the Electoral System Shaped the Outcome', in Robert Ford, Tim Bale, Will Jennings and Paul Surridge, *The British General Election of 2019* (Basingstoke: Palgrave Macmillan, 2021), 461.

22 John Curtice, Stephen Fisher and Patrick English, 'The Geography of a Brexit Election: How Constituency Context and the Electoral System Shaped the Outcome', in Robert Ford, Tim Bale, Will Jennings and Paul Surridge, *The British General Election of 2019* (Basingstoke: Palgrave Macmillan, 2021), 467.

23 Andrew Blick, *Getting Brexit Undone* (London: Federal Trust, 2022), 17, accessed 19 March 2023, https://fedtrust.co.uk/wp-content/uploads/2022/07/Getting-Brexit-Undone-Andrew-Blick.pdf.

Firmly placing themselves on one side of the divide, the Conservatives secured a House of Commons majority of 80, the party's largest since 1987. They were able to convert an increase in vote share of just 1.3 percent (42.3 percent to 43.6) into a net gain of 48 seats (7.4 percent of the total in the Commons, 650). In the context of the Single Member Plurality (or 'First-Past-the-Post') voting system employed, it is not only the number of votes received but where they are cast that is crucial. The Brexit issue and its divisive quality helped the Conservatives create the necessary compound. The Conservative stance, encapsulated in the slogan 'Get Brexit Done',[24] was arguably central to their success in areas that had produced leave majorities in 2016 and which had previously been held by Labour. While shedding some remain supporters in 2019, the Conservatives were more than compensated by the leave voters they secured, and by expanding their support in opportune areas. People who voted Conservative at the 2015 General Election accounted for 40 percent of leave voters at the referendum the following year (and 31 percent of remain voters).[25] In 2017, the Conservatives gained an increased share of leave voters, at 65 percent (and 25 percent of remain voters).[26] In 2019, the party expanded this proportion further, to 74 percent (with its percentage of remain voters down again to 19).[27] Of the 57 seats the Conservatives gained in 2019 (absolute, not net), 55 had leave majorities in 2016.[28]

Some Conservatives saw Brexit as entailing the ascendancy of objectionable ideas, methods and people within the party. Alan Duncan supported remain at the referendum. But he had been a longstanding Eurosceptic. He describes how, in his view, '[s]omewhere along the line from the early 1990s the cause of honest and thoughtful Euroscepticism' had 'mutated into a form of simplistic nationalism that strikes me as ugly and demeaning.' While they might have sought reform of

---

24 For example, the title of the 2019 Conservative manifesto was *Get Brexit Done: Unleash Britain's Potential.* Conservative and Unionist Party, *Get Brexit Done: Unleash Britain's Potential* (Conservative and Unionist Party, London, 2019), 47–48, accessed 11 March 2023, https://assets-global. website-files.com/5da42e2cae7ebd3f8bde353c/5dda924905da587992a064ba_Conservative%202019% 20Manifesto.pdf.

25 Lord Ashcroft, 'How the United Kingdom voted on Thursday . . . and why', *Lord Ashcroft Polls*, 24 June 2016, accessed 19 March 2023, https://lordashcroftpolls.com/2016/06/how-the-united-kingdom-voted-and-why/.

26 See: YouGov survey results, accessed 19 March 2023, https://d25d2506sfb94s.cloudfront.net/cu mulus_uploads/document/kug7qzc4lh/InternalResults_170615_VoteSwitchers_W.pdf.

27 Adam McDonnell and Chris Curtis, 'How Britain voted in the 2019 General Election', *YouGov*, 17 December 2019, accessed 19 March 2023, https://yougov.co.uk/topics/politics/articles-reports /2019/12/17/how-britain-voted-2019-general-election.

28 Andrew Blick, *Getting Brexit Undone* (London: Federal Trust, 2022), 16, accessed 19 March 2023, https://fedtrust.co.uk/wp-content/uploads/2022/07/Getting-Brexit-Undone-Andrew-Blick.pdf.

the EU and different terms of membership for the EU, 'too many Eurosceptics re-treated to crude sloganeering.' There existed, Duncan believed, 'a rational and pragmatic case to be made for leaving the EU'. Yet 'few bothered to make it.' Al-luding to the UKIP leader Nigel Farage, Duncan described how 'we faced a wave of populist nonsense, emotive platitudes and downright lies: a barrage of Farage.' While such tactics were 'to be expected from a fringe party like UKIP', they, 'should never have entered the mainstream of the Conservative Party.' He regretted a ten-dency 'to suggest that highly complex questions have easy answers or that there are no trade-offs between national sovereignty and economic well-being.' Duncan re-counted how, in his view, 'during and after the 2016 referendum the increasingly swivel-eyed Brexiteer ultras in the Conservative Party mounted a determined effort to resist the encroachment of reality into their worldview. Inconvenient facts were dismissed as scaremongering, and necessary compromises condemned as betrayals.' There followed '[t]oxic stalemate . . . until finally those who clung to reason were purged and the high priests of the new religion took their place.' The Conservatives then 'won an election on another simplistic slogan' and 'finally managed to "Get Brexit Done".' Yet, Duncan concluded, writing in 2021, 'the day of reconciling a false prospectus with hard truths seems further away than ever.'[29]

Brexit polarisation had a perverse impact on Labour. Jeremy Corbyn, the party leader from 2015–2020, had a prior record of opposing the European integration proj-ect, but was a remain advocate at the referendum (though how effectively he ful-filled this role was a subject of debate).[30] While nearly all Labour MPs[31] and most of its voters[32] had supported remain, the party displayed a reluctance to appear to dis-respect the 2016 vote. The section of the 2017 Labour General Election manifesto on 'Negotiating Brexit' opened with the words: 'Labour accepts the referendum result'.[33] It went on to discuss the type of deal it would seek, and its approach to obtaining it. At the 2019 General Election, following internal party pressure, the position had

---

29 Alan Duncan, *In The Thick Of It: the private diaries of a minister* (London: William Collins, 2021), 2–3.

30 Jonathan Este, 'Labour's Brexit policy explained', *The Conversation*, 19 November 2019, ac-cessed 18 March 2023, https://theconversation.com/labours-brexit-policy-explained-127380.

31 Jim Edwards, 'This is the size of the majority in the House of Commons against Brexit', *Busi-ness Insider*, 3 November 2016, accessed 18 March 2023, https://www.businessinsider.com/major ity-house-of-commons-against-brexit-2016-11?r=US&IR=T.

32 For analysis of this issue see: John Curtice and Victoria Ratti, *Culture Wars: keeping the Brexit divide alive?* (London: National Centre for Social Research, 2022), 25, accessed 19 March 2023, https://www.bsa.natcen.ac.uk/media/39478/bsa39_culture-wars.pdf.

33 Labour Party, *For The Many Not The Few: the Labour Party manifesto 2017* (London: Labour Party, 2017), 24, accessed 18 March 2023, https://labour.org.uk/wp-content/uploads/2017/10/labour-manifesto-2017.pdf.

shifted away from this acceptance of Brexit, but not to a complete rejection of it. Labour pledged that '[w]ithin three months of coming to power, a Labour government will secure a sensible deal. And within six months, we will put that deal to a public vote alongside the option to remain.'[34]

There is strong evidence that Brexit was a factor in the loss by Labour of seats – especially in 2019 – previously regarded as safe territory for the party, which voted leave in 2016. These constituencies came to be labelled collectively the 'Red Wall'.[35] As one group of authors puts it:

> Brexit . . . helped break down traditional but often already frayed party loyalties, particularly among older, white socially conservative voters who in 2016 voted to leave the EU and who once made up a substantial part of Labour's core vote. Indeed, it was the geographical concentration of such voters in many former industrial towns in the North, the Midlands and Wales that had voted heavily for Leave that enabled the Tories to break through Labour's "Red Wall" in 2019 . . . Labour was well aware of its problems in such seats during the Parliament and the campaign, and indeed well before this, but never found an effective response.[36]

Overall, in 2019, Labour lost 60 seats, 52 of which had voted leave in 2016.[37] In December 2019, as we have seen, of the two main parties, the Conservatives appealed decisively, and successfully, to one side of the Brexit divide; while Labour did not. At this election Labour lost not only leave but also remain voters. Its share of the former group fell from 24 percent in 2017 to 14 percent in 2019; and of the latter from 55 percent to 49 percent.[38] Overall, with the party taking only 202 of 650 seats in the Commons, it was the worst Labour performance at a General Election since 1935.[39] This election did more than simply seal UK exit from the EU by providing the Conservative government under Johnson with the Commons majority it needed. It is reasonable to conclude that the manner of the December 2019 defeat, in particular the loss of the 'Red Wall' seats, and the desire to reverse it, helped drive La-

---

34 Labour Party, *It's Time For Real Change: the Labour Party manifesto 2019* (London: Labour Party, 2019), 89, accessed 18 March 2023, https://labour.org.uk/wp-content/uploads/2019/11/Real-Change-Labour-Manifesto-2019.pdf.

35 James Kanagasooriam and Elizabeth Simon, 'Red Wall: The Definitive Description', *Political Insight* 12, no. 3 (2021), 8–11.

36 Robert Ford, Tim Bale, Will Jennings and Paul Surridge, *The British General Election of 2019* (Basingstoke: Palgrave Macmillan, 2021), 495–496.

37 Andrew Blick, *Getting Brexit Undone* (London: Federal Trust, 2022), 17, accessed 19 March 2023, https://fedtrust.co.uk/wp-content/uploads/2022/07/Getting-Brexit-Undone-Andrew-Blick.pdf.

38 Adam McDonnell and Chris Curtis, 'How Britain voted in the 2019 General Election', *YouGov*, 17 December 2019, accessed 19 March 2023, https://yougov.co.uk/topics/politics/articles-reports /2019/12/17/how-britain-voted-2019-general-election.

39 Andrew Blick, *Getting Brexit Undone* (London: Federal Trust, 2022), 17, accessed 19 March 2023, https://fedtrust.co.uk/wp-content/uploads/2022/07/Getting-Brexit-Undone-Andrew-Blick.pdf.

bour towards presenting itself as accepting of, even positive about, Brexit, and other connected policies discussed below.[40]

Keir Starmer succeeded Corbyn shortly after the General Election, in April 2020. Starmer had been a notable enthusiast for EU membership; and when seeking election as Labour leader said in January 2020 that '[w]e have to make the case for freedom of movement'. When asked if he would restore it were he to come to office, Starmer said '[y]es, of course. Bring back, argue for, challenge'.[41] But as leader he developed a different stance. An important speech on this subject came in July 2022. Presenting himself as reconciled with the referendum result which Labour had in 2019 offered the possibility of reversing, Starmer held that '[i]n 2016, the British people voted for change.' As he put it '[t]he very narrow question that was on the ballot paper – leaving or remaining in the EU – is now in the past.' Starmer insisted that '[u]nder Labour, Britain will not go back into the EU. We will not be joining the single market or the customs union'. He also ruled out the restoration of freedom of movement that he had previously seemed to favour. But how would he differentiate his Brexit from that of the Conservatives? Part of this approach was, within the limits to which he had chosen to commit himself, 'to tear down unnecessary barriers' to trade. Starmer also sought to depict Brexit in socially progressive terms, referring to 'the hope that underpinned' the referendum result: 'the desire for a better, fairer future for our country'. Rather than a 'return to freedom of movement to create short term fixes', he went on, 'we will invest in our people and our places, and deliver on the promise our country has.'[42] We will return to this Starmer variant on Brexit below.

The approach Labour adopted under Starmer showed that the very cleavage that helped make Brexit possible, and which the referendum accentuated, had the effect of reinforcing Brexit and tendencies to which it was connected. While there was polarisation, rather than reflecting it in a symmetrical sense, both main parties in the UK (or rather Great Britain) became committed in principle to Brexit. Between them, especially after 2019 and following formal UK departure from the EU, they failed to provide voters who were not supporters of it with a proper outlet –

---

40 For an account of post-2019 General Election focus groups analysing attitudes in the 'Red Wall' that seems to have been influential upon Starmer-era Labour, see: Deborah Mattinson, *Beyond the Red Wall: Why Labour lost, how the Conservatives won and what will happen next?* (London: Biteback, 2020), chap. 15.

41 Lizzy Buchan, 'We have to make the case for freedom of movement', *Independent*, 31 January 2020, accessed 27 April 2023, https://www.independent.co.uk/news/uk/politics/labour-leadership-keir-starmer-brexit-freedom-movement-a9310996.html.

42 'Keir Starmer sets out Labour's 5-point plan to Make Brexit Work', 4 July 2022, accessed 15 March 2023, https://labour.org.uk/press/keir-starmer-sets-out-labours-5-point-plan-to-make-brexit-work-2/.

arguably a proposition meriting democratic concern. Both the Conservatives and Labour presented the question of UK membership of the EU as settled. But opinion research suggested that a significant proportion of the public took, or came to take, a different view. Opinion polling conducted in February 2023, for instance, showed that, when asked whether they thought the matter was resolved and should be kept closed, 44 percent said they did, while 43 percent replied they did not.[43]

Alongside the impact on parties and their voter support, Brexit was connected to territorial differences and other associated discrepancies. Wales and England both produced leave majorities (of 52.5 percent and 53.4 percent respectively); while Scotland and Northern Ireland favoured remaining (by 62 percent and 55.8 percent respectively). Within England, London produced a clear remain result (by 59.9 percent). There were significant variations in voting patterns according to the extent to which someone identified as English or British. Those who identified as English not British voted leave by a 79 percent majority; more English than British were 66 percent leave; equally English and British were 51 percent leave; more British than English were 63 percent remain; and British not English were 60 percent remain. In Northern Ireland, underneath the overall remain outcome was another, prior, distinction. The Catholic/Nationalist community was strongly supportive of remain (85 and 88 percent within these respective groups voting remain), while the Protestant/Unionist community was – by a smaller margin – inclined towards leave (60 and 66 percent within these respective categories voting leave).[44]

Age was another means of differentiation. In the 18–24 age group, 73 percent of those who voted backed remain; for ages 25–34 the proportion was 62 percent; and for ages 35–44, 52 percent. Above this age group, the majorities were for leave: for 45–54 year olds, there was a 56 percent leave majority; for 55–64, 57 percent leave; and for ages 65 and above, 60 percent leave. Ethnicity was a significant predictor. People identifying as black voted remain by a majority of 73 percent; and among those placing themselves in the Asian category, 67 percent were remain. Those defining themselves as white voted leave by a majority of 53 percent.[45] Divisions also manifested themselves in accordance with levels of educational attain-

43 John Curtice, 'Is the Brexit debate really over? Perhaps not', *UK in a changing Europe*, 10 March 2023, accessed 19 March 2023, https://ukandeu.ac.uk/is-the-brexit-debate-really-over-perhaps-not/.

44 John Garry, *The EU Referendum Vote in Northern Ireland: Implications for our understanding of citizens' political views and behaviour* (Queens University, Belfast, 2017), accessed 18 March 2023, https://www.qub.ac.uk/brexit/Brexitfilestore/Filetoupload,728121,en.pdf.

45 'How the United Kingdom voted on Thursday . . . and why', *Lord Ashcroft Polls*, 24 June 2016, accessed 19 March 2023, https://lordashcroftpolls.com/2016/06/how-the-united-kingdom-voted-and-why/.

ment and social grade. Those who had reached no more than the GCSE level were 69 percent leave; while people with a first degree or higher were 69 percent remain.[46] Another poll showed 81 percent of people who were taking part in full-time education at the time of the referendum as being remain voters. The AB grade of intermediate and senior managers, administrators and professionals produced a 57 percent remain majority. All the other grades favoured leave: C1 (supervisors and junior administrators, managers and professionals, and clerical staff) were 51 percent leave; C2 (skilled manual workers) were 64 percent leave; and DE (semi-skilled and unskilled workers; casual workers; lowest grade workers; retired people on state pensions; and unemployed people on state benefits) were also 64 percent leave.[47]

Support for leave within the C2 and DE groups was politically significant. It can be seen as being prefigured by the shift in campaigning focus taken by UKIP late in the previous decade. As a study of the party notes, from the 1990s onwards, UKIP had initially concentrated 'on appealing to middle-class, Southern and Euro-sceptic Conservatives, who were angry after the Maastricht Treaty and felt disconnected from their natural political home.' The party perceived itself 'as a pressure group, who existed to convert the Conservative Party to hard Euroscepticism.' But after 2009, the approach changed: UKIP:

> began appealing to disadvantaged voters, including those from traditionally Labour voting groups: white, working-class people whose traditional loyalty to the centre left had eroded, and who stayed at home on election days or flirted with the extreme right BNP [British National Party]. To attract these voters, UKIP began fusing their hard Eurosceptic message with stronger nationalist, anti-elite and anti-immigration elements.[48]

The Brexit experience encouraged a perception that Labour had somehow lost its appeal to traditional sources of support. Opponents felt able to criticise Labour for failure in this regard. As the Conservative politician Penny Mordaunt and her co-author Chris Lewis put it in a 2021 book, the 2008 'financial crisis' impacted most seriously on 'the most vulnerable', whose 'reasonable conclusion was that parts of the country were being neglected. The bottom third felt ignored – worse than that, actually: patronised or despised'. Labour, Mordaunt and Lewis went

46 Elizabeth Simon, 'Educational attainment and referendum voting: questions and connections', *UK in a changing Europe*, 16 March 2022, accessed 19 March 2023, https://ukandeu.ac.uk/educational-attainment-referendum-voting/.
47 'How the United Kingdom voted on Thursday . . . and why', *Lord Ashcroft Polls*, 24 June 2016, accessed 19 March 2023, https://lordashcroftpolls.com/2016/06/how-the-united-kingdom-voted-and-why/.
48 Robert Ford and Matthew Goodwin, *Revolt on the Right: Explaining support for the radical right in Britain* (Abingdon: Routledge, 2014), 108.

on, rather than setting out 'to understand these regions' – which provided an electoral base for the party – 'subjected them instead to a sort of middle-class Munchism. They variously mocked (and were shocked by) their "bigotry" and their England-flag-football patriotism. They called them "stupid"'.[49]

Within Labour, those who advocated acceptance of Brexit – some of whom had already taken up such a position before the 2019 General Election – tended to place particular interpretations upon it that fitted with their political orientation. They might, for instance, depict the vote as being a response to socio-economic and political marginalisation by excluded groups. In such accounts, it might be possible to harness the movement for a leftist programme, that would at the same time manage to reconcile itself with nationalist or patriotic sentiments. Nandy was a prominent advocate of such positions, describing in a 2022 book how:

> Many of the places where a majority voted to leave the EU were places where, over four decades, industries had been lost and with them a sense of place and pride. Towns that within living memory had powered the world through the mines, mills and factories of Britain had experienced decades of economic decline . . . This is the impact that decisions of recent decades have had on our communities and our sense of belonging, sweeping away the familiar . . . But in the political arena, it was barely up for discussion.[50]

Nandy recalled that 'During the EU referendum I came to feel that too many of the arguments we put forward as part of the Remain campaign were driven by a sense of pessimism. At their heart was the idea that as a small country we had little to offer, unable to shape the world beyond our shores.'[51] In such a landscape, there was scope for divisive populism to gain in traction; her prescription was for a 'quiet patriotism' that could supplant it.[52]

The former Labour Cabinet member, Shadow Leader of the Opposition, and subsequently a member of the Starmer Shadow Cabinet, Ed Miliband, wrote of Brexit in 2021 that:

> Wherever you stand on the issue itself, I think that vote – and the discontent it signified – tells us something profoundly important. The discontent was partly grounded in people's view about our relationship with the EU, but I am convinced it goes deeper. I learned this from many conversations in my constituency in Doncaster, which voted Leave by one of the largest margins in the country. So many people who voted for Brexit said similar things to me. 'I'm voting for a better future for my children.' 'Things need to change.' 'Things can't get

49 Penny Mordaunt and Chris Lewis, *Greater: Britain after the storm* (London: Biteback, 2021), 90–91.
50 Lisa Nandy, *All In: How We Build a Country That Works* (Manchester: HarperNorth, 2022), 52–53.
51 Lisa Nandy, *All In: How We Build a Country That Works* (Manchester: HarperNorth, 2022), 67.
52 Lisa Nandy, *All In: How We Build a Country That Works* (Manchester: HarperNorth, 2022), 60.

any worse.' This discontent cannot be divorced from the aftermath of the financial crash – austerity and stagnant wages – but nor can it be separated from longer-term trends: the ongoing economic and social shock of deindustrialisation, the deeply exploitative world of work that many people face and fears about prospects for the next generation. Meeting this deep-seated wish for change, for something better, is certainly not going to happen without a significant transformation.[53]

More overtly enthusiastic about Brexit, and less connected to senior Labour decision makers, the Labour Peer Maurice Glasman, in his 2022 book *Blue Labour: The Politics of the Common Good*, expressed the view that:

> Leaving the EU allows Labour to implement a radical economic programme outside of the constraints of the single market and the stringent conditions of the Lisbon Treaty concerning state aid and competition law. Labour could have won the war of position in the Brexit interregnum by leading the movement to leave and articulating the possibilities for national renewal that it opened up . . . Instead it became the defender of the old order and of globalization.[54]

As we have seen, despite his positioning prior to becoming Labour leader, in the post, Starmer shifted to a position of accepting Brexit, upon which he sought to place a distinctive Labour interpretation. A speech Starmer delivered at the beginning of 2023 expanded upon the latter approach. In it, he called for 'a huge power shift out of Westminster' to 'transform our economy, our politics and our democracy.' Starmer sought to link this approach 'back to Brexit.' He explained that 'a whole host of issues were on that ballot paper. But as I went around the country, campaigning for Remain, I couldn't disagree with the basic case so many Leave voters made to me.' He recalled encountering '[p]eople who wanted public services they could rely on. High streets they could be proud of. Opportunities for the next generation. And all of this in their town or city.' He then went as far as to appropriate the main slogan of the leave campaign, asserting: 'It's not unreasonable for us to recognise the desire for communities to stand on their own feet. It's what Take Back Control meant. The control people want is control over their lives and their community.' Starmer therefore promised to 'embrace the Take Back Control message. But we'll turn it from a slogan to a solution.' The 'new approach to growth and our economy' he envisaged, bringing about more even territorial distribution of opportunity, dealt with another concern that 'was part of the Brexit moment as well. Working people want their town or city to prosper by

---

53 Ed Miliband, *Go Big: How To Fix Our* World (London: The Bodley Head, 2021), 4.
54 Maurice Glasman, *Blue Labour: The Politics of the Common Good* (Cambridge: Polity, 2022), 105.

standing on their own feet. They want growth from the grassroots. To create wealth on their terms and in their way.'[55]

But how plausible was it to treat Brexit as a progressive political movement? Further analysis of opinion research suggests a need for doubt on this point.[56] Perhaps the best way of differentiating the two groups of voters and identifying them each as a coherent group was through outlooks on a range of cultural issues. Depending on the side they favoured in the referendum, someone was likely to subscribe to a broad set of stances. Leave voters by large majorities felt that the following phenomena were a 'force for bad': multiculturalism (81 percent); social liberalism (80 percent); feminism (74 percent); the 'Green movement' (78 percent); globalisation (69 percent); immigration (80 percent).[57] Substantial – albeit not quite as large – majorities of remain voters were favourable towards each of the same tendencies.[58] These findings suggested that the Brexit issue was connected to a wider public division between groups of people who differed over a cluster of social attitudes.

This observation calls into question the idea that Labour could meaningfully channel the leave movement for leftist purposes, as it seemingly sought to do. We will return to the subject of where its efforts in this regard led Labour in the next chapter. While Labour hoped that its acceptance of Brexit might be a means of advancing its political cause, the Conservatives seemingly sought to capitalise on the realignment it had achieved at the 2019 General Election for their own purposes. They seemed to do so through exploiting the cultural divisions Brexit had helped expose. Here might be a central motive for interventions, for instance over trans rights, that some commentators have perceived collectively as the waging of 'culture wars.'[59] On a basis of their analysis of public attitudes in this field, John Curtice and Victoria Ratti wrote in 2022 that:

> attitudes towards 'culture war' issues vary between different demographic groups and between social liberals and social conservatives in much the same way as attitudes towards

55 Keir Starmer, 'Keir Starmer's New Year's speech', 25 January 2023, accessed 15 March 2023, https://labour.org.uk/ press/keir-starmer-new-years-speech/.

56 For example, Maria Sobolewska and Robert Ford, *Brexitland* (Cambridge: Cambridge University Press, 2020), 323–324.

57 Lord Ashcroft, 'How the United Kingdom voted on Thursday . . . and why', Lord Ashcroft Polls, 24 June 2016, accessed 19 March 2023, https://lordashcroftpolls.com/2016/06/how-the-united-kingdom-voted-and-why/.

58 'Lord Ashcroft, How the United Kingdom voted on Thursday . . . and why', Lord Ashcroft Polls, 24 June 2016, accessed 19 March 2023, https://lordashcroftpolls.com/2016/06/how-the-united-kingdom-voted-and-why/.

59 For example, Pippa Crerar and Libby Brooks, 'Rishi Sunak blocks Scotland's gender recognition legislation', *Guardian*, 16 January 2023, accessed 19 March 2023, https://www.theguardian.com/world/2023/jan/16/rishi-sunak-blocks-scotlands-gender-recognition-legislation.

the EU. Indeed, we can show that Remain and Leave supporters themselves have different views – as do Conservative and opposition party supporters. In short, there does appear to be the potential for 'culture war' issues to maintain the electoral division between Remainers and Leavers that was central to how people voted in the 2019 general election.[60]

Yet Curtice and Ratti expressed doubts about how successful electorally an effort to utilise this division might prove to be over time.[61] They noted, for instance, that the balance of public opinion had become more favourable regarding the impact of immigration over the preceding decade.[62] There was also evidence of an accelerating tendency for the public in growing numbers to view leaving the EU as the wrong decision. Regular polling conducted from August 2016 showed, between this point and November 2022, a drop of 14 percent among those thinking Brexit was right, and a rise of 14 percent among those who judged it was wrong. (This shift, however, was partly attributable to generational change, with older people tending towards leave passing on, and younger people of a remain inclination reaching voting age.)[63] However, aside from such general developments, both the Conservatives and Labour continued to these treat these issues as of political significance – perhaps taking the view that they were particularly important in parliamentary constituencies over which they were directly competing. The Conservatives seemed to see cultural issues as a mobilising tool they should continue to deploy;[64] while the Labour response might suggest it regarded itself as vulnerable on the same front, as is discussed later.

As a polarising episode, then, Brexit raised democratic deterioration issues in a number of ways. In itself, it prompted systemic instability, through, for instance, strains placed on the principle of collective Cabinet responsibility, and in other areas discussed below. At the popular level, it instigated the appearance of two self-identifying

---

60 For analysis of this issue see: John Curtice and Victoria Ratti, *Culture Wars: keeping the Brexit divide alive?* (London: National Centre for Social Research, 2022), 25, accessed 19 March 2023, https://www.bsa.natcen.ac.uk/media/39478/bsa39_culture-wars.pdf.

61 For analysis of this issue see: John Curtice and Victoria Ratti, *Culture Wars: keeping the Brexit divide alive?* (London: National Centre for Social Research, 2022), 25, accessed 19 March 2023, https://www.bsa.natcen.ac.uk/media/39478/bsa39_culture-wars.pdf.

62 For analysis of this issue see: John Curtice and Victoria Ratti, *Culture Wars: keeping the Brexit divide alive?* (London: National Centre for Social Research, 2022), 25, accessed 19 March 2023, https://www.bsa.natcen.ac.uk/media/39478/bsa39_culture-wars.pdf.

63 Joris Larik, Juho Harkonen and Simon Hix, 'Will support for Brexit become extinct?', *UK in a changing Europe*, 20 November 2022, accessed 23 May 2023, https://ukandeu.ac.uk/will-support-for-brexit-become-extinct/.

64 For the Conservatives, see e.g.: Adam Forrest, 'Lee Anderson says Tories should fight election on "culture wars and trans debate"', *Independent*, 14 February 2023, accessed 19 March 2023, https://www.independent.co.uk/news/uk/politics/lee-anderson-tories-election-trans-b2282185.html.

groups, leavers and remainers, pitted against each other. It was an issue over which compromise was difficult to achieve. Brexit polarisation saw radical Eurosceptic forces gain in authority within the Conservative Party, particularly with the arrival of Johnson in the leadership. The Conservatives were able, at the General Election of 2019, to exploit this division to their advantage. They did so to Labour's cost, which lost appeal not only to the leave side but also among remainers. Following this experience, and after exit from the EU had taken place, Labour depicted itself as reconciled with Brexit, as part of an effort to enhance its support among alienated social groups. Consequently, the party system failed to provide a full outlet for those who persisted in their dislike of Brexit. The Brexit cleavage linked to a series of further divisions. Perhaps most clearly, the two groups could be characterised by their tendency to hold fundamentally opposing positions on a range of cultural issues: where one side was likely to regard, for instance, trans rights, as positive, the other tended to perceive the same point as negative. This pattern had further democratic consequences because it created a perceived advantage in pursuing policies – for instance, over asylum seekers – that themselves generated democratic concerns. This latter point is discussed further below.

Populist Tendencies

Brexit had populist dimensions. David Cameron, who as premier brought about the 2016 referendum in which he sought a remain outcome, has written of the campaign that '[e]very trait of this age of populism – the prominence of social media, the emergence of fake news, anti-establishment sentiment, growing unease with globalisation, frustration over the level of immigration – appeared to conspire against out cause'.[65] The broad, even disparate, collection of groups and individuals that achieved Brexit between them exhibited aspects of the populist templates discussed above. Such movements tend to target supranational organisations, depicting them as imposing their own agendas and threatening the autonomy of member states. The EU has often figured in campaigns of this sort, in the UK as elsewhere. A UKIP leaflet from the 2016 referendum campaign, for instance, presented the EU as exerting increasing legal and policy control over the UK, and as pursuing the objective of 'a United States of Europe.' It was, the publication held, 'destroying Britain as an independent, democratic nation'.[66] The general

---

65 David Cameron, *For the Record* (London: William Collins, 2019), 658.
66 'Who Governs Britain?', 1–2, accessed 19 March 2023, https://digital.library.lse.ac.uk/objects/lse:nij973dof/read/single#page/1/mode/1up.

idea of a battle against an elite cartel – another populist-type image – featured repeatedly in accounts provided by advocates of Brexit. Alongside the EU, they targeted various other institutions, groups and categories such as experts. Writing about the 2016 referendum campaign, for example, the Conservative MP Mark Francois, a prominent proponent of Brexit, averred that it was:

> hardly a fair fight. Pitched on the side of Remain were the four established political Parties in Britain, the Conservatives, the Labour Party and the Liberal Democrats – whilst in Scotland, the Scottish Nationalist [sic] Party were also very firmly in favour of Remaining in the EU. This position was also supported by almost the entire British Establishment from the Confederation of British Industry (the CBI), through to the Trade Union Congress (the TUC), the BBC, SKY, and a number of national newspapers ranging from *The Times* through to the *Guardian, Independent* and the *Mirror*.[67]

From this perspective, the result of the vote was a victory for 'the people' (however defined) over a coalition of domestic and international elites. As Brendan O'Neill, a journalist connected to the *Spiked* website, remarked days after the referendum:

> Hell hath no fury like an establishment spurned. If you didn't know this already, you certainly know it now, following the British people's vote for Brexit. A whopping 17.4 million of us voted to cut our nation's ties with the European Union, against 16.1 million who voted to stay. And we did so against the advice of most of the political class, media experts, the Brussels bureaucracy, the International Monetary Fund, President Barack Obama, and virtually every other Western leader. Most shockingly of all, against the advice of celebs . . . We defied them all. We rejected every EU-loving overture from the great and good and well-educated. And boy, are they mad.[68]

Another proposition associated with populism was the idea of an elite conspiracy to frustrate the democratic will of the people once expressed. Conforming to this pattern, The Brexit Party's *Contract with the People*, published in advance of the 2019 General Election, complained of '[t]he way the political Establishment has conspired to frustrate democracy over Brexit'.[69] Among the supposed culprits were the BBC, the Civil Service, the judiciary, and Parliament.[70]

---

67 Mark Francois, *Spartan Victory: the inside story of the battle for Brexit by The Rt Hon Mark Francois MP* (privately published, 2021), 153.

68 Brendan O'Neill, 'The Fury of the Elites', *Reason*, 27 June 2016, in Brendan O'Neill, *Anti Woke* (London: Connor Court, 2018), 99.

69 The Brexit Party, *Contract with the People* (London: The Brexit Party, 2019), 4, accessed 19 March 2023, https://www.thebrexitparty.org/wp-content/uploads/2019/11/Contract-With-The-People.pdf.

70 The Brexit Party, *Contract with the People* (London: The Brexit Party, 2019), 1, accessed 19 March 2023, https://www.thebrexitparty.org/wp-content/uploads/2019/11/Contract-With-The-People.pdf.

Populism is known for manifesting itself across different parts of the political spectrum. Similarly, Brexit had advocates of varied political dispositions that might be difficult to reconcile with each other. There were supporters of what was known as 'Lexit', exponents of which saw the EU as an imposer of a free market or 'neoliberal' agenda.[71] The hard left Trade Union and Socialist Coalition campaigned for leave in 2016. Speaking at one of its events, in London on 2 June 2016, the General Secretary of the RMT transport union, Mick Cash,[72] described the EU as having come to pursue: 'neo-liberalism, pro-privatisation, austerity, deregulation. We're pro-European but anti-EU. It's a body for the rich and powerful.'[73] Sometimes Brexit was presented as connected to the attainment of a more equal territorial distribution of wealth and opportunity within the UK. In January 2022, the UK government published *The Benefits of Brexit: How the UK is taking advantage of leaving the EU.* In this paper, which provided an overview of the opportunities supposedly arising from the cessation of EU membership, it claimed that, now outside the organisation: 'we can simplify processes, including for subsidies and procurement, and will have more freedom over how we spend our money to support local and regional growth, helping to level up the country.'[74] It could also appear as facilitating economic deregulation: what is sometimes known as the 'Singapore on Thames' variant of Brexit.[75] As well as confirming that Brexit never amounted to a single, clear prospectus (calling into question what, if anything, those voting for it actually endorsed, collectively or individually), this amorphous quality is supportive of the idea that it had a populist dimension. Brexit could meld with orientations that differed radically on important matters such as the respective roles of markets and of the public sector; and on the need for more

---

71 Joe Guinan, 'Lexit: the EU is a neoliberal project, so let's do something different when we leave it', *New Statesman*, 20 July 2017, accessed 20 March 2023, https://www.newstatesman.com/politics/brexit/2017/07/lexit-eu-neoliberal-project-so-lets-do-something-different-when-we-leave-it.
72 Not to be confused with his successor Mick Lynch, who was of similar disposition.
73 'The Socialist case against the EU: TUSC tour continues', *Socialist Party*, 8 June 2016, accessed 19 March 2023, https://www.socialistparty.org.uk/articles/22984/08-06-2016/the-socialist-case-against-the-eu-tusc-tour-continues/.
74 H M Government, *The Benefits of Brexit: How the UK is taking advantage of leaving the EU* (London: Stationery Office, January 2022), 34–35, accessed 19 March 2023, https://assets.publishing.service.gov.uk/government/uploads/system/uploads/attachment_data/file/1054643/benefits-of-brexit.pdf.
75 See e.g.: Joel Reland, 'Does Liz Truss want to build Singapore on Thames?', *UK in a changing Europe*, 18 October 2022, accessed 19 March 2023, https://ukandeu.ac.uk/does-liz-truss-want-to-build-singapore-on-thames/.

closed or more open borders (though one view – for instance, the desire tightly to control immigration – might predominate).[76]

Among supporters of Brexit, a premium tended to be placed on the concept of rejecting external interference, and restoring a domestic autonomy that had supposedly been lost as a consequence of EU membership: an outlook that might chime with populism. The powerful 'Take Back Control' slogan employed by Vote Leave, the official nominated lead campaign group on the leave side for the 2016 referendum, conveyed this idea.[77] Following exit, during negotiations that ultimately led to the Trade and Cooperation Agreement between the EU and UK, those responsible on the UK side depicted themselves as prioritising UK sovereignty in the face of an alleged reluctance on the part of the EU properly to recognise it. Lord (David) Frost, the UK Chief Negotiator, emphasised this theme frequently, including in a report on discussions he issued on 10 September 2020, in which he stated that: 'a number of challenging areas remain and the divergences on some are still significant.' The UK had, he explained, 'been consistently clear from the start of this process about the basis on which agreement is possible between us . . . open and fair competition, on the basis of high standards, in a way which is appropriate to a modern free trade agreement between sovereign and autonomous equals.'[78] The stressing of the primacy of self-government was also central to UK objections to the Northern Ireland Protocol of the EU Withdrawal Agreement. The UK government soon reached the view that – despite initially presenting it in a positive light – the way this arrangement worked in practice was unsatisfactory.[79] In doing so, it placed emphasis on the idea of the right of the UK to control its internal affairs,[80] and visibly planned action that might in its own account go as far as the breach of international law.[81]

---

76 Chris Bickerton, 'What happens after Brexit is up to us. Why not open our borders to non-EU workers?', *LSE blog*, 25 May 2016, accessed 19 March 2023, https://blogs.lse.ac.uk/brexit/2016/05/25/what-happens-after-brexit-is-up-to-us-why-not-open-our-borders-to-non-eu-workers/.

77 See: 'Why Vote Leave', accessed 19 March 2023, http://www.voteleavetakecontrol.org/why_vote_leave.html.

78 Lord Frost: 'Statement after round 8 of the negotiations', *No 10 media blog*, 10 September 2020, accessed 19 March 2023, https://no10media.blog.gov.uk/2020/09/10/lord-frost-statement-after-round-8-of-the-negotiations/.

79 HM Government, *Northern Ireland Protocol: the way forward*, CP 502 (London: Cabinet Office, July 2021), accessed 20 March 2023, https://assets.publishing.service.gov.uk/government/uploads/system/uploads/attachment_data/file/1008451/CCS207_CCS0721914902-005_Northern_Ireland_Protocol_Web_Accessible_1_.pdf.

80 'Lord Frost: Observations on the present state of the nation', 12 October 2021, accessed 20 March 2023, https://www.gov.uk/government/speeches/lord-frost-speech-observations-on-the-present-state-of-the-nation-12-october-2021.

81 679, Parl.Deb. H.C., 8 September 2020, col. 509.

Analysis of populism identifies it as inclined to favour the use of referendums. The 2016 referendum and its result were essential inciting incidents of the Brexit phenomenon. The idea that the question of membership should be settled by a public vote was crucial to the platform of those who wanted to leave, some of whom were advocates of the use of referendums more generally.[82] Once the 'leave' result was attained, those who believed it should (in whatever form) be implemented held that it was an irresistible instruction from below. In her conference speech of 5 October 2016, Theresa May asserted that it was now necessary to 'stop quibbling, respect what the people told us on the 23rd of June – and take Britain out of the European Union'. Such arguments often included scenarios in which the public were pitted against the elite. Accordingly, May – who, as already noted, had herself been a remainer at the referendum – added that 'it took that typically British quiet resolve for people to go out and vote as they did: to defy the establishment, to ignore the threats, to make their voice heard.'[83] Even many of those who continued after the referendum to favour remaining tended to accept the general premise that the vote had created a firm obligation. Their participation in a campaign for a further referendum could be interpreted as recognition of the force of the previous vote.[84]

However, there was some dissent regarding the idea of an overriding obligation that could only be overturned – if at all – by another referendum. This resistance existed at popular and elite level. In 2019 a petition to Parliament demanding that the process of leaving be halted, without holding another vote, obtained 6,103,056 signatories – perhaps the highest such total in UK history.[85] Exhorting representatives to 'Revoke Article 50 and remain in the EU', it noted that '[t]he government repeatedly claims exiting the EU is "the will of the people". We need to put a stop to this claim by proving the strength of public support now, for remaining in the EU. A People's Vote may not happen – so vote now.' The government response of 26 March 2019 was that it would 'not revoke Article 50. We will honour the result of the 2016 referendum and work with Parliament to deliver a deal that ensures we

---

82 UKIP, *Believe in Britain* (London: UKIP, 2015), 71, 35, accessed 20 March 2023, https://d3n8a8p ro7vhmx.cloudfront.net/ukipdev/pages/1103/attachments/original/1429295050/UKIPManifesto2015.pdf.

83 Theresa May, Conservative conference speech, 5 October 2016, accessed 20 March 2023, https://www.independent.co.uk/news/uk/politics/theresa-may-speech-tory-conference-2016-in-full-transcript-a7346171.html.

84 See: 'What was the People's Vote Campaign?', *UK in a changing Europe*, 24 September 2020, accessed 20 March 2023, https://ukandeu.ac.uk/the-facts/what-is-the-peoples-vote-campaign/.

85 'Article 50 petition to cancel Brexit passes 6m signatures', *Guardian*, 31 March 2019, accessed 30 March 2023, https://www.theguardian.com/politics/2019/mar/31/article-50-petition-to-cancel-brexit-passes-6m-signatures.

leave the European Union.'[86] Another example of support for the idea that implementation of Brexit could cease without another popular vote came from the Liberal Democrats. Their 2019 General Election manifesto, for instance, suggested that the forthcoming contest could provide the necessary legitimacy for such an action. It held that:

> [t]he election of a Liberal Democrat majority government on a clear stop Brexit platform will provide a democratic mandate to stop this mess, revoke Article 50 and stay in the EU. In other circumstances, we will continue to fight for a people's vote with the option to stay in the EU, and in that vote we would passionately campaign to keep the UK in the EU.[87]

How sustainable was the proposition that the referendum was the source of a transcendent obligation? Numerous politicians, of different parties and on opposing sides of the debate, inside and outside Parliament, presented the vote, prior to its being held, as being a means of resolving the question of membership decisively;[88] as did other official communications. For instance, the leaflet issued by the UK government supporting its remain position appeared to present the referendum in this light when stating that '[o]n Thursday, 23rd June there will be a referendum. It's your opportunity to decide if the UK remains in the European Union . . . It's a big decision. One that will affect you, your family and your children for decades to come.'[89] But, such statements notwithstanding, there are various grounds for questioning the supposed irresistible binding authority claimed for the vote. The referendum result certainly lacked legal force.[90] Moreover, claims about the possibility of there being a definite public verdict were undermined by the absence of a single, clear account offered to voters of what Brexit would achieve. The government was reluctant for any such plan to come to the attention of the public, to the point that it avoided devising one. Suzanne Heywood, wife of the then-Cabinet Secretary, the late Jeremy Heywood, writes that

---

86 See https://petition.parliament.uk/archived/petitions/241584.

87 Liberal Democrats, *Stop Brexit, Build a Brighter Future: Manifesto 2019* (London: Liberal Democrats, 2019), 11, accessed 20 March 2023, https://www.libdems.org.uk/policy/2019-liberal-democrat-manifesto.

88 See e.g.: Andrew Blick, *Stretching the Constitution: the Brexit shock in historic perspective* (Oxford: Hart/Bloomsbury, 2019), 56.

89 HM Government, *Why the Government believes that voting to remain in the European Union is the best decision for the UK* (London: HM Government, 2016), 2, accessed 20 March 2023, https://assets.publishing.service.gov.uk/government/uploads/system/uploads/attachment_data/file/515068/why-the-government-believes-that-voting-to-remain-in-the-european-union-is-the-best-decision-for-the-uk.pdf.

90 The European Union Referendum Act 2015, which provided for the holding of the vote, includes no reference to implementation of the result.

Cameron 'told Jeremy that he didn't want the Civil Service to do any work on the consequences of a "no" vote since the government wasn't obliged to work on something that wasn't its policy. In any case, if such preparations were leaked, they would be seized on by the Leave campaign.'[91] On the other side, advocates of leaving, as we have seen, had diverse, sometimes seemingly incompatible, motives and visions of what would follow departure. Furthermore, as is discussed below, various dubious claims were made to voters about its likely benefits (alongside doubtful assertions on the remain side).

Notwithstanding possible doubts about the referendum as a definitive basis for action, the result came to be widely acceded to by senior politicians as creating a fixed obligation, especially after the December 2019 General Election (soon followed by actual exit from the EU in January of the following year). There was a degree of credence attached to the notion that any reversal of leaving was precluded either permanently or for an indeterminate though lengthy period; and that there was an obligation to take the steps necessary to ensuring full realisation of the potential gains (whatever they might be) that Brexit offered. This tendency is confirmed by the previously discussed stances taken by Labour politicians who previously advocated remain and supported another public vote. For example, Starmer told BBC Radio Newcastle in February 2022 that: '[w]e have exited the EU and we are not going back – let me be very clear in the North East about that. There is no case for rejoining. What I want to see now is not just Brexit done in the sense that we're technically out of the EU, I want to make it work. I want to make sure we take advantage of the opportunities and we have a clear plan for Brexit.'[92] Ed Miliband had already said in a broadcast interview in June 2021 that 'Brexit is a big idea. I didn't support it but I think it is a big idea . . . I've got to embrace it because that argument is over.'[93] Miliband wrote separately that 'the Brexit argument' was 'settled by the result of the 2019 election'.[94]

Former remainer politicians, then, came to declare that they were reconciled with and accepting of UK withdrawal from the EU. Yet claims about various elite groups seeking to circumvent Brexit, which were made regularly during the period from 2016, persisted even after many former remainers conceded their

---

91 Suzanne Heywood, *What Does Jeremy Think? Jeremy Heywood and the making of modern Britain* (London: William Collins, 2021), 451.

92 Andrew Blick, *Getting Brexit Undone* (London: Federal Trust, 2022), 7, accessed 19 March 2023, https://fedtrust.co.uk/wp-content/uploads/2022/07/Getting-Brexit-Undone-Andrew-Blick.pdf.

93 Sam Scholli, 'Ed Miliband: "The argument is over, I've got to embrace Brexit"', *LBC*, 3 June 2021, accessed 20 March 2023, https://www.lbc.co.uk/radio/presenters/matt-frei/ed-miliband-the-argument-is-over-ive-got-to-embrace-brexit/.

94 Ed Miliband, *Go Big: How To Fix Our World* (London: The Bodley Head, 2021), 4.

cause. One target was the Civil Service. In July 2022, Suella Braverman – a Conservative MP and serving minister in the UK government, then holding the post of Attorney General – was reported in a press interview stating that 'some of the biggest battles you face as a minister are, in the nicest possible way, with Whitehall and internally with civil servants, as opposed to your political battles in the chamber'. Officials, she claimed, suffered from 'an inability to conceive of the possibility of life outside of the EU'. Braverman went on 'What I have seen time and time again, both in policymaking and in broader decision making, [is] that there is a Remain bias. I'll say it. I have seen resistance to some of the measures that ministers have wanted to bring forward'.[95] In April 2023, Dominic Raab left office as Deputy Prime Minister and Secretary of State for Justice and Lord Chancellor, after having been found by an investigation to have bullied officials. In his resignation letter, he raised objections regarding the behaviour of civil servants, in particular during his time as Foreign Secretary 'in the context of Brexit negotiations over Gibraltar, when a senior diplomat breached the mandate agreed by Cabinet'.[96] Complaints about supposed elite machinations post-departure could take on the character of a conspiracy theory, as when Boris Johnson referred in the House of Commons in July 2022 to a 'deep state' seeking to reverse Brexit.[97]

There was an overall tendency to identify Brexit with democracy. As the Brexit Party put it in 2019: '[o]ur priority is to Leave the European Union and deliver the Brexit that 17.4m voted for in 2016. Acting on the biggest popular mandate in British history is crucial to restore faith in our democracy. What sort of democratic society do we live in, if a few Parliamentarians can defy the expressed will of the people?'[98] But it was a certain version of democracy: a project to reassert this form of government at the level at which it supposedly could truly be realised: that of a single country; the justification for which itself came from what was depicted as an exercise of democracy in its purest, direct, form, that took priority over the representative variety and the institutions and rules associated with it (such as courts and the legal principles they were responsible for upholding). Mick Hume, editor-at-large of the *Spiked* website and a weekly columnist for

---

95 Beckie Smith, 'Attorney General's "Remain bias" jibe "damaging to civil service morale"', *Civil Service World*, 4 July 2022, accessed 20 March 2023, https://www.civilserviceworld.com/professions/article/unsubstantiated-criticism-damaging-civil-service-morale-after-attorney-general-slams-re main-bias.

96 Dominic Raab to Rishi Sunak, 31 April 2023, accessed 6 May 2023, https://www.bbc.co.uk/news/uk-politics-65333734.

97 718, Parl.Deb. H.C., 18 July 2022, col.732.

98 The Brexit Party, *Contract with the People* (London: The Brexit Party, 2019), 1, accessed 19 March 2023 https://www.thebrexitparty.org/wp-content/uploads/2019/11/Contract-With-The-People.pdf.

The Times for a decade, published in 2017 book entitled *Revolting! How the establish-ment are undermining democracy and what they're afraid of.* In it he wrote that:

> We live at a strange moment in the history of democratic politics. Today, perhaps for the first time, every serious politician and thinker in the Western world will declare support for democracy in principle. Yet in practice the authorities are seeking to limit democratic deci-sion-making and separate power from the people.
>
> They invest authority in unelected institutions, from the courts to the European Commis-sion. Elected politicians act as a professional elite, divorced from those they are supposed to represent. And everywhere, the intellectual fashion is to question whether voters are really fit or qualified to make democratic decisions on major issues, such as membership of the European Union or the Presidency of the United States.[99]

This logic could help generate a context in which governments felt able to over-ride constitutional norms in pursuit of objectives directly or indirectly connected to Brexit, and perhaps spilling over into their more general approach. The at-tempted prorogation of Parliament of 2019, for instance, seems to have been moti-vated by a desire on the part of Johnson to lessen the obstacles to making good on his pledge to leave the EU by 31 October of that year.[100] Upon taking office as Prime Minister in September 2022, Liz Truss set about implementing a fiscal agenda that, in her analysis, was an extension of the Brexit project. It was accompanied by irreg-ular actions including the removal of the Permanent Secretary to the Treasury, Tom Scholar; and the resistance of full scrutiny of the new package brought forward.[101] Brexit turbulence helped elevate certain politicians, who might not otherwise have attained such levels of advancement, who exhibited tendencies to violate norms. Most obviously, it helped secure for Johnson, whose qualities are discussed in more detail below, the post of Foreign Secretary and then Prime Minister. Other such ad-vancements to which Brexit seemed to contribute included that of Nadine Dorries, who became Secretary of State for Digital, Culture, Media and Sport under Johnson in September 2021 (leaving with Johnson a year later). While holding this office, Dor-ries behaved in ways that prompted objections. They included a complaint by a se-

---

99 Mick Hume, *Revolting! How the establishment are undermining democracy and what they're afraid of* (London: William Collins, 2017), e-book, locs 56–60.

100 Jen Kirby, 'Boris Johnson just suspended Parliament over Brexit', *Vox*, 28 August 2019, ac-cessed 20 March 2023, https://www.vox.com/2019/8/28/20836579/boris-johnson-brexit-parliament prorogue.

101 For a sympathetic contemporary view of the Truss project, see: Walter Russell Mead, 'Liz Truss's Big Gamble on the U.K. Economy', *Wall Street Journal*, 26 September 2022, accessed 20 March 2023, https://www.wsj.com/articles/liz-trusss-big-gamble-on-the-u-k-economy-british-eu-reform-prime-minister-brexit-protocol-good-friday-agreement-11664220025.

lect committee that she had made claims to it about a Channel 4 documentary in which she participated being faked that it found to be not 'credible'.[102]

The idea that the referendum had yielded an overriding popular directive, while presented as democratic in nature, could – from another point of view – be regarded as democratically restrictive. It encouraged the view, which gained wide currency, that the issue of UK membership of the EU was – for an indeterminate but long period of time, or perhaps permanently – removed from the agenda. Even the point at which a further referendum might be permitted – if ever – was unclear. To seek to reverse Brexit by representative routes was even less acceptable a proposition. The implication seemed to be that, regardless of any evidence regarding possible negative impact from Brexit, or significant changes to the wider context, or changes in patterns of public opinion, a revisiting of the decision was indefinitely excluded. From 2016 onwards the Conservative Party was in principle decisively committed to this tenet. After vacillations, Labour under Starmer came firmly, in its public pronouncements, to share it. Yet to remove such an important matter from the field of political contestation might be seen as severely to limit the possibility of change, particularly in response to public outlooks, that is key to democracy. This tension revealed a way in which populist-type democracy could become difficult to reconcile with its more conventional, representative variants.

To present a project as embodying 'the will of the people'[103] encourages the question: who are the people? There is a populist tendency to apply an exclusive definition, leaving out supposed alien elements. The referendum itself took place on a franchise that did not extend to EU citizens. In this sense, before the vote had even been held, this arrangement implicitly accepted the standpoint of those on the leave side who rejected the concept of supranational citizenship. While members of this excluded group could not vote in UK general elections, they were part of the franchise for local authorities, and for the Scottish independence referendum of 2014 (which also allowed participation by people aged 16 and 17 – another group excluded from the 2016 vote). So it was at least possible to make a case for European citizens being given the vote in 2016.[104] The decision not to en-

---

102 House of Commons Committee on Digital, Culture, Media and Sport, *Rt Hon Nadine Dorries MP*, Fourth Special Report of Session 2022–2023 (London: House of Commons, 20 October 2022), H.C. 801, 3, accessed 20 March 2023, https://committees.parliament.uk/publications/30386/docu ments/175488/default/.

103 For this phrase see e.g.: The Brexit Party, *Contract with the People* (London: The Brexit Party, 2019), 1, accessed 19 March 2023, https://www.thebrexitparty.org/wp-content/uploads/2019/11/Contract-With-The-People.pdf.

104 Andrew Blick, *Stretching the Constitution: the Brexit shock in historic perspective* (Oxford: Hart/Bloomsbury, 2019), 88–89.

franchise this group meant that those who arguably had the greatest interest in the outcome of the referendum were prohibited from taking part in it.

Alongside this exclusion, the subject of people coming to the UK from outside and the claimed domestic consequences played a central part in the pro-Brexit campaign. In the words of Suzanne Heywood, 'Jeremy had always felt that immigration was Remain's weakest point. Successive governments had thought that if they didn't talk about the issue, it would go away. But that had never worked.'[105] Leave campaigners appeared to share the assessment made by the Cabinet Secretary. In 2018, the House of Commons Digital, Culture, Media and Sport Committee remarked how it had been told by Aaron Banks, co-founder of Leave.EU (the campaign group that had backing from Nigel Farage as leader of UKIP), about the approach the group took to the referendum. Banks described social media as a 'firestorm that, just like a bush fire . . . blows over the whole thing. Our skill was creating bush fires and then putting a big fan on and making the fan blow.' Banks went on: 'the immigration issue was the one that set the wild fires burning.'[106] Further evidence of the degree and nature of the prominence attached to this subject during the campaign is provided by a leaflet issued in the lead up to the referendum by Vote Leave.[107] Vote Leave was the officially designated lead pro-leave group, in which a cross party group of parliamentarians, including Johnson, participated. Lionel Barber, then editor of the *Financial Times*, describes being told in March 2016 by Dominic Cummings, the Vote Leave campaign director, 'that the two issues voters care about are immigration and money.'[108] The Vote Leave leaflet reflects this perception, and links the two subjects together. Describing itself as providing 'official information', it has the purported purpose of assisting readers in their deliberations about which way to vote. Stressing the issue of 'fair access to services', the leaflet then claims that 'the official bill for EU membership' amounted to '£350 million every week – the cost of a new hospital.' (It later qualifies this point in a backhanded sense by stating that 'We get less than half of this back') The leaflet then refers to five countries that were 'in the queue to join the EU', listing 'Albania, Macedonia, Montenegro, Serbia, Turkey.' It sug-

105 Suzanne Heywood, *What Does Jeremy Think? Jeremy Heywood and the making of modern Britain* (London: William Collins, 2021), 454.
106 House of Commons Digital, Culture, Media and Sport Committee, *Disinformation and 'fake news': Interim Report*, Fifth Report of Session 2017–2019 (London: House of Commons, 29 July 2019), H.C. 363, 40.
107 See: 'Vote Leave Campaign Committee', accessed 3 April 2023, http://www.voteleavetakecontrol.org/campaign.html.
108 Lionel Barber, *The Powerful and the Damned: life behind the headlines in the financial times* (London: Penguin, 2020), diary entry for 14 March 2016, 313.

gests that '[y]ou have to decide whether this will help Britain, Europe, and fair access to public services'.[109] Behind the limited effort to convey neutrality, the purpose was to frame the issue in terms of a choice between underfunded public services subjected to increasing strain by new arrivals from a rapidly expanding EU (remain); or better funded public services with less demands on their use (leave). Over three pages, the leaflet drives home points about a quarter of a million people coming to the UK from within the EU every year, and how the accession of more states would grant the right to do so to many more.[110]

Claims such as those included in this leaflet were misleading,[111] and were suggestive of a communications effort intended to provoke unfounded concerns about the scale and consequences of people coming from other parts of the EU to the UK. Some observers detected an impact that extended beyond simply influencing (or trying to influence) the way in which people voted. As one author, Emmy van Deurzen, who 'grew up in the Netherlands' and later moved to the UK, subsequently put it: 'the 2016 Brexit referendum unleashed a nasty tide of xenophobia, racism and bigotry in the UK, in a way that I had never imagined possible in the country I had adopted because of its gentleness, openness, fairness and progressiveness'.[112] Seemingly concerned about the tone of the campaign in this regard and events following the result, appearing before the Commons for the first time after the referendum, Cameron expressed regret that:

> [i]n the past few days, we have seen despicable graffiti daubed on a Polish community centre, and verbal abuse hurled against individuals because they are members of ethnic minorities. Let us remember that these people have come here and made a wonderful contribution to our country. We will not stand for hate crime or attacks of this kind. They must be stamped out.[113]

---

109 For a guarded approach to this subject that nonetheless repeatedly seeks to place the image of huge numbers of arrivals in the UK in the mind of the reader, see the Vote Leave campaign leaflet: *The European Union and your family: the facts*, 1, accessed 20 March 2023, https://digital.library.lse. ac.uk/objects/lse:jiq913sox/read/single#page/1/mode/1up.

110 For a guarded approach to this subject that nonetheless repeatedly seeks to place the image of huge numbers of arrivals in the UK in the mind of the reader, see the Vote Leave campaign leaflet: *The European Union and your family: the facts*, 2–3, accessed 20 March 2023, https://digital. library.lse.ac.uk/objects/lse:jiq913sox/read/single#page/1/mode/1up.

111 Anthony Reuben and Peter Barnes, 'Reality Check: Checking the Vote Leave leaflet', *BBC News*, 11 April 2016, accessed 3 April 2023, https://www.bbc.co.uk/news/uk-politics-eu-referendum-36014941.

112 Emmy van Deurzen, 'The Brexit vote unleashed a nasty tide of xenophobia, racism and bigotry in the UK – I no longer felt welcome', *Independent*, 22 June 2021, accessed 3 April 2023, https://www.independent.co.uk/voices/brexit-xenophobia-racism-nazi-uk-b1869927.html.

113 612 Parl.Deb. H.C., 27 June 2016, col. 22.

The subject of people coming to the UK from outside retained political salience after departure had occurred, as we will see. For instance, when seeking to assert the Brexit-embracing stance it developed under the leadership of Keir Starmer, Labour specifically precluded its ever seeking to revive freedom of movement.[114]

Constitutional and Territorial Destabilisation

Brexit arose from an exercise in direct democracy. But implementation fell to a representative system the personnel of which clearly leant more towards remain than the electorate, and would never have embarked on such a course of action without the pressure produced by a referendum result. As of the day before the vote, on 22 June 2016, a clear majority of MPs (more than 70 per cent) had publicly declared in favour of continued membership. Inside the two main parties, re-mainers outnumbered leavers by 185 to 138 in the Conservatives; and by 218 to 10 in Labour. At Cabinet level, there were 24 remainers and 6 leavers.[115] Beyond Par-liament, it can reasonably be assumed that substantial numbers within other insti-tutions, such as the judiciary and Civil Service, were inclined towards remaining, given factors such as their level of educational attainment.

Here we can detect a basis for the theme promoted by Brexit advocates of elite resistance to the will of the people. It must be the case that many within po-sitions of authority in the UK who played various parts within the events that fol-lowed the 2016 vote were privately unconvinced about the desirability of the decision to leave. But the notion that – acting individually or together – they worked determinedly to undermine the Brexit project is difficult to sustain. A chief problem with such theses, aside from the fact that they involve casting col-lective aspersions on the professionalism of a considerable body of public serv-ants – arises from the Brexit programme itself, such as it is. There was never a single clear account of what – beyond leaving itself – it meant. As time has pro-gressed Brexit advocates have begun to differ more clearly in public about the appropriate way forward.[116] Furthermore, as is discussed below, a number of the

---

114 'Keir Starmer: Immigration not quick fix to NHS problems', *BBC News*, 6 November 2022, ac-cessed 15 March 2023, https://www.bbc.co.uk/news/uk-scotland-63526167.

115 'EU vote: Where the cabinet and other MPs stand', *BBC News*, 22 June 2016, accessed 20 March 2023, https://www.bbc.co.uk/news/uk-politics-eu-referendum-35616946.

116 Rowena Mason, 'Flagship post-Brexit Australia trade deal "not actually very good", MPs hear', *Guardian*, 14 November 2022, accessed 20 March 2023, https://www.theguardian.com/politics/2022/nov/14/flagship-post-brexit-australia-trade-deal-not-actually-very-good-george-eustice.

assertions made regarding the potential and reality of Brexit have been ill-founded. How is it possible to be guilty of resisting a project of such nebulosity?

A more fundamental problem for the representative system, then, was that it was being expected to deliver on a prospectus that was never coherently defined; but that was associated with various claims that appeared lacking in plausibility – and as time progressed, were increasingly exposed as such.[117] It was not so much whether politicians and officials assigned with implementing Brexit might on balance have preferred not to be doing so. The fundamental problem lay in the nature of the undertaking, which did not allow for its own satisfactory realisation. As already discussed, there was a wide divergence among advocates of leaving the EU regarding the nature and objectives of such a project. Even if we concentrate on the governing Conservative Party, or perhaps more specifically still on the period from the Johnson ascendancy onwards, significant discrepancies can be detected, over matters such as the approach taken towards the status of Northern Ireland.[118]

The lack of a single agreed rationale for the project, combined with unreliable assertions connected to it, offered a weak basis for coherent action. In its pursuit of Brexit, the UK found itself in contorted postures. For instance, it insisted on particular positions in negotiations with the EU that pointed clearly to heightened trade barriers between the UK and the EU. The Trade and Cooperation Agreement (TCA) that came into force after the post-departure transition period reflected this stance. Yet subsequently, the UK, under the same political leadership that had been in place at the time the TCA was reached, then delayed implementing at the UK end aspects of the measures contained in the TCA, on the grounds that they would make importing more difficult – a prospect that was a direct outcome of the previous insistences of the UK.[119]

The diary of Michael Barnier, the EU chief Brexit negotiator, is revealing in this regard. At the official commencement of Brexit negotiations on 19 June 2017, Barnier records asking his UK counterpart, the Secretary of State for Exiting the European Union, David Davis:

---

117 For such claims made on both sides during the campaign, see: Jon Stone, 'Brexit lies: The demonstrably false claims of the EU referendum campaign', *Independent*, 17 December 2017, accessed 20 March 2023, https://www.independent.co.uk/infact/brexit-second-referendum-false-claims-eu-referendum-campaign-lies-fake-news-a8113381.html.

118 David Gauke, 'Northern Ireland protocol shows how Brexit is still destroying the Tory Party', *New Statesman*, 16 June 2022, accessed 20 March 2023, https://www.newstatesman.com/comment/2022/06/northern-ireland-protocol-shows-how-brexit-is-still-destroying-tory-party.

119 'British government delays import checks for the fourth time since Brexit', *Speciality Food Magazine*, 13 May 2022, accessed 20 March 2023, https://www.specialityfoodmagazine.com/news/british-government-delays-import-checks-for-the-fourth-time-since-brexit.

'Can you confirm that the United Kingdom wants to leave the European Union and also wants to leave the Single Market and the Customs Union?' To this threefold question, his answer is a clear 'yes'. Apart from his concern to hold to the commitments of the referendum, is he fully aware of all the consequences of this triple withdrawal?

Another question is whether he really has a clear mandate to implement this form of 'hard Brexit'. Judging from the political debate in the UK – and even within the government itself, between [Chancellor of the Exchequer] Phillip Hammond and [Foreign Secretary] Boris Johnson – I don't think he does. But today, that is the choice they are making. So we are going to implement it, even if some argue that the door should remain open for the UK to backpedal on its decision.[120]

Regardless of the difficulties inherent in the project itself, UK governments from 2016 onwards presented themselves as keepers of the referendum mandate.[121] The way in which they approached the task they took upon themselves led them into difficult areas of law; and brought them into tension with the UK Parliament and devolved institutions. The first Miller case (Miller I), resolved in the Supreme Court early in 2017, ruled that the triggering of Article 50 of the Treaty on European Union, commencing the process by which a state could leave the EU, could only take place once the government had received specific authorisation to do so through an Act of Parliament. Fundamental matters were involved: the power of the executive; the limitations upon it; the relationship between it and different branches of the constitution; and the status of the referendum result. As the majority judgment put it:

some of the most important issues of law which judges have to decide concern questions relating to the constitutional arrangements of the United Kingdom. These proceedings raise such issues . . . because they concern (i) the extent of ministers' power to effect changes in domestic law through exercise of their prerogative powers at the international level, and (ii) the relationship between the UK government and Parliament on the one hand and the devolved legislatures and administrations of Scotland, Wales and Northern Ireland on the other.[122]

---

120 Michael Barnier, *My Secret Brexit Diary: A Glorious Illusion* (Cambridge: Polity, 2021), diary entry for 21 19 June 2017, 56–57.
121 Andrew Blick, *Taking Back Control? The EU referendum, Parliament and the 'May Doctrine'* (London: Federal Trust for Education and Research, 2016), accessed 21 March 2023, https://fedtrust. co.uk/taking-back-control/.
122 R (on the application of Miller and another) (Respondents) *v.* Secretary of State for Exiting the European Union (Appellant), [2017] UKSC 5, Judgment given on 27 January 2017, 4–5, accessed 21 March 2023, https://www.supremecourt.uk/cases/docs/uksc-2016-0196-judgment.pdf.

The majority found that:

> the referendum of 2016 did not change the law in a way which would allow ministers to withdraw the United Kingdom from the European Union without legislation. But that in no way means that it is devoid of effect. It means that, unless and until acted on by Parliament, its force is political rather than legal. It has already shown itself to be of great political significance.[123]

Miller I saw the judiciary drawn to the centre of the Brexit controversy. As we have seen, in populist-flavoured anti-EU narratives, judges could be painted as members of a manipulative, anti-democratic elite. The Divisional Court was a particular target, finding against the government in November in 2016, which then appealed and lost at the Supreme Court in January 2017. Brenda Hale, a Supreme Court justice at the time of Miller I who would later become its president, describes: 'the vitriol heaped upon the Divisional Court, consisting of the Lord Chief Justice, the Master of the Rolls . . . and Lord Justice Sales, a distinguished Court of Appeal judge . . . their photographs appeared in the *Daily Mail* under the banner headline "Enemies of the People".' Hale held that such a depiction was completely unfounded and that '[b]y asserting the fundamental principles of the constitution which governs us all, [the Divisional Court] were standing up for the people and for Parliament.' Regrettably, Hale went on, 'the Lord Chancellor, Liz Truss, who had sworn an oath to protect the rule of law and the independence of the judiciary, did not instantly leap to their defence.'[124]

With the second Miller case (Miller II), of autumn 2019, the Supreme Court ruled that the attempt the Johnson government had made to prorogue Parliament was unlawful and went as far as to deem that it had not taken place. As previously, circumstances were politically fraught, and the judiciary itself was under scrutiny. One issue the Court had to consider was the extent of its own remit with respect to matters involving Parliament.[125] In a unanimous judgment, it confirmed that, as with the previous Miller case, it was dealing with questions of considerable weight, such as the nature of electoral mandates and the limits on executive power:

123 R (on the application of Miller and another) (Respondents) *v.* Secretary of State for Exiting the European Union (Appellant), [2017] UKSC 5, Judgment given on 27 January 2017, 40, accessed 21 March 2023, https://www.supremecourt.uk/cases/docs/uksc-2016-0196-judgment.pdf.

124 Brenda Hale, *Spider Woman: Lady Hale, a life* (London: Vintage, 2022), 230–231.

125 R (on the application of Miller) (Appellant) *v.* The Prime Minister (Respondent) Cherry and others (Respondents) *v.* Advocate General for Scotland (Appellant) (Scotland), [2019] UKSC 41, Judgment given on 24 September 2019, 22–24, accessed 21 March 2023, https://www.supremecourt.uk/cases/docs/uksc-2019-0192-judgment.pdf.

Let us remind ourselves of the foundations of our constitution. We live in a representative democracy. The House of Commons exists because the people have elected its members. The Government is not directly elected by the people (unlike the position in some other democracies). The Government exists because it has the confidence of the House of Commons. It has no democratic legitimacy other than that. This means that it is accountable to the House of Commons – and indeed to the House of Lords – for its actions, remembering always that the actual task of governing is for the executive and not for Parliament or the courts. The first question, therefore, is whether the Prime Minister's action had the effect of frustrating or preventing the constitutional role of Parliament in holding the Government to account . . . The answer is that of course it did.[126]

This passage shows the Supreme Court asserting representative democratic principles. It does so against the possibility of a more populist version of democracy. In this alternative model which the Supreme Court seeks to resist, the executive assumes for itself a special authority, asserting supremacy over other institutions, even those that – unlike it, in the UK context – are directly elected.

During the year of the Miller II case, 2019, the UK government – which had lost its overall Commons majority at the 2017 General Election – suffered a series of defeats in the House of Commons unprecedented in their scale and frequency. They included the rejection – on three successive occasions – of the withdrawal agreement May had reached with the EU.[127] The executive had become unable to proceed with its core policy programme. There were consequences for the process of withdrawal from the EU, and a danger that the UK would find itself outside the EU without replacement arrangements in place – a 'no deal' Brexit. To avoid this outcome, the UK secured in total three extensions to the two-year negotiating period provided for under Article 50 of the Treaty on European Union, after which removal from the EU would automatically occur. After two of these postponements had occurred, in September 2019, Parliament took steps independently of the government to try to ensure that the UK sought a further extension if necessary to avoid a 'no deal' outcome, which many in Parliament thought would be an economic and political disaster. At the time it acted the exit date was set for 31 October 2019; and the Johnson government was presenting itself as willing to countenance leaving without having reached an agreement, if its negotiating objectives were not agreed to by the EU.

---

126 R (on the application of Miller) (Appellant) *v.* The Prime Minister (Respondent) Cherry and others (Respondents) *v.* Advocate General for Scotland (Appellant) (Scotland), [2019] UKSC 41, Judgment given on 24 September 2019, 20, accessed 21 March 2023, https://www.supremecourt.uk/cases/docs/uksc-2019-0192-judgment.pdf.

127 Jonathan Este, 'Theresa May loses another Brexit vote', *The Conversation*, 29 March 2019, accessed 21 March 2023, https://theconversation.com/theresa-may-loses-another-brexit-vote-heres-why-april-12-is-now-the-key-date-to-watch-114543.

The European Union (Withdrawal) (No. 2) Act 2019 created a legal requirement for the Prime Minister to seek a further prolongation of the Article 50 period. Introduced as a Private Member's Bill by Hilary Benn MP, a Labour former
Cabinet minister, working with colleagues including the Conservative MP, Oliver
Letwin, it was forced through by a parliamentary majority united around the
goal of avoiding 'no deal', determined to impose itself on a minority government.
As Benn put it to the Commons:

> The purpose of the Bill is simple: to ensure that the United Kingdom does not leave the Euro-
> pean Union on 31 October without an agreement. The Bill has wide cross-party support . . .
> The Bill is backed by Members who have very different views on how the matter of Brexit
> should be finally resolved, including Members who until very recently were senior members
> of the Cabinet. People could describe this as a somewhat unlikely alliance, but what unites us
> is a conviction that there is no mandate for no deal, and that the consequences for the econ-
> omy and for our country would be highly damaging.[128]

The legislation and the manner of its coming into being amounted to an extraordinary reversal of ingrained constitutional practices. The established position
was that governments were responsible for the conduct of diplomacy, for which
Parliament held them to account, but did not seek to supplant them in the actual
formation and implementation of policy. Now the legislature was forcing a course
of action upon the executive. As Alan Duncan, no longer a minister, expressed it
in a diary entry for 4 September 2019:

> [t]he first day of the Letwin-Benn government! . . . The Bill passes all its stages, with a ma-
> jority of twenty-eight at third reading. The government is now completely at the mercy of
> the Commons. As if to prove the point, PM Johnson then proposes another motion for an
> early election and is again defeated. He personifies the definition of being trapped in office
> but not in power.[129]

Brexit, once again, had upended constitutional understandings. Both the May and
Johnson governments struggled to control and maintain the meaningful support
of Parliament, and in particular of the House of Commons. As Duncan noted, on
4 September 2019 (after the 'Benn Bill' had secured the approval of the Commons),
Johnson sought to resolve the dispute through triggering a General Election
under the terms of the Fixed-term Parliaments Act 2011. But he did not secure the
level of support from MPs necessary for him to do so. Johnson subsequently by-
passed the 2011 Act through legislation passed at the end of October, leading to

---

128 664 Parl.Deb. H.C., 4 September 2019, col.215.
129 Alan Duncan, *In The Thick Of It: the private diaries of a minister* (London: William Collins,
2021), diary entry for 4 September 2019, 508–509.

the General Election of 12 December. This period of struggle between Parliament and government was brought on by a particular conjunction of factors, including the divisive nature of Brexit, the post-June 2017 Commons arithmetic, and the time limits imposed by the Article 50 process. The public spectacle it created was readily incorporated into populist-type narratives. Those espousing such outlooks could depict Parliament as an elite institution resisting the implementation of the referendum result and therefore opposed to democracy.[130] A particularly curious outcome was that the party of government should attack the institution out of which governments are formed. The Conservative Party 2019 General Election manifesto referred to '[t]he failure of Parliament to deliver Brexit – the way so many MPs have devoted themselves to thwarting the democratic decision of the British people in the 2016 referendum'.[131] In the next chapter we will see how such depictions could form part of more general programmes that extended beyond the specific issue of Brexit.

Lying at the centre of heightened controversy, MPs became a target for threats and sometimes actual attacks. As previously noted, Jo Cox – a pro-remain Labour MP – was murdered by a far-right extremist during the referendum campaign. Lisa Nandy has described how, subsequently:

> [i]n the aftermath of the EU Referendum of 2016, MPs were pulled apart by a tug of war between two opposing groups in the country, half of whom wanted to remain and half of whom wanted to leave . . . Every day I – like so many others – would wake up to find new death threats in my inbox, at my office and at my home. On one occasion a man arrived in my constituency office threatening my staff with a hammer. Terms like 'traitor' and 'betrayal', largely unheard in British political debate, came to dominate our discourse inside Parliament and were then reflected back to us in the streets of Britain. At a rally in Parliament Square . . . I was surrounded by a mob and physically threatened as I tried to get inside to vote.[132]

Another Labour MP, Jess Phillips, describes a conversation held with a man who had 'tried to kick in the door of my office while aggressively shouting insults at my staff and some of my constituents who were inside.'[133] As part of a 'restorative justice'

---

130 The Brexit Party, *Contract with the People* (London: The Brexit Party, 2019), 1, accessed 19 March 2023, https://www.thebrexitparty.org/wp-content/uploads/2019/11/Contract-With-The-People.pdf.

131 Conservative and Unionist Party, *Get Brexit Done: Unleash Britain's Potential* (London: Conservative and Unionist Party, 2019), 47, accessed 11 March 2023, https://assets-global.website-files.com/5da42e2cae7ebd3f8bde353c/5dda924905da587992a064ba_Conservative%202019%20Manifesto.pdf.

132 Lisa Nandy, *All In: How We Build a Country That Works* (Manchester: HarperNorth, 2022), 50–51.

133 Jess Phillips, *Everything You Really Need To Know About Politics: My Life as an MP* (London: Gallery Books, 2021), 190.

exercise, he subsequently told Phillips 'that he had read online that I hated people like him and I had said that people who voted for Brexit were thick. He told me he had read online that I had turned a blind eye to grooming gangs.' He was wrong on numerous counts. Phillips, for instance, had – when speaking to a mass demonstration in favour of a further referendum on Brexit – 'explicitly said "I ask you all never to never treat my constituents who voted for Brexit as if they are stupid."'[134] It should be recorded that MPs of other parties and those who were assertive supporters of Brexit, were also targeted. Among them, on September 2018, anarchists shouted abuse at the Conservative MP Jacob Rees-Mogg and his children, an incident that prompted condemnation from across the political spectrum.[135] Threats to the security of MPs continued. On October 15, 2021, a man acting on ideological and religious motivations murdered the Conservative MP, Sir David Amess.[136]

Brexit involved the whole of the UK leaving the EU (though not, as we will see, on entirely uniform terms), on a basis of a majority of votes cast throughout the country. Matters involving external relations are principally the business of the UK government and Parliament. However, Brexit had significant implications for the internal governance of the UK. They arose partly because the EU had responsibilities in areas, such as agriculture, that came within the remit of devolved authorities in Wales, Scotland and Northern Ireland. Departing from the EU had implications both for the substantive content of policy in these fields, and for the way it would be made and by whom. The devolved authorities therefore took a close interest in the implementation of Brexit. Tensions that developed reflected the important matters that were involved, including concerns about the overriding of constitutional principles, and the inappropriate concentration of authority.[137] Brexit was, therefore, a source of instability in the territorial constitution.

If there is a disagreement between the UK legislature and one or more of its devolved counterparts, then ultimately the Parliament in Westminster has the ability to impose its will, should it choose to do so. However, it exercises its power subject to political realities. It also does so in the context of understandings about what

---

134 Jess Phillips, *Everything You Really Need To Know About Politics: My Life as an MP* (London: Gallery Books, 2021), 191.

135 Pippa Crerar, 'Jacob Rees-Mogg and his family harassed by activists', *Guardian*, 12 September 2018, accessed 29 April 2023, https://www.theguardian.com/politics/2018/sep/12/jacob-rees-mogg-and-his-family-harassed-by-activists.

136 'Man who fatally stabbed MP Sir David Amess sentenced to whole-life tariff', *Crown Prosecution Service*, 13 April 2022, accessed 15 June 2023, https://www.cps.gov.uk/cps/news/update-man-who-fatally-stabbed-mp-sir-david-amess-sentenced-whole-life-tariff.

137 For an overview, see: Alison L. Young, 'What impact has Brexit had upon devolution?', *Constitutional Law Matters*, 5 May 2022, accessed 29 April 2023, https://constitutionallawmatters.org/2022/05/devolution-what-impact-has-brexit-had-on-devolution/.

constitutes proper behaviour, sometimes known as constitutional conventions. A key consideration in the relationship between the UK and devolved legislatures is known (at least in its application to Scotland) as the Sewel Convention. According to this rule, as set out in the *Scotland Act 2016*, 'it is recognised that the Parliament of the United Kingdom will not normally legislate with regard to devolved matters without the consent of the Scottish Parliament.'[138] The same principle applies for Wales (also included in a statute, the *Wales Act 2017*) and Northern Ireland.

This convention is constitutionally significant because it is a means of protecting the autonomy of the devolved institutions from the power of the UK Parliament, normally implementing the legislative agenda of the UK executive. In systems elsewhere in the world, the division of responsibilities between different tiers of governance might be set out in a constitutional text. If such an instrument existed in the UK, limitations of the type addressed by the Sewel Convention might be enforced by an independent umpire in the form of the judiciary. In the UK, an Act of the Westminster Parliament, whether or not it amounts to a unilateral interference in devolved business, cannot be annulled by a court. The Sewel convention and its equivalents in theory allow for dialogue between the UK and devolved institutions aimed at ensuring outcomes that meet the objectives of the former while being acceptable to the latter. It implies a territorial constitution operating on a basis of consensus. If for some reason it ceases to function satisfactorily, then in its place is a system under which the UK executive and Parliament impose themselves.

Brexit saw the convention become subject to significant pressure. On multiple occasions, Acts were passed by the UK Parliament notwithstanding objections from one or more of the territorial legislatures. One such instance came in January 2020. The legislatures of Wales, Scotland and Northern Ireland had all withheld consent to the European Union Withdrawal Agreement Bill, but the UK government nonetheless proceeded to take it through the Westminster Parliament to become an Act. The convention allows for some departure from proceeding only subject to consent by inclusion of the word 'normally'. Brexit, it could be held, was not a regular event. To diverge from the usual practice was therefore arguably within the scope of the rule itself.[139] However, to legislate repeatedly regardless of objections, even when such a course was one theoretically allowed for, carried with it the risk of undermining the credibility of a convention which was important to the operation of the UK constitution. It might also make similar actions in the future, even if not clearly connected to Brexit, easier to contemplate.

---

138 Scotland Act 2016, c.11, § 2.
139 Akash Paun, Jess Sargeant, Elspeth Nicholson and Lucy Rycroft, 'Sewel convention', *Institute for Government*, 16 January 2018, accessed 22 March 2023, https://www.instituteforgovernment. org.uk/explainers/sewel-convention.

The Sewel Convention and its equivalents were a means of maintaining a territorial power balance within the UK political system. Brexit had upset it, implying a tilt towards the UK tier. Departure from the EU provided the potential for such a concentration of responsibility in another way. Prior to leaving, measures intended to maintain regulatory uniformity across the EU had served to ensure that – as part of the EU – the UK had a single market. To avoid the possibility, after exit from the EU, of non-tariff barriers restricting trade within the UK (or Great Britain), UK policymakers were concerned to ensure some degree of regulatory consistency across different territories within the country. But the way in which they pursued this priority could, from the devolved standpoint, appear to be power-hoarding. There was discussion of how decisions about the use of various key powers should be made, and by whom. Measures such as the *United Kingdom Internal Market Act 2020* have been criticised by some as creating the potential for the UK government unilaterally to impose decisions that were supposed to be within the remit of the devolved institutions.[140]

Events connected to Brexit served to demonstrate that EU membership had been a means of binding the UK together, providing a basis for shared rules and principles. It was always likely that replacements for them would lead to claims of UK- or English-level aggrandisement.[141] A more dramatic test for the cohesion of the UK came in Scotland, which had produced a remain majority, and where the prospect and then reality of departure from the EU contributed to a revival in the independence movement. In September 2014, a referendum had been held on this subject. A key argument offered by the (victorious) pro-Union side against Scottish departure from the UK was that, in leaving the UK, Scotland would forfeit EU membership; that swift admission in its own right was not guaranteed; and that this outcome would be damaging. Brexit reversed this logic. The Scottish National Party (SNP) could now claim that being part of the UK entailed Scotland being forced out of the EU, on harsh terms, despite a majority in the 2016 vote in Scotland having opposed such an outcome.[142]

---

140 Andrew Blick (ed.), *The Constitution in Review: Second Report from the United Kingdom Constitution Monitoring Group, For period 1 July – 31 December 2021* (London: Constitution Society, February 2022), 35–36, accessed 1 April 2023, https://consoc.org.uk/wp-content/uploads/2022/02/UK-Constitution-Monitoring-Group-Second-Report.pdf.

141 See: David Torrance, 'EU powers after Brexit: "Power grab" or "power surge"?', *House of Commons Library*, 29 July 2020, accessed 29 April 2023, https://commonslibrary.parliament.uk/eu-powers-after-brexit-power-grab-or-power-surge/.

142 '"Brexit changed everything": revisiting the case for Scottish independence', *Guardian*, 3 July 2021, accessed 29 April 2023, https://www.theguardian.com/books/2021/jul/03/brexit-changed-everything-revisiting-the-case-for-scottish-independence.

Brexit, in any form, would be difficult to reconcile with the requirements of the Northern Ireland peace process, the main expression of which was the Belfast/Good Friday Agreement of 1998. Brexit implied the insertion of a new barrier of some kind between the EU and its former member state, the UK. The UK post-departure might take on the ability to diverge from EU regulations; and the EU would need to protect its single market against the entry of goods that did not conform to its standards. These competing imperatives could create particular sensitivities for Northern Ireland, since the EU and UK had a land border (their only one) on the island of Ireland. The EU would need a way of checking products entering the Republic of Ireland via Northern Ireland. But a central component of the peace in Northern Ireland was the ability of people and goods to pass without hindrance back and forth between Northern Ireland and the Republic. The dilemma was reflected in and heightened by voting patterns in the referendum. Northern Ireland as a whole had produced a remain result, in contrast to the overall UK outcome by which it was forced to abide. On the Catholic/Nationalist side there had been a large remain majority; while the Protestant/Unionist grouping had favoured – though less decisively – leave. Finding a solution that was politically viable as well as likely to be practicable was a vexing task.[143]

The issue helped bring down the May government. Part of the problem was that, following the General Election of June 2017, May became dependent upon the parliamentary support of the Democratic Unionist Party (DUP), a Northern Ireland party that was as firmly supportive of Brexit as it was hostile to any agreement that might – in its perception – create differences between it and the remainder of the UK.[144] Further difficulties arguably arose because of a gap between the expectations promoted by some proponents of Brexit within the Conservative Party and the practical realities involved in the realisation of the project. Barnier records in his diary for 22 October 2018 holding an 'interesting meeting' with the Conservative MPs from the ERG, describing them as 'hard-line Brexiteers' who were 'pushing for a hard Brexit and a permanent exit from the Single Market and the Customs Union.' Barnier describes how:

> [a]t length, and with the help of several experts, they argue for a fully technological solution to implementing border controls in Northern Ireland. Like all Brexiteers and DUP politicians, they are opposed to any division of the British customs territory and therefore to the backstop. I tell them that we will never be able to control the health of cows entering our internal market with drones!

---

143 For a contextual overview, see: Katy Hayward, *What Do We Know and What Should We Do About the Irish Border* (London: Sage, 2021).

144 Dan Stewart, 'This Is the Fateful Decision That Led to Theresa May's Downfall', *Time*, 24 May 2019, accessed 29 April 2023, https://time.com/5595424/theresa-may-brexit-downfall/.

Barnier concluded: '[t]hese characters have their convictions, though.'[145]

Brought to power partly by this issue, Johnson negotiated in 2019 what became the Northern Ireland Protocol of the Withdrawal Agreement on the basis of which the UK left the EU on 31 January 2020. The Protocol avoided a physical border within the island of Ireland by introducing a barrier between Northern Ireland and the other parts of the UK. One exceptional feature of this arrangement was that it made UK authorities responsible for carrying out checks within their own territory on behalf of an external body, the EU. Objections to the Protocol came from within the Unionist community in Northern Ireland, within which there was fierce dislike of the idea that it entailed divergence from Great Britain. Johnson and the UK government were criticised for behaving in ways that added to the controversy. Johnson initially claimed, incorrectly, that there would be no checks on goods moving in either direction between Great Britain and Northern Ireland; and his administration came to object to the Protocol, or at least the way the EU interpreted it. In seeking to enable itself unilaterally to override the Protocol, or perhaps to pressurise the EU into adopting different measures, the UK government produced proposals that seemed to threaten a breach of treaty obligations and the violation of international law. On one occasion, the then-Northern Ireland Secretary, Brandon Lewis, stated to the Commons on 8 September 2020 that provisions intended for inclusion in the Internal Market Bill 'break international law in a very specific and limited way'.[146]

Eventually, under Sunak, the EU and the UK reached an accord on 23 February 2023 in the form of the Windsor Framework. But the ongoing controversy had caused considerable disruption, which continued notwithstanding the EU and UK in theory arriving at an understanding. The DUP, which rejected the Windsor Framework, had declined to participate in the Northern Ireland Executive since May 2022, following an election in which the republican Sinn Fein party had supplanted it as the largest party in the Northern Ireland Assembly. As a consequence, (albeit not for the first time) the power-sharing requirements of the Belfast/Good Friday Agreement could not be fulfilled. Devolution could no longer function properly. For a prolonged period, Northern Ireland was denied its own democratic form of government, with civil servants taking on key responsibilities.[147]

---

145 Michael Barnier, *My Secret Brexit Diary: A Glorious Illusion* (Cambridge: Polity, 2021), diary entry for 22 October 2018, 192–193.

146 Andrew Blick and Peter Hennessy, *The Bonfire of the Decencies: Repairing and Restoring the British Constitution* (London: Haus, 2022), 86–87, 102.

147 See e.g.: Melissa Dando, 'Northern Ireland Still Doesn't Have An Executive, What Happens Now?', *PoliticsHome*, 5 August 2022, accessed 29 April 2023, https://www.politicshome.com/news/article/northern-ireland-still-doesnt-have-an-executive-what-happens-now.

A further area of Brexit-generated uncertainty related to the considerable part, over a period of nearly half a century, that the EU and precursors had played in shaping the legal environment of the UK. It was not possible, even if deemed desirable, fully to replicate the pre-existing legal environment without membership of the organisation underpinning it. Moreover, even were it plausible to do so, to seek to preserve previous arrangements in their entirety and in perpetuity would be difficult to reconcile with the project of leaving of the EU, calling its purpose into doubt. The question was not whether there would be change, but how much; what form precisely it would take; over what timeframe it would occur; and who would determine the processes to be used.

Initially, as discussed above, the UK pursued broad continuity after departure. It did so through the creation of a category of 'Retained EU Law' through the European Union (Withdrawal) Act 2018. Later, the Conservative government – encouraged and pressurised by some of the same forces that had driven the Brexit project up to this point – developed plans designed to trigger substantial divergence from European law. On 22 September 2022, the then-Secretary of State for Business, Energy and Industrial Strategy, Jacob Rees-Mogg MP (himself a leading figure within the ERG), introduced the Retained EU Law (Revocation and Reform) Bill into Parliament. It was drafted to ensure that, by a deadline set for 31 January 2023, all EU-derived law would lapse unless actively retained or altered by ministers. The Bill was criticised on a number of grounds, including the arbitrary time limit it created; the expansive uncertainties it would entail for the legal system; the difficulties involved in identifying all the relevant measures, which were extensive in number; the complications it would bring about for the courts in resolving disputes; and the considerable discretion it would afford to UK ministers, with a minimal role for the UK Parliament in the process.[148] In May 2023 the plans as set out in the Bill were considerably reduced in their scope.[149] But that such a measure was contemplated at all, especially in its initial more extreme form, is notable.

Fundamentally, EU membership had provided the UK with what was in some ways the equivalent of a 'written' or 'codified' constitution. Within the EU, should the domestic legislation of a member state conflict with European law, then the

---

148 Andrew Blick (ed.), *The Constitution in Review: Fourth Report from the United Kingdom Constitution Monitoring Group, For period 1 August – 31 December 2022* (London: Constitution Society, March 2023), 42–43, accessed 1 April 2023, https://consoc.org.uk/wp-content/uploads/2023/03/Constitution-in-Review-4-1.pdf.

149 'Schedule of retained EU law', *Gov.uk*, 17 May 2023, accessed 15 June 2023, https://www.gov.uk/government/publications/schedule-of-retained-eu-law#:~:text=On%2010%20May%20an%20amendment,at%20the%20end%20of%202023.

former must give way to the latter. In the UK, this principle meant that even an Act of Parliament could be disapplied by a court, in as far as it was incompatible with European law, regardless of whether the Act of Parliament had been passed before or after the European measure came into force. This proposition represented a challenge to the long-established constitutional principle of parliamentary 'sovereignty', according to which no source of law (even traditionally an earlier Act of Parliament) took priority over an Act of Parliament, and no body could rule it invalid. The debate was a complex one. For instance, European law was incorporated into the UK system by an Act of Parliament (the European Communities Act 1972), and from the domestic perspective, therefore, Parliament might be seen to have retained its position of supremacy. Indeed, it could (and ultimately did) repeal the 1972 Act. Yet, at the very least, the workings of European law had required a considerable refinement of legal understandings. Brexit saw this newer system come to an end for the UK.[150] But what would take its place?

It was UK-level ministers who were best placed to determine what the answer would be. It is not surprising, then, that the emergent post-EU legal order of the UK suggested an augmentation of the UK executive. This tendency manifested itself partly in relation to the UK Parliament, with the prospect of ministers wielding strengthened delegated law-making capacity, subject to circumscribed potential for oversight from the legislature. It also potentially entailed a relative tilt towards the UK and away from the devolved tier, as discussed above. Tendencies connected to the legal impact of Brexit, then, raise various issues of concern to this work: disruption and destabilisation of established arrangements; an accretion of authority to the UK executive; and the removal of constitutional limitations and protections.

Communication

Both the substantive content of political messages and the means by which they are communicated are subjects of interest in the literature assessed above. The Brexit phenomenon is connected to much significant material in this regard. Campaign claims are subject only to limited legal limitations, and the Electoral Commission plays no part in their formal regulation. In advance of the vote, both sides promulgated misleading assertions. On 14 June 2016 a letter appeared in the press, signed by more than 200 academics, holding that '[a] referendum result is

---

150 For a discussion of these issues, see: Vernon Bogdanor, *Beyond Brexit: towards a British constitution* (London: I. B. Tauris, 2019), 257–278.

democratically legitimate only if voters can make an informed decision.' It went on to caution that 'the level of misinformation in the current campaign is so great that democratic legitimacy is called into question.' The authors held that '[b]oth sides are making misleading claims', with 'official communications . . . dropping through letter boxes – at taxpayers' expense – in recent days.' On the one hand, in its leaflet, Vote Leave had led 'with the claim that EU membership costs the UK £350 million a week – repeatedly exposed by independent authorities as a blatant falsehood.' On the other hand, the lead remain group, Britain Stronger in Europe, had produced a 'leaflet [that began] by saying that "over three million UK jobs are linked to our exports to the EU". Though this is in line with independent analyses, not all these jobs would go in the event of Brexit.' The letter emphasised that: '[p]ropagating falsehoods, with support from the public purse, distorts the public communication upon which democracy depends.'[151]

Concerns of this nature also existed at the highest level within the Civil Service. Suzanne Heywood recalls that, shortly before referendum period began, Heywood 'heard that the Treasury was about to publish [a] document, this time on the immediate economic impact of leaving the EU. When he tracked down a copy of this, he was startled by its conclusion – a vote to leave would push the country into recession and destroy between half a million and 800,000 jobs. This felt extreme, particularly since this impact was based only on a decision to leave, not by the exit itself.' He 'rang the Treasury to discuss their analysis' but 'was told it was too late to make any changes.' Heywood was 'incredibly frustrated'. While sharing the Treasury view 'that leaving the EU would harm Britain's economy and that people should understand this . . . if the government put out material that was seen as being too dramatic, it risked making the Civil Service look political and made it easy for pro-Leave campaigners to dismiss it – as they did after this second paper was published, labelling it "Project Fear".'[152] During the campaign the very concept of neutral expertise became controversial.[153]

There is also evidence of willingness at high level in the leave campaign to prioritise strategic gain over precise accuracy of claims. Leadsom records being asked to join the Vote Leave board, and agreeing to do so 'on the proviso that the campaign dropped its high-profile campaign slogan that Britain "sends £350 million a

151 Isobel White and Neil Johnston, *Referendum campaign literature* (London: House of Commons Library, 2016), 9–10, accessed 2 April 2023 https://researchbriefings.files.parliament.uk/documents/CBP-7678/CBP-7678.pdf.

152 Suzanne Heywood, *What Does Jeremy Think? Jeremy Heywood and the making of modern Britain* (London: William Collins, 2021), 452–453.

153 Henry Mance, 'Britain has had enough of experts, says Gove', *Financial Times*, 3 June 2016, accessed 10 May 2023, https://www.ft.com/content/3be49734-29cb-11e6-83e4-abc22d5d108c.

week" to the EU, which I felt was misleading.' Leadsom 'raised the issue with Dominic Cummings'. She recounts that Cummings told her: '[t]hat's not my problem. I'm here to win the campaign and we're not changing the wording.' Cummings, Leadsom felt, appeared to have 'no interest in that technical detail.' She declined to join the board.[154] Lionel Barber describes in his diary a visit to his *Financial Times* office by the Vote Leave senior team on 14 March 2016. On the subject of the '£350m a week' claim, Barber records that:

> [w]e all know this figure is misleading but Cummings says that as long as Leave and Remain are arguing how much it costs to be a member of the EU, Leave is winning. The precise figure does not matter. If the debate turns to trade and the economy, then Remain is winning. He refuses to discuss what comes after the UK leaves the EU . . . Cummings says he has no idea what damage such a shock might do. The figure is unknowable and the ordinary person in the street would have little understanding anyway.[155]

In his memoir, in addition to complaining about the £350 million claim, Cameron objected to references to possible Turkish membership of the EU, stating that '[T]here was no prospect of Turkey joining the EU for decades, if ever. It had merely applied, and was in talks . . . We were no longer in the realms of bending or stretching the truth, but ditching it altogether. Leave were lying.'[156]

Aside from the content of messages, there were other kinds of complaints about the use of communications in the referendum campaign. That the government – having adopted a particular line on Brexit – promoted its support for remain to the population in addition to the work of campaign groups, was controversial. A total of 221,866 people signed a petition which included the complaint that: 'Prime Minister David Cameron plans to spend British taxpayers' money on a pro-EU document to be sent to every household in the United Kingdom in the run up to the EU referendum. We believe voters deserve a fair referendum – without taxpayer-funded biased interceptions by the Government.'[157]

The literature review noted the concerns about the role of digital communication in democratic processes. Scrutiny of this type has focused on the 2016 referen-

---

154 Andrea Leadsom, *Snakes and Ladders: navigating the ups and downs of politics* (London: Biteback, 2022), 68–69.

155 Lionel Barber, *The Powerful and the Damned: life behind the headlines in the financial times* (London: Penguin, 2020), diary entry for 14 March 2016, 313.

156 David Cameron, *For the Record* (London: William Collins, 2019), 668–669.

157 UK Government and Parliament, Petition, 'Stop Cameron spending British taxpayer's money on Pro-EU Referendum leaflets', debate 9 May 2016, accessed 2 April 2023, https://petition.parliament.uk/archived/petitions/116762.

dum. One aspect of this form of campaigning was that it enabled 'microtargeting':[158] that is, the focusing via social media (described by Banks as a 'firestorm'[159]) of messages dealing with specific topics, directed to individuals considered susceptible to influence in respect of the issues they addressed. This practice was controversial partly because it implied that different voters could make the same decision on a basis of divergent, even contradictory, claims (in addition to those claims possibly being simply false or misleading). The possibility of a clear mandate for a specific objective was thereby called into question.[160] Online campaigning figured in the activities of Vote Leave which subsequently led the Electoral Commission to decide that it had violated the law in relation to referendum spending.[161] There was also concerned interest in the use made of personal data for online campaigning on the leave side.[162] The possible employment of digital communications during the 2016 campaign by hostile external forces is discussed below. After the referendum, public concerns developed that digital communications were a factor in various irregularities in the conduct of politics. They fed into wider discussion, in the UK and internationally, about the democratic impact of the Internet, and the challenges it posed. Investigations on this subject by the House of Commons Digital, Culture Media and Sport Committee attracted widespread domestic and international attention, and mo-

---

158 Peter Pomerantsev, *This Is Not Propaganda: Adventures in the War Against Reality* (London: Faber and Faber, 2019), loc. 2930.

159 House of Commons Digital, Culture, Media and Sport Committee, *Disinformation and 'fake news': Interim Report*, Fifth Report of Session 2017–2019 (London: House of Commons, 29 July 2019), H.C. 363, 40.

160 Andrew Blick, *Stretching the Constitution: the Brexit shock in historic perspective* (Oxford: Hart/Bloomsbury, 2019), 32. For selection of microtargeted Facebook adverts from the 2016 referendum campaign, see: Patrick Worrall, 'Vote Leave's "dark" Brexit ads', *Channel Four FactCheck*, 27 July 2018, accessed 2 April 2023, https://www.channel4.com/news/factcheck/factcheck-vote-leaves-dark-brexit-ads. For discussion of microtargeting, see also: The Electoral Commission, *Digital campaigning: Increasing transparency for voters* (London: The Electoral Commission, 2018), 10–11, accessed 3 April 2023, https://www.electoralcommission.org.uk/sites/default/files/pdf_file/Digital-campaigning-improving-transparency-for-voters.pdf.

161 See: The Electoral Commission, 'Investigation: Vote Leave Ltd, Mr Darren Grimes, BeLeave, and Veterans for Britain', various dates, accessed 2 April 2023, https://www.electoralcommission.org.uk/who-we-are-and-what-we-do/our-enforcement-work/investigations/investigation-vote-leave-ltd-mr-darren-grimes-beleave-and-veterans-britain; and The Electoral Commission, 'Statement on the Metropolitan police's investigation into Vote Leave and Darren Grimes', 8 May 2020, accessed 2 April 2023, https://www.electoralcommission.org.uk/media-centre/statement-metropolitan-polices-investigation-vote-leave-and-darren-grimes.

162 House of Commons Digital, Culture, Media and Sport Committee, *Disinformation and 'fake news': Final Report*, Eighth Report of Session 2017–2019 (London: House of Commons, London, 18 February 2019), H.C. 1791, 43–44, accessed 15 March 2023, https://publications.parliament.uk/pa/cm201719/cmselect/cmcumeds/1791/1791.pdf.

tivated proposed legislative changes to bring about more satisfactory online regulation.[163]

Concerns about Brexit-related deceit persisted after the vote. Inevitably, given that the leave side won, attention focused more on claims made in support of departure than those advanced in favour of continued membership. The £350 million claim continued to surface. In September 2017, David Norgrove, Chair of the UK Statistics Authority, wrote publicly to Johnson, at the time Foreign Secretary, stating that:

> I am surprised and disappointed that you have chosen to repeat the figure of £350 million per week, in connection with the amount that might be available for extra public spending when we leave the European Union.
>
> This confuses gross and net contributions. It also assumes that payments currently made to the UK by the EU, including for example for the support of agriculture and scientific research, will not be paid by the UK government when we leave.
>
> It is a clear misuse of official statistics.[164]

Alongside the repetition of earlier dubious assertions, new ones were generated: for example, that – as the Secretary of State for Health and Social Care, Matt Hancock, put it in December 2020 – it had been possible to approve the Pfizer Covid vaccine more swiftly '[b]ecause of Brexit'.[165] Various other Conservative politicians made statements to similar effect. Informed assessments showed that they did not properly reflect reality.[166] In January 2022, the government published a document entitled *The Benefits of Brexit: How the UK is taking advantage of leaving the EU*. In a part of the text entitled 'Our Achievements so far', there is reference to: '£57 billion more for our NHS. We are spending more money on our NHS. By the 2024–2025 financial year our yearly expenditure on our NHS is projected to be £57 billion higher in cash terms than we spent in 2016–2017, or over £1 billion more per week.'[167] It is notable that the text stops short of asserting that Brexit was a direct

---

163 For a consideration of these issues, see: Andrew Blick, *Electrified Democracy: the Internet and the United Kingdom Parliament in history* (Cambridge: Cambridge University Press, 2021).

164 Sir David Norgrove, Chair of the UK Statistics Authority, to Rt Hon Boris Johnson MP, Foreign Secretary, 17 September 2017, accessed 2 April 2023, https://uksa.statisticsauthority.gov.uk/wp-content/uploads/2017/09/Letter-from-Sir-David-Norgrove-to-Foreign-Secretary.pdf.

165 Pippa Allen-Kinross, 'Vaccine approval isn't quicker because of Brexit', *Full Fact*, 4 December 2020, accessed 2 April 2023, https://fullfact.org/health/coronavirus-vaccine-brexit/.

166 Pippa Allen-Kinross, 'Vaccine approval isn't quicker because of Brexit', *Full Fact*, 4 December 2020, accessed 2 April 2023, https://fullfact.org/health/coronavirus-vaccine-brexit/.

167 HM Government, *The Benefits of Brexit: How the UK is taking advantage of leaving the EU* (London: HM Government, January 2022), 8, accessed 2 April 2023 https://assets.publishing.ser

cause or enabler in full of such a funding increase.[168] But the inclusion of this content in such a document suggests the intention of creating this impression. Scrutiny of other aspects of *The Benefits of Brexit* seemed to reveal that a degree of nuance was lacking from the publication.[169] In November 2022, the Secretary of State for Levelling Up, Michael Gove, stated in a tweet that 'We've secured new free trade deals with over 70 countries since 2016. That's over £800 billion worth of new global trade.' Yet the £800 billion figure was in fact roughly the value of all trade with those parties (among them the EU itself) with which the UK had agreements; many of which largely replicated deals already in place before departure from the EU. To claim them all as new was questionable; and to attribute all trade to the deals themselves would also be misleading.[170]

The External Dimension

At its core, Brexit involved the self-removal of the UK from a supranational organisation in which, in different incarnations, it had been a participant since 1973. The overall process was about more than external relations. But nonetheless there were extensive ramifications for the relationship between the UK and the outside world, which are pertinent to the issues already identified for the purposes of this work. Leaving the EU meant rejecting continued participation in a project of deepening cooperation between states that had historically tended towards fierce rivalry and often military conflict. It is important to be realistic about how far the EU and its individual components adhere to its professed principles in practice, and we should never exclude the pursuit of narrower self-interest by particular Member States.[171] But it remains noteworthy that the EU commits itself to the goals of promoting norms, within and beyond the territories

---

vice.gov.uk/government/uploads/system/uploads/attachment_data/file/1054643/benefits-of-brexit. pdf.

168 'Boosterism blinds us to the possible benefits of Brexit', *Nuffield Trust*, 3 March 2022, accessed 2 April 2023, https://www.nuffieldtrust.org.uk/news-item/boosterism-blinds-us-to-the-possible-benefits-of-brexit.

169 Joe Marshall and Dan Goss, 'What "benefits of Brexit" does the government claim?', *Institute for Government*, 1 April 2022, accessed 2 April 2023, https://www.instituteforgovernment.org.uk/article/explainer/what-benefits-brexit-does-government-claim.

170 Hannah Smith, '"New" UK trade deals don't account for "over £800 billion worth of new global trade"', *Full Fact*, 3 November 2022, accessed 14 January 2023, https://fullfact.org/economy/post-Brexit-trade-deals-Gove/#actions.

171 For an historic perspective on this point, see: Alan Milward, *The European Rescue of the Nation State* (Abingdon: Routledge, 1999).

it covered, such as democracy, the rule of law – international and domestic – and human rights.[172]

Eurosceptic political groupings across Europe are often inclined to be hostile towards established liberal democratic values as well as to the EU.[173] While it would be incorrect to claim that support for Brexit is synonymous with authoritarian leanings, there could be an association between the two as outlooks and as political movements. In 2009, in an attempt to affirm his Eurosceptic credentials within his party, the then Leader of the Opposition David Cameron withdrew the Conservatives in the European Parliament from the moderate right European People's Party, the members of which included the German Christian Democrats. Establishing a new grouping brought the Conservatives into cooperation with such entities as the Polish Law and Justice Party, which came to figure prominently in subsequent accounts of democratic disruption, discussed in the literature review above.[174] The next chapter will identify connections between the Brexit experience and further democratic difficulties in the UK. For instance, it will discuss the role of politicians such as Johnson whose careers, words and actions were associated with both; and successive governments from 2016, shaped or brought into being by Brexit, which pursued controversial approaches in other areas.

Some Brexit supporters seemed to hope and expect that UK exit would presage further such departures by other Member States, and perhaps a collapse of the EU itself.[175] Others presented scenarios in which the UK could form a close relationship of some kind with a continuing EU, from the outside – a position advanced by Johnson.[176] But, unsurprisingly, support for leaving the EU often in-

---

172 For a classic statement of the EU as a 'normative power', see: Ian Manners, 'Normative power Europe: a contradiction in terms?', *Journal of Common Market Studies* 40, no. 2 (2002), 235–258.

173 For extremism and its connection to Euroscepticism, see e.g.: Harun Karcic, 'Democratic backsliding in Europe: Who is to blame?', *RUSI*, 11 May 2021, accessed 3 April 2023, https://rusi. org/explore-our-research/publications/commentary/democratic-backsliding-europe-who-blame; Catherine E. De Vries and Erica E. Edwards, 'Taking Europe to its extremes: Extremist parties and public Euroscepticism', *Party Politics* 15, no. 1 (2009), 5–28.

174 Kate Fall, *The Gatekeeper* (London: HQ, 2020), 247.

175 Mat Dathan, 'Now he's going for the domino effect: Nigel Farage pledges to use his time to help other EU nations win their own independence after quitting as UKIP leader', *Mail Online*, 6 July 2016, accessed 2 April 2023, https://www.dailymail.co.uk/news/article-3676746/Now-s-going-domino-effect-Nigel-Farage-pledges-use-time-help-EU-nations-win-independence-quitting-Ukip-leader.html.

176 Boris Johnson, 'Uniting for a Great Brexit: Foreign Secretary's speech', *gov.uk*, 14 February 2018, accessed 2 April 2023, https://www.gov.uk/government/speeches/foreign-secretary-speech-uniting-for-a-great-brexit.

volved hostile depictions of the European project. Johnson, for example, despite sometimes striking a friendly tone, could also make harsh allegations against the EU. For instance, in May 2016, he said in a campaign speech that 'if you want an example of EU foreign policy making on the hoof – in the EU's pretension to run EU defence policy that has caused real trouble – then look at what has happened in Ukraine.'[177] The implication that fault for the Russian invasion of 2014 lay with the EU attracted – and continues to attract – criticism. At the time, in a tweet, Carl Bildt, the former Swedish Prime Minister, referred to Johnson as an '[a]pologist for Putin'.[178] Hostility towards the EU could extend to denial of its intrinsic legitimacy as a project. In July 2019, newly-elected Brexit Party Members of the European Parliament seemed to convey this outlook when they turned their backs in the Chamber as the EU anthem was played.[179] Antagonistic postures towards the EU continued after departure had taken place, including at government level over matters such as the Northern Ireland Protocol.[180] In an article written in May 2023 for the heavily-Eurosceptic *Daily Express*, Starmer, describing his intention of making a success of Brexit, claimed that, under the post-membership arrangements reached by the Conservatives 'our European friends and competitors aren't just eating our lunch – they're nicking our dinner money as well.'[181]

Even when it did not entail overt hostility, Brexit could be perceived as a challenge to the viability of the EU. Some supporters of Brexit had seemed to anticipate that they could negotiate deals separately with individual Member States.[182] Had that assumption proved correct, there would have been serious consequences for the integrity of the bloc. As it transpired, EU solidarity held, and the UK had to negotiate solely with the EU as a single entity. Moreover, the concessions the UK appeared to seek were hard for the EU to entertain. Visiting Brussels in October 2016, Lionel Barber noted in his diary being told by an 'EU veteran' that: '[p]eople in London do not

---

177 'Johnson accused of being Putin apologist', *Sky News*, 9 May 2016, accessed 2 April 2023, https://news.sky.com/story/johnson-accused-of-being-putin-apologist-10275259.
178 'Johnson accused of being Putin apologist', *Sky News*, 9 May 2016, accessed 2 April 2023, https://news.sky.com/story/johnson-accused-of-being-putin-apologist-10275259.
179 Jennifer Rankin, 'Brexit party MEPs turn backs on Ode to Joy at European parliament', *Guardian*, 2 July 2019, accessed 3 April 2023, https://www.theguardian.com/politics/2019/jul/02/brexit-party-meps-turn-their-backs-european-anthem-ode-to-joy.
180 'Brexit: Lord Frost accuses EU of "ill will" over UK exit', *BBC News*, 8 March 2021, accessed 2 April 2023, https://www.bbc.co.uk/news/uk-politics-56311605.
181 For commentary, see: Xander Elliards, *The National*, 'Keir Starmer claims Europe is "nicking UK's dinner money" in Express', 31 May 2023, accessed 15 June 2023, https://www.thenational.scot/news/23558096.keir-starmer-claims-europe-nicking-uks-dinner-money-express/.
182 Andrew Blick, *Stretching the Constitution: the Brexit shock in historic perspective* (Oxford: Hart/Bloomsbury, 2019), 291.

understand how Brexit is viewed in Brussels as an existential threat to the EU. A special deal for the Brits is off the table because it would incite copycat Brexits.'[183] There seems to have been a perception that the UK was simply being unreasonable in its demands; and that it had to be rebutted. On 15 March 2018, Barnier wrote in his diary that 'we must give a clear response to the British attempts at cherry-picking. A few days ago, Luxembourg's Prime Minister Xavier Bertel summed up the situation as follows: "Before, they were in and had many opt-outs; now they want to be out with many opt-ins."'[184]

Brexit saw an agenda previously more associated with political extremism[185] become a mainstream phenomenon in the UK, which came to be embraced, or at least accepted, by both of its two most prominent parties, the Conservatives and Labour. In practice, observation of the UK experience post-2016 seemingly led politicians in states that were still members of the EU who had previously been more critical of it to soften their stances on the matter.[186] In this sense, Brexit produced an outcome which was the opposite to that which some expected and perhaps hoped it would. Rather than undermining the EU, it had perhaps lessened the internal threats to it. Nonetheless, in some respects Brexit brought the UK into alignment with forces that were less than supportive of democracy and stability in the region and indeed the wider world. The stance the UK government took over the Northern Ireland Protocol might be regarded as a challenge to the concept of international rule of law generally. As far as individual politicians were concerned, Donald Trump specifically identified with Brexit and depicted the referendum and his ascendancy as part of the same pattern[187] (as did others, such as Nigel Farage).[188]

---

183 Lionel Barber, *The Powerful and the Damned: life behind the headlines in the financial times* (London: Penguin, 2020), diary entry for 10 October 2016, 328.

184 Michael Barnier, *My Secret Brexit Diary: A Glorious Illusion* (Cambridge: Polity, 2021), diary entry for 15 March 2018, 128.

185 Catherine E. De Vries and Erica E. Edwards, 'Taking Europe to its extremes: Extremist parties and public Euroscepticism', *Party Politics* 15, no. 1 (2009), 5–28.

186 John Henley, 'Support for Eurosceptic parties doubles in two decades across EU', *Guardian*, 2 March 2020, accessed 2 April 2023, https://www.theguardian.com/world/2020/mar/02/support-for-eurosceptic-parties-doubles-two-decades-across-eu.

187 Ewen MacAskill, 'Donald Trump arrives in UK and hails Brexit vote as "great victory"', *Guardian*, 24 June 2016, accessed 2 April 2023: https://www.theguardian.com/us-news/2016/jun/24/donald-trump-hails-eu-referendum-result-as-he-arrives-in-uk.

188 Graeme Massie, 'Nigel Farage praises Trump at rally after being introduced as one of Europe's "most powerful men"', *Independent*, 29 October 2020, accessed 2 April 2023, https://www.independent.co.uk/news/world/americas/us-election-2020/trump-farage-rally-arizona-election-brexit-b1405731.html.

Another leader to whom diminution and disruption of the EU was surely welcome was Vladimir Putin. It is reasonable to conclude that the 2016 'leave' result and its aftermath were considered beneficial by Russian policy-makers.[189] They created a challenge for European unity (though one which the EU seemed to withstand[190]); and were a source of strains between the UK and states that were its longstanding allies. During her successful Conservative leadership election campaign, in August 2022, Liz Truss made a comment that exemplified the existence of such tensions and their roots in the political dynamics of the Brexit-era Conservative Party. When asked whether the French President Emmanuel Macron was a 'friend or foe', Truss replied that the 'jury' was 'still out'.[191]

We cannot exclude the possibility that the referendum campaign was a target for Russian interference (though, if real, whether it made a substantial difference to the outcome is more difficult to establish). In 2019, for example, the House of Commons Digital, Culture, Media and Sport Committee described how 'Kremlin-aligned media published significant numbers of unique articles about the EU referendum.' The Committee referred to analysis of 'the most shared of the articles' that had 'identified 261 with a clear anti-EU bias to the reporting . . . The articles that went most viral had the heaviest anti- EU bias.' The Committee went on:

> The social reach of these anti-EU articles published by the Kremlin-owned channels was 134 million potential impressions, in comparison with a total reach of just 33 million and 11 million potential impressions for all content shared from the Vote Leave website and Leave.EU website respectively. The value for a comparable paid social media campaign would be between £1.4 and 4.14 million.[192]

While willing to recognise that Russia posed a threat in general, the government – which had come into being in its then-present incarnation because of the referendum result, and which was committed to implementing the leave outcome – was resistant to acknowledging that there might have been interference in relation to

---

189 Andrew Roth, 'Putin tells May to "fulfil will of people" on Brexit', *Guardian*, 20 December 2018, accessed 2 April 2023, https://www.theguardian.com/politics/2018/dec/20/vladimir-putin-theresa-may-brexit-fulfil-will-of-the-people.

190 Roch Dunin-Wasowicz, 'Knowing Me, Not Knowing EU: how misunderstanding the EU means misunderstanding the UK (and makes it harder to leave)', *LSE blog*, 8 October 2019, accessed 2 April 2023, https://blogs.lse.ac.uk/brexit/2019/10/08/knowing-me-not-knowing-eu-how-misunderstanding-the-eu-means-misunderstanding-the-uk-and-makes-it-harder-to-leave/.

191 'Tory leadership: Truss criticised for Macron "jury is out" remark', *BBC News*, 26 August 2022, accessed 2 April 2023, https://www.bbc.co.uk/news/uk-politics-62682448.

192 House of Commons Digital, Culture, Media and Sport Committee, *Disinformation and 'fake news': Final Report*, Eighth Report of Session 2017–2019 (London: House of Commons, 18 February 2019), H.C. 1791, 70.

the 2016 public vote on EU membership. As the Committee put it: 'The Government has been very ready to accept the evidence of Russian activity in the Skripal [poisoning] case, an acceptance justified by the evidence. However, it is reluctant to accept evidence of interference in the 2016 Referendum in the UK.'[193] A report by the Intelligence and Security Committee of Parliament published – after a long delay seemingly contrived by the government – in July 2020 stated that: '[t]here have been widespread public allegations that Russia sought to influence the 2016 referendum on the UK's membership of the EU. The impact of any such attempts would be difficult – if not impossible – to assess, and we have not sought to do so.' Nonetheless, the committee held, 'it is important to establish whether a hostile state took deliberate action with the aim of influencing a UK democratic process, irrespective of whether it was successful or not.' It complained of 'the extreme caution amongst the intelligence and security Agencies at the thought that they might have any role in relation to the UK's democratic processes, and particularly one as contentious as the EU referendum.' The committee held 'that this attitude is illogical; this is about the protection of the process and mechanism from hostile state interference, which should fall to our intelligence and security Agencies.'[194]

Johnson (and his successors) made much of having supplied support for Ukraine against the Russian invasion. The UK did provide genuine assistance. But, as we have seen, his desire to criticise the EU had in 2016 led Johnson towards a stance that could be viewed as that of a Putin apologist. He had prior form for making dilemmas relating to Russia a basis for criticism of the EU. In June 2000 (the month after Putin first became President) Johnson published an article in the *Spectator*, of which he was editor, holding that the EU was excessively exclusive in its attitude regarding appropriate future member states. In reenforcing this point, he held that the case for Russian admission into Nato and the EU was 'unanswerable'.[195] Following the 2022 invasion, opposition to Russia – specifically for its invasion of Ukraine – became a clear goal for Johnson. But in his rhetorical advocacy of this project, Johnson once again depicted the EU in an extremely unfavourable light, when in a March 2022 speech he likened the Ukranian struggle

193 House of Commons Digital, Culture, Media and Sport Committee, *Disinformation and 'fake news': Final Report*, Eighth Report of Session 2017–2019 (London: House of Commons, 18 February 2019), H.C. 1791, 71.

194 Intelligence and Security Committee of Parliament, *Russia*, H.C. 632 (London: House of Commons, 21 July 2020), 12–13.

195 'Bill Clinton is right', 10 June 2000, reproduced in Boris Johnson, *Lend me your ears* (London: HarperCollins, 2004), 295.

against Russia to Brexit – in the process arguably also belittling the suffering of Ukraine (which had in fact applied to join the EU).[196]

Boris Johnson's final speech as Prime Minister, 6 September 2022[197]
Excerpts with commentary

Excerpts

Well this is it folks
thanks to all of you for coming out so early this morning
In only a couple of hours from now I will be in Balmoral to see Her Majesty The Queen
and the torch will finally be passed to a new Conservative leader
the baton will be handed over in what has unexpectedly turned out to be a relay race
they changed the rules half-way through but never mind that now
and through that lacquered black door a new Prime Minister will shortly go to meet a fantastic group of public servants
the people who got Brexit done
the people who delivered the fastest vaccine roll out in Europe
and never forget – 70 per cent of the entire population got a dose within 6 months, faster than any comparable country
that is government for you – that's this conservative government
the people who organised those prompt early supplies of weapons to the heroic Ukrainian armed forces,
an action that may very well have helped change the course of the biggest European war for 80 years
And because of the speed and urgency of what you did – everybody involved in this government
to get this economy moving again from July last year in spite of all opposition, all the naysayers
we have and will continue to have that economic strength
to give people the cash they need to get through this energy crisis that has been caused by Putin's vicious war
. . .
and if Putin thinks that he can succeed by blackmailing or bullying the British people then he is utterly deluded
and the reason we will have those funds now and in the future is because we Conservatives understand the vital symmetry between government action
and free market capitalist private sector enterprise
we are delivering on those huge manifesto commitments
making streets safer – neighbourhood crime down 38 per cent in the last three years
13,790 more police on the streets

---

196 Andrew Blick and Peter Hennessy, *The Bonfire of the Decencies: Repairing and Restoring the British Constitution* (London: Haus, 2022), 86.

197 Boris Johnson, 'Boris Johnson's final speech as Prime Minister: 6 September 2022', *gov.uk*, accessed 7 May 2023, https://www.gov.uk/government/speeches/boris-johnsons-final-speech-as-prime-minister-6-september-2022.

(continued)

---

building more hospitals – and yes we will have 50,000 more nurses by the end of this parliament
and 40 more hospitals by the end of the decade
putting record funding into our schools and into teachers' pay
giving everyone over 18 a lifetime skills guarantee so they can keep upskilling throughout their lives
3 new high speed rail lines including northern powerhouse rail
colossal road programmes from the Pennines to Cornwall,
the roll-out of gigabit broadband up over the last three years, since you were kind enough to elect
me, up from 7 per cent of our country's premises having gigabit broadband to 70 per cent today.
And we are of course providing the short and the long term solutions for our energy needs
and not just using more of our own domestic hydrocarbons but going up by 2030 to 50 GW of wind
power, that is half this country's energy electricity needs from offshore wind
alone, a new nuclear reactor every year
and looking at what is happening in this country, the changes that are taking place,
that is why the private sector is investing more venture capital investment than China itself
more billion pound tech companies sprouting here than in France, Germany and Israel combined
and as a result unemployment as I leave office, down to lows not seen since I was about ten years
old and bouncing around on a space hopper
and on the subject of bouncing around and future careers
let me say that I am now like one of those booster rockets that has fulfilled its function
and I will now be gently re-entering the atmosphere and splashing down invisibly in some remote
and obscure corner of the pacific
And like Cincinnatus I am returning to my plough
and I will be offering this government nothing but the most fervent support
. . .
I say to my fellow Conservatives it is time for the politics to be over folks
and it's time for us all to get behind Liz Truss and her programme
. . .
I am proud to have discharged the promises I made my party when you were kind enough to choose
me,
. . .
ensuring that Britain is once again standing tall in the world
speaking with clarity and authority
from Ukraine to the AUKUS pact with America and Australia
because we are one whole and entire United Kingdom whose diplomats, security services and armed
forces are so globally admired
and as I leave I believe our union is so strong that those who want to break it up, will keep trying
but they will never ever succeed
. . .
Together we have laid foundations that will stand the test of time
whether by taking back control of our laws or putting in vital new infrastructure

---

(continued)

Commentary

The tone of this speech is not what one might expect from a senior office-holder who has been forced out of his post by his own senior party colleagues, having repeatedly failed to live up to expected standards of conduct. Johnson appears to question the legitimacy of his removal by stating that 'they changed the rules half-way through but never mind that now'. He also implies that his removal was a matter of skulduggery, when stating that 'it is time for the politics to be over folks'. His promise of loyalty in future did not prevent him from voting against the deal Rishi Sunak reached with the EU over Northern Ireland in 2023. When praising the performance of his 'public servants', he does not note their participation – along with him – in gatherings that violated Covid restrictions; or the high turnover of senior officials during his tenure. Johnson makes a series of claims about his achievements. Fact-checking of this list made at the time suggested that it contained misleading aspects to it:[198] a continuation of a pattern long associated with Johnson. The programme he outlines is aimed at the electoral coalition the Conservatives assembled under his leadership in 2019.

Boris Johnson's statement in Downing Street, 7 July 2022[199]
Excerpts with commentary

Excerpts

It is now clearly the will of the Parliamentary Conservative party that there should be a new leader of that party
and therefore a new Prime Minister
and I have agreed with Sir Graham Brady
the chairman of our backbench MPs
that the process of choosing that new leader should begin now
and the timetable will be announced next week
and I have today appointed a cabinet to serve – as I will – until a new leader is in place
so I want to say to the millions of people who voted for us in 2019 – many of them voting Conservative for the first time
thank you for that incredible mandate
the biggest Conservative majority since 1987
the biggest share of the vote since 1979
and the reason I have fought so hard for the last few days to continue to deliver that mandate in person

---

198 See e.g.: Andrew Woodcock, 'Boris Johnson speech factchecked: How do the former PM's claims about his legacy stack up?', *Independent*, 6 September 2022, accessed 9 May 2023, https://www.independent.co.uk/news/uk/politics/boris-johnson-legacy-fact-check-b2160660.html.
199 Boris Johnson, 'Prime Minister Boris Johnson's statement in Downing Street: 7 July 2022', *gov*.uk, accessed 7 May 2023, https://www.gov.uk/government/speeches/prime-minister-boris-johnsons-statement-in-downing-street-7-july-2022.

(continued)

was not just because I wanted to do so
but because I felt it was my job, my duty, my obligation to you to continue to do what we promised in 2019
and of course I am immensely proud of the achievements of this government
from getting Brexit done and settling our relations with the continent after half a century
reclaiming the power for this country to make its own laws in parliament
getting us all through the pandemic
delivering the fastest vaccine rollout in Europe
the fastest exit from lockdown
and in the last few months leading the west in standing up to Putin's aggression in Ukraine
and let me say now to the people of Ukraine that I know that we in the UK will continue to back your fight for freedom for as long as it takes
and at the same time in this country we have at the same time been pushing forward a vast programme of investment in infrastructure, skills and technology
the biggest for a century
because if I have one insight into human beings
it is that genius and talent and enthusiasm and imagination are evenly distributed throughout the population
but opportunity is not
and that is why we need to keep levelling up
keep unleashing the potential of every part of the United Kingdom
and if we can do that in this country, we will be the most prosperous in Europe
and in the last few days I have tried to persuade my colleagues that it would be eccentric to change governments
when we are delivering so much
and when we have such a vast mandate and when we are actually only a handful of points behind in the polls
even in mid term after quite a few months of pretty unrelenting sledging
and when the economic scene is so difficult domestically and internationally
and I regret not to have been successful in those arguments
and of course it is painful not to be able to see through so many ideas and projects myself
but as we've seen at Westminster, the herd is powerful and when the herd moves, it moves and
and my friends in politics no one is remotely indispensable
And our brilliant and Darwinian system will produce another leader equally committed to taking this country forward through tough times
not just helping families to get through it but changing and improving our systems, cutting burdens on businesses and families
and – yes – cutting taxes
because that is the way to generate the growth and the income we need to pay for great public services
and to that new leader I say, whoever he or she may be, I will give you as much support as I can
and to you the British people I know that there will be many who are relieved
but perhaps quite a few who will be disappointed
and I want you to know how sad I am to give up the best job in the world
but them's the breaks

(continued)

. . .
I want to thank the peerless British civil service for all the help and support that you have given
. . .
I want to thank the wonderful staff here at Number Ten and of course at chequers and our fantastic protforce detectives – the one group, by the way, who never leak
and above all I want to thank you the British public for the immense privilege you have given me
and I want you to know that from now until the new Prime Minister is in place, your interests will be served and the government of the country will be carried on
. . .

Commentary

The tone and content of this speech do not reflect the manner in which Johnson was forced out of office, including mass resignations by ministers. He seems to imply the existence of a personal mandate which he had a duty to honour by remaining in office. Despite his removal being a consequence of problems with his conduct, he feels able to appoint a new Cabinet and continue in office until a successor is identified. He dwells on his usual policy points.

Boris Johnson's speech following victory in 2019 General Election, 13 December 2019[200]
Excerpts and commentary

Excerpts

---

members of our new one nation government – a people's government – will set out from constituencies that have never returned a Conservative MP for 100 years
and yes they will have an overwhelming mandate, from this election, to get Brexit done
and we will honour that mandate by Jan 31
and so in this moment of national resolution I want to speak directly to those who made it possible
and to all those who voted for us, for the first time,
all those whose pencils may have wavered over the ballot
and who heard the voices of their parents and their grandparents whispering anxiously in their ears
I say thank you for the trust you have placed in us and in me
and we will work round the clock to repay your trust and to deliver on your priorities
with a parliament that works for you
and then I want to speak also to those who did not vote for us or for me
and who wanted and perhaps still want to remain in the EU
and I want you to know that we in this one nation conservative government will never ignore your good and positive feelings – of warmth and sympathy towards the other nations of Europe
because now is the moment – precisely as we leave the EU – to let those natural feelings find renewed expression

---

200 Boris Johnson, 'PM statement in Downing Street: 13 December 2019', *gov*.uk, accessed 7 May 2023, https://www.gov.uk/government/speeches/pm-statement-in-downing-street-13-december-2019.

(continued)

---

in building a new partnership, which is one of the great projects for next year
and as we work together with the EU
as friends and sovereign equals

. . .

I frankly urge everyone on either side of what after three and a half years after all an increasingly
arid argument I urge everyone to find closure and to let the healing begin

. . .

and if you ask yourselves what is this new government going to do, what is he going to do with his
extraordinary majority
I will tell you that is what we are going to do we are going to unite and level up – unite and level up
bringing together the whole of this incredible United Kingdom
England, Scotland, Wales, Northern Ireland together
taking us forward unleashing the potential of the whole country delivering opportunity across the
entire nation

. . .

I want everyone to go about their Christmas preparations happy and secure in the knowledge that
here in this people's government the work is now being stepped up
to make 2020 a year of prosperity and growth and hope and to deliver a Parliament that works for
the people

Commentary

This speech claims that the General Election has delivered a mandate for Brexit. It makes a reference
to 'our new one nation government – a people's government' that is of a populist flavour. The
references to maintaining good relations with the EU are difficult to reconcile with some of Johnson's
past statements and future actions (in relation to the Northern Ireland Protocol in particular). The
hopes expressed about uniting the multi-national UK might be regarded as excessively optimistic
given the territorially divisive nature of Brexit. The rhetoric is of reconciliation. However, the political
project with which Johnson was associated, and which brought him to high office, sought to exploit
and magnify differences, rather than overcome them.

Boris Johnson's first speech as Prime Minister, 24 July 2019[201]
Excerpts with commentary

Excerpts

I have just been to see Her Majesty the Queen who has invited me to form a government and I have accepted
I pay tribute to the fortitude and patience of my predecessor
and her deep sense of public service
but in spite of all her efforts it has become clear that there are pessimists at home and abroad
who think that after three years of indecision
that this country has become a prisoner to the old arguments of 2016
and that in this home of democracy we are incapable of honouring a basic democratic mandate
And so I am standing before you today to tell you
the British people
that those critics are wrong
The doubters, the doomsters, the gloomsters – they are going to get it wrong again
The people who bet against Britain are going to lose their shirts
because we are going to restore trust in our democracy
and we are going to fulfil the repeated promises of parliament to the people and come out of the EU on October 31
no ifs or buts
and we will do a new deal, a better deal that will maximise the opportunities of Brexit while allowing us to develop a new and exciting partnership with the rest of Europe
based on free trade and mutual support
I have every confidence that in 99 days' time we will have cracked it
. . .
And I will tell you something else about my job.
It is to be Prime Minister of the whole United Kingdom
and that means uniting our country
answering at last the plea of the forgotten people
and the left behind towns
by physically and literally renewing the ties that bind us together
so that with safer streets and better education and fantastic new road and rail infrastructure and full fibre broadband
we level up across Britain
. . .
because it is time we unleashed the productive power not just of London and the South East
but of every corner of England, Scotland, Wales and Northern Ireland
the awesome foursome that are incarnated in that red white and blue flag

201 Boris Johnson, 'Boris Johnson's first speech as Prime Minister: 24 July 2019', *gov.uk*, accessed 7 May 2023, https://www.gov.uk/government/speeches/boris-johnsons-first-speech-as-prime-minister-24-july-2019.

(continued)

. . .

and for the values we stand for around the world
Everyone knows the values that flag represents
It stands for freedom and free speech and habeas corpus and the rule of law
and above all it stands for democracy
and that is why we will come out of the EU on October 31
because in the end Brexit was a fundamental decision by the British people that they wanted their laws made by people that they can elect
and they can remove from office
and we must now respect that decision
and create a new partnership with our European friends – as warm and as close and as affectionate as possible

. . .

And next I say to our friends in Ireland, and in Brussels and around the EU
I am convinced that we can do a deal
without checks at the Irish border, because we refuse under any circumstances to have such checks
and yet without that anti-democratic backstop
and it is of course vital at the same time that we prepare for the remote possibility
that Brussels refuses any further to negotiate
and we are forced to come out with no deal
not because we want that outcome – of course not
but because it is only common sense to prepare
and let me stress that there is a vital sense in which those preparations cannot be wasted
and that is because under any circumstances we will need to get ready
at some point in the near future
to come out of the EU customs union and out of regulatory control
fully determined at last to take advantage of brexit
because that is the course on which this country is now set
with high hearts and growing confidence we will now accelerate the work of getting ready
and the ports will be ready and the banks will be ready
and the factories will be ready
and business will be ready
and the hospitals will be ready
and our amazing food and farming sector will be ready and waiting to continue selling
ever more not just here but around the world
and don't forget that in the event of a no deal outcome we will have the extra lubrication of the £39 bn

. . .

but if there is one thing that has really sapped the confidence of business over the last three years
it is not the decisions we have taken
it is our refusal to take decisions
and to all those who say we cannot be ready
I say do not underestimate this country

(continued)

Commentary

In this speech, Johnson emphasises his purpose of driving through Brexit, and to classifies those who are opposed to him as 'people who bet against Britain'. He speaks with his wider policy agenda to the electoral coalition he hopes to mobilise. Johnson seeks to rely on the idea that Brexit is self-evidently a democratic project.

Chapter Four
Wider Tendencies

The previous chapter considered how far the ongoing Brexit phenomenon has raised general issues of democratic concern in the UK. We now perform the same task in relation to other developments in the Brexit era of 2016 onwards. We begin with a discussion of political leaders, parties and their ideas, considering the evidence that they might since 2016 have served to undermine democracy. Next we examine rules and institutions, asking whether they have been undermined or altered in ways which serve to compromise core principles. Finally we assess the key component of democracy: the people. What role have the public played in the events evaluated in this work? How are they communicated with, and how do they communicate and engage? What is their relationship with those who govern them? What do they think? Are these characteristics and relationships changing, and if so in what ways and to what effect?

In addressing these questions, it is worth contemplating some of the political background against which they are assessed. In the period since 2016 there has been a degree of turbulence at high political level. Four prime ministers, all of whom led Conservative administrations, left office. None of them did so following a General Election; rather, it was the internal dynamics of their own party that led to their exit. Cameron seemed to judge that his position was about to become untenable, and the next three – May, Johnson and Truss – were all forced out more directly. The Johnson departure in particular spoke to issues relevant to this book, pertaining to the failure to adhere to basic norms by holders of public office. The immediate trigger for his removal in July 2022 was that he had given an inaccurate account of his prior knowledge of the conduct of a minister accused of improper behaviour.[1] Multiple resignations from his own government eventually convinced him that he had to go. It was not the first and would not be the last time that his conduct had been called into question.

Johnson was not the only person forced to leave post during the period following scrutiny of their own conduct. For example, the Deputy Prime Minister (and Secretary of State for Justice and Lord Chancellor), Dominic Raab resigned in April 2023 after an inquiry found that he had bullied civil servants.[2] Nadhim Zahawi, a former Chancellor of the Exchequer, exited his role as Conservative Party

---

1 Andrew Blick and Peter Hennessy, *The Bonfire of the Decencies: Repairing and Restoring the British Constitution* (London: Haus, 2022), 21.

2 'Dominic Raab: Resignation letter and Rishi Sunak's response in full', *BBC News*, 21 April 2023, accessed 30 April 2023, https://www.bbc.co.uk/news/uk-politics-65333734.

https://doi.org/10.1515/9783110735925-004

chair in January 2023, having been found to have failed to make necessary declara-
tions about an investigation into his tax arrangements.[3] Such incidents, disruptive in
themselves, were also indicative of broader trends relevant to themes covered in this
book, including the failure to live up to accepted standards.

Attention should also be given to wider tendencies impacting on the UK and
other countries internationally. Most notable is the global pandemic that began in
2020. It had the broadest of consequences for the functioning of society, including
the democratic system itself. There were many aspects to this tendency. Some of
them involved political culture. The journalist, Isabel Hardman, noted in 2022
that 'Johnson believed that ending the deadlock over Brexit would draw the poi-
son out of politics. For a while, there was indeed a contraction in the number of
protestors outside Parliament who would sometimes follow and intimidate MPs.
But Brexit has since been replaced by the anti-vax movement, with its acolytes
mobbing leading politicians such as Sir Keir Starmer.'[4]

There were also constitutional consequences. In a 2021 report, the House of
Lords Select Committee on the Constitution captured just some of them, noting
that, in response to the emergency, government had 'introduced a large volume
of new legislation, much of it transforming everyday life and introducing unprecedented restrictions on ordinary activities.' However, 'parliamentary oversight of
these significant policy decisions has been extremely limited'. Part of the problem
had been that '[t]he vast majority of new laws, including the most significant and
wide-reaching, have come into effect as secondary legislation, often without prior
approval from Parliament.'[5] Connected to this minimisation of legislative oversight and executive dominance were issues involving the intelligibility, consistency, fairness and effectiveness of law. The Committee found that:

> [L]egal changes introduced in response to the pandemic were often set out in guidance, or
> announced in media conferences, before Parliament had an opportunity to scrutinise them.
> On a number of occasions, the law was misrepresented in these public-facing forums. The
> consequence has been a lack of clarity around which rules are legally enforceable, posing

---

3 'In full: the letters between Nadhim Zahawi, Rishi Sunak and his ethics adviser', *Guardian*,
29 January 2023, accessed 8 May 2023, https://www.theguardian.com/uk-news/2023/jan/29/in-full-
the-letters-between-nadhim-zahawi-rishi-sunak-and-his-ethics-adviser.
4 Isabel Hardman, *Why We Get the Wrong Politicians* (London: Atlantic, 2022), 174.
5 House of Lords Select Committee on the Constitution, *COVID-19 and the use and scrutiny of
emergency powers*, 3rd Report of Session 2021–2022 (London: House of Lords, 10 June 2021),
H.L. 15, 2, accessed 12 March 2023, https://committees.parliament.uk/publications/6212/documents/
69015/default/.

challenges for the police and local government, leading to wrongful criminal charges, and potentially undermining public compliance.[6]

The pandemic, then, drove – at least in the short term – a variety of serious democratic slippages, understandable in the context of the time, but nonetheless concerning. But have they also encouraged further such negative developments – and perhaps provided camouflage to those that were underway for different reasons?

Leadership, Parties and Ideas

A recurring feature of the literature analysed earlier in this book pertains to the role of certain often very charismatic individuals, such as Donald Trump: within the elite yet denouncing it and rejecting its rules, mores and conventions. How far such people are themselves the primary source of difficulties, or how far they are a consequence of other underlying factors, is not a straightforward question to answer.[7] But that they can play a prominent part in episodes of democratic turbulence is clear. The way in which they operate is important in itself, but also for what it reveals about the framework of government of which they are a part and to which they contribute. When considering this tendency in the context of the UK since 2016, it is useful to refer to a number of politicians, all of whom took on positions of party leadership. Most prominent among them is Boris Johnson, Conservative Prime Minister from 2019–2022. Johnson himself invites consideration in this light, for instance through the public admiration he expressed in his journalistic output for the Italian leader Silvio Berlusconi.[8] The Johnson ascent is a demonstration of how the Brexit episode, discussed in the previous chapter, has helped facilitate a wider disruption of UK democracy. His attainment of a Cabinet post under May (serving as Foreign Secretary from 2016–2018), then the premiership, became possible in the exceptional circumstances generated by the referendum result. Johnson had – opportunistically rather than on principle, it seems – attached his already

---

6 House of Lords Select Committee on the Constitution, *COVID-19 and the use and scrutiny of emergency powers*, 3rd Report of Session 2021–2022 (London: House of Lords, 10 June 2021), H.L. 15, 3, accessed 12 March 2023, https://committees.parliament.uk/publications/6212/documents/69015/default/.

7 A vast literature exists by authors seeking to explain Trump, for an introduction see e.g.: Michael Bernhard and Daniel O'Neill, 'Trump: causes and consequences', *Perspectives on Politics* 17, no. 2 (2019), 317–324.

8 Ben Worthy and Mark Bennister, 'Comparing Boris Johnson's premiership to Silvio Berlusconi's', *LSE Blog*, 21 July 2022, accessed 16 July 2023, https://blogs.lse.ac.uk/europpblog/2022/07/21/comparing-boris-johnsons-premiership-to-silvio-berlusconis/.

considerable public profile to the leave cause; and was able to capitalise on the turbulence that followed.[9] During his term at No.10, apprehension about the condition
of democracy in the UK visibly grew. Prominent figures from across the political
spectrum voiced concerns. They included the outgoing Labour Peer and renowned
filmmaker, David Putnam, and the former Conservative Prime Minister, John
Major, who made widely publicised speeches respectively in October 2021 and February 2022. Putnam referred to 'the multiple dangers faced by democracy'; while
Major cautioned that democracy in the UK was not 'in a state of grace'.[10]

A defining feature of Johnson as a politician, and of the public persona he
seemed intentionally to project, has been a readiness to test understandings, standards and even the law. It is a long-established trait of his. In his career as a journalist and media personality he was prone to making controversial and potentially
unsavoury statements. An instance of this kind of behaviour came in a 10 January 2002 *Daily Telegraph* article in which Johnson referred to: 'flag-waving picaninnies' of the Commonwealth; and to the 'tribal warriors' with 'watermelon smiles' of
'the Congo'.[11] (Johnson subsequently apologised for this particular article, though in
a qualified way.[12]) The habit – demonstrated on this occasion – Johnson had of disregard for regular standards was a vulnerability that eventually contributed to his
loss of office in 2022 and then departure from Parliament in 2023. But it was also
perhaps a calculated part of his public appeal, and a means of obtaining objectives.
As someone wont to operate outside the more accepted boundaries of behaviour,
Johnson was perceived with apprehension within his own parliamentary party. It
only accepted him as leader in the desperate circumstances of mid-2019, shortly
after the European elections in May in which the Conservatives finished in fifth
place in the UK. The diaries of Sasha Swire, wife of the Conservative MP Hugo Swire,
provide a glimpse of how Johnson was able to charm those who were aware of his
flaws into excusing them, partly through his personality, partly through his perceived political usefulness. Recording a conversation she had with Johnson when sitting next to him at a small dinner at No.10, Swire wrote in a 20 August 2019 entry:

> Dinner is amusing. Boris is about the best placement you can get. Cheeky. Flippant. Enthusi-
> astic. Bombastic. Ebullient. Energetic. We have a good laugh . . . Boris is, in many ways, an

---

9 Andrew MacAskill, 'Factbox: Die-hard eurosceptic or opportunist? Johnson's views on the EU',
Reuters, 23 July 2019, accessed 3 April 2023, https://www.reuters.com/article/britain-eu-leader-
johnson-europe-idINKCN1UI1AE.

10 Andrew Blick and Peter Hennessy, *The Bonfire of the Decencies: Repairing and Restoring the
British Constitution* (London: Haus, 2022), 56–57.

11 Harry Mount (ed.), *The Wit and Wisdom of Boris Johnson* (London: Bloomsbury, 2019), 16.

12 Owen Bowcott and Sam Jones, 'Johnson's "picaninnies" apology', *Guardian*, 23 January 2008,
accessed 30 April 2023, https://www.theguardian.com/politics/2008/jan/23/london.race.

island, a spinning, mad island . . . And even though he is an island he seems, like Trump, to be much more in touch with the people and the provinces . . . Yes he is an alley cat, but he has a greatness of soul, a generosity of spirit, a desire to believe the best in people, a lack of pettiness and envy which is pretty uncommon in politics, and best of all a wonderful comic vision of the human condition. He is not like any politician I have ever encountered before, and I have met many. You can't quite believe he is there. In that job! But he is and it's going to be a hell of a ride.[13]

Both the hopes and concerns held about him in senior Conservative circles were confirmed: the party won its largest General Election victory since 1987 before the end of the year; less than three years after that, Johnson was forced out of office, and less than four years later, he had ceased to be an MP. Gavin Barwell, a former Conservative MP and Chief of Staff to Theresa May as Prime Minister from 2017–2019 noted of Johnson in 2022, before his fall but when he was experiencing difficulties, that:

[n]ormally a prime minister gets into political trouble because they pursue a policy which the British people don't support . . . because they are the victim of events beyond their control . . . or . . . because they fall out with a significant chunk of their own party about a key issue. But Boris's problems are entirely the result of his personal behaviour. The character flaws that Number 10 . . . so cruelly magnified were all apparent during his time as foreign secretary . . . : a lack of seriousness, a belief that the rules don't apply to him, a lack of honesty when challenged about his behaviour and a preference for courtiers over people who would tell him what he needs to hear.[14]

There was resistance to Johnson at elite level, and eventually his repeated contravention of expected patterns of conduct led him into conflict with regulatory mechanisms. But Johnson had a source of political strength and claim to legitimacy via his perceived popular appeal (as noted by Swire). In January 2022, when Johnson was being investigated over lockdown gatherings, Jacob Rees-Mogg argued his removal as premier would necessitate a General Election.[15] This posture was hard to reconcile with the UK constitutional system. There are numerous examples of changes of Prime Minister taking place between elections, with one party leader handing over to their successor as leader of the same party. The critical requirement is whether a leader can command the confidence of the House

13 Sasha Swire, *Diary of an MP's Wife: Inside and outside power* (London: Abacus, 2021), diary entry for 20 August 2019, 510.

14 Gavin Barwell, *Chief of Staff: An insider's account of Downing Street's most turbulent years* (London: Atlantic Books, 2022), 16.

15 Adam Forrest, 'Jacob Rees-Mogg says general election needed if Boris Johnson ousted', *Independent*, 26 January 2022, accessed 30 April 2023, https://www.independent.co.uk/news/uk/politics/boris-johnson-general-election-mogg-b2000833.html.

of Commons, which in practice derives from the party balance in that Chamber.[16] Yet Rees-Mogg held that 'we have moved, for better or worse, to essentially a presidential system and . . . therefore the mandate is personal rather than entirely party, and . . . any [new] prime minister would be very well advised to seek a fresh mandate.'[17] While Rees-Mogg seemed to imply a broader change, it is notable that his argument was advanced in the specific context of a defence of Johnson.

In assessing Johnson as a Prime Minister, it is useful to turn to his own words. As a journalist and broadcast performer, words were important to him. By considering some of his spoken interventions at selected key moments during his premiership, and the responses they generated, we can obtain insight into his approach and its implications. On 25 September 2019, the day after the Supreme Court had found his attempted prorogation unlawful, Johnson told the Commons that: 'I think that the court was wrong to pronounce on what is essentially a political question, at a time of great national controversy.'[18] In his position as the most senior and publicly visible figure within the executive, and leader of the largest group inside the legislature, he showed a willingness to question the legitimacy of the judiciary as interpreter of the law. The Supreme Court had in fact attempted to deal with such criticism in its judgment, stating that:

> although the courts cannot decide political questions, the fact that a legal dispute concerns the conduct of politicians, or arises from a matter of political controversy, has never been sufficient reason for the courts to refuse to consider it . . . almost all important decisions made by the executive have a political hue to them. Nevertheless, the courts have exercised a supervisory jurisdiction over the decisions of the executive for centuries. Many if not most of the constitutional cases in our legal history have been concerned with politics in that sense.[19]

In a Commons debate on the same day, Johnson participated in a way which suggested disregard for Parliament and the way it described its own legislation; and for the wider implications of the use of hostile language. He repeatedly misnamed

---

16 Jonathan Este, 'Boris Johnson's claim of a "mandate" from the people isn't accurate – here's how prime ministers really get power', *The Conversation*, 8 July 2022, accessed 3 April 2023 https://www.reuters.com/article/britain-eu-leader-johnson-europe-idINKCN1UI1AE >, last.

17 Adam Forrest, 'Jacob Rees-Mogg says general election needed if Boris Johnson ousted', *Independent*, 26 January 2022, accessed 30 April 2023 https://www.independent.co.uk/news/uk/politics/boris-johnson-general-election-mogg-b2000833.html.

18 664 Parl.Deb H.C. (21 September 2019), col. 775.

19 R (on the application of Miller) (Appellant) *v.* The Prime Minister (Respondent) Cherry and others (Respondents) *v.* Advocate General for Scotland (Appellant) (Scotland), [2019] UKSC 41, Judgment given on 24 September 2019, 12, accessed 21 March 2023, https://www.supremecourt.uk/cases/docs/uksc-2019-0192-judgment.pdf.

a bill being passed (against the wishes of his government) to preclude a no-deal Brexit. Johnson (and others) insisted on calling it the 'Surrender Act', rather than using its real title, the European Union (Withdrawal) (No. 2) Bill. The Labour MP, Lucy Powell, was one of those who objected to this invective. Referring to the murder of Jo Cox during the 2016 referendum campaign, Powell said:

> I just wanted to remind the House that Jo's murder did not happen in a vacuum. It happened in a context—a context that is not dissimilar to the context we find ourselves in today. I have heard from Jo's family this evening, and they have been very distressed by watching this place today. I know others have said it, but it has come from one side of the House: the language of 'surrender', of 'betrayal' and of 'capitulation'. This is the kind of language and the context that led to the murder of an MP leaving her surgery of an evening in a small market town by somebody from the far right, and we cannot forget that context when we conduct ourselves. I just wanted to put that on the record.[20]

Another Labour MP, Paula Sherriff, had been applauded earlier after explaining that:

> Many of us in this place are subject to death threats and abuse every single day. Let me tell the Prime Minister that they often quote his words—surrender Act, betrayal, traitor—and I, for one, am sick of it. We must moderate our language, and that has to come from the Prime Minister first, so I should be interested in hearing his opinion. He should be absolutely ashamed of himself.[21]

Johnson responded to Sherriff that 'I have to say that I have never heard such humbug in all my life.' After describing what he presented as the negative implications of the bill, he appeared to place responsibility for this alarming scenario on its victims and others in Parliament who had supported this measure and were resisting his agenda. He suggested that '[i]f I may say so respectfully to Opposition Members who are getting very agitated about this, the best way to get rid of the surrender Act is not to have voted for it in the first place, to repeal it, and to vote for the deal that we are going to do. That is the way forward.'[22]

One of a plethora of episodes in which his conduct came under scrutiny took place in April 2021, while Johnson was campaigning in the Hartlepool by-election. It saw a gain for the Conservatives at the expense of Labour, arguably representing the peak of his 'Red Wall' success. At the time the media were showing interest in the substance of leaked texts between him and the entrepreneur James Dyson, and the question of who had been the source for the leak. The story raised questions about his integrity and that of members, past and present, of his inner

---

20 664 Parl.Deb. H.C. (25 September 2019), col. 825.
21 664 Parl.Deb. H.C. (25 September 2019), col. 794.
22 664 Parl.Deb. H.C. (25 September 2019), col. 794.

group. When asked by a broadcast journalist about the subject, Johnson replied that 'I don't think people give a monkey's about this issue, what they care about is what we'll be doing to protect the health of the British public'.[23] This comment suggested an attitude on the part of Johnson that he could violate regular standards of conduct while avoiding negative electoral consequences. The result in Hartlepool suggested that such an assessment– whether palatable or objectionable – might be correct. That Johnson was willing openly to avow this view was remarkable. In fact he had already exhibited a tendency to offer views of the calculations that underlay his mode of operation – indeed doing so appeared itself to be an intended part of his appeal. One notable instance of such a habit had come in a 25 March 2013 BBC interview when he told the journalist Michael Cockerell that '[a]s a general tactic in life, it is often useful to give the slight impression that you are deliberately pretending not to know what is going on – because the reality may be that you don't know what's going on, but people won't be able to tell the difference.'[24]

Johnson was also subject to criticism for an unfounded slur made against Starmer in Parliament in February 2022. It related to a deceased celebrity who had evaded prosecution for serial sex offences, and Starmer's time as Director of Public Prosecutions.[25] Following the comment, an incident occurred in which Starmer was surrounded by a group of individuals describing him as a 'paedophile protector'. Starmer was quoted in the press saying that: 'The PM knew exactly what he was doing. It is a conspiracy theory of violent fascists that has been doing the rounds for some time . . . I have never been called a paedophile protector before. That happened . . . for the first time in my life. If others want to argue that this is unconnected with precisely what the PM said one week before then let them make that case. But they'll never persuade me that there is no link.'[26]

On 19 April 2022 Johnson made his first Commons appearance after becoming the first sitting Prime Minister to be found to have committed a crime: violation of Covid laws introduced by his own government. Johnson, who had resisted calls to resign, made a statement that could be perceived as suggestive of a reluctance

---

23 LBC, 'Boris Johnson: British public "don't give a monkey's" about Downing Street leaks', 24 April 2021, accessed 10 March 2023, https://www.lbc.co.uk/news/boris-johnson-denies-blocking-inquiry-carrie-symonds-dominic-cummings/.

24 Harry Mount (ed.), *The Wit and Wisdom of Boris Johnson* (London: Bloomsbury, 2019), 12–13.

25 Isabel Hardman, *Why We Get the Wrong Politicians* (London: Atlantic, 2022), 174.

26 Matthew Weaver, 'Starmer blames PM's Savile slur for inciting mob that accosted him', *Guardian*, 10 February 2022, accessed 30 April 2023, https://www.theguardian.com/uk-news/2022/feb/10/keir-starmer-blames-pm-boris-johnson-savile-slur-inciting-mob.

meaningfully to accept responsibility for his actions, even when his wrongdoing had been formally confirmed. He said:

> [L]et me begin in all humility by saying that on 12 April, I received a fixed penalty notice relating to an event in Downing Street on 19 June 2020. I paid the fine immediately and I offered the British people a full apology, and I take this opportunity, on the first available sitting day, to repeat my wholehearted apology to the House. As soon as I received the notice, I acknowledged the hurt and the anger, and I said that people had a right to expect better of their Prime Minister, and I repeat that again in the House now.
>
> Let me also say—not by way of mitigation or excuse, but purely because it explains my previous words in this House—that it did not occur to me, then or subsequently, that a gathering in the Cabinet Room just before a vital meeting on covid strategy could amount to a breach of the rules. I repeat: that was my mistake and I apologise for it unreservedly. I respect the outcome of the police's investigation, which is still under way. I can only say that I will respect their decision making and always take the appropriate steps. As the House will know, I have already taken significant steps to change the way things work in No. 10.[27]

Part of Johnson's motivation in claiming ignorance of his wrongdoing appears to have been a desire to rebut any claim that he had knowingly misled the Commons when asked about incidents at No.10. But including this qualification in a statement of apology prompted one Labour MP, Mick Whitley, when participating in the debate that followed, to remark that 'the Prime Minister stands before us today as the first resident of No. 10 to be found guilty of breaking the law while serving in public office. While he has finally apologised today, it has been accompanied by the absurd caveat that the man who set the rules could not understand them.'[28]

A further scandal, prompting mass resignations from his Cabinet, finally forced Johnson by 7 July 2022 to recognise that he had to leave office. Yet immediately before this point, there were some concerns that he might contemplate seeking a General Election to pre-empt his removal. The journalist, Sebastian Payne, reported that senior figures within the Civil Service, the Palace, and the Conservative Party had discussed measures that could prevent the request being put to the monarch.[29] On 18 July, with his exit from No.10 now preordained, Johnson generated yet more controversy through his remarks to the Commons, which included the following passage:

> Some people will say, as I leave office, that this is the end of Brexit. Listen to the deathly hush on the Opposition Benches! The Leader of the Opposition and the deep state will prevail in their plot to haul us back into alignment with the EU as a prelude to our eventual

27 712 Parl.Deb. H.C. (19 April 2022), col. 48.
28 712 Parl.Deb. H.C. (19 April 2022), col. 55.
29 Sebastian Payne, *The Fall of Boris Johnson* (London: Macmillan, 2022), 207–209.

return. We on this side of the House will prove them wrong, won't we? . . . Some people will say that this is the end of our support for Ukraine . . . That is exactly the analysis. The champanskoye corks have allegedly been popping in the Kremlin, just as the Islington lefties are toasting each other with their favourite 'Keir Royale'. But I have no doubt that whoever takes over in a few weeks' time will make sure that we keep together the global coalition in support of our Ukrainian friends.[30]

In this passage, Johnson appeared to suggest his removal was part of a sinister, high-level plot to undo Brexit, but that might also be welcome to the Russian government, who in turn had parallels of some kind with North London-based Starmer supporters. Among this collection of ideas that were difficult both to offer credence to individually, and to reconcile with one another, he employed a term – 'deep state' – that had been promoted by Trump and had come to be associated with QAnon conspiracy theories about 'elite paedophiles'.[31] One writer, Morgan Jones, commented:

> While the sentiment might be Johnson's usual fare about protecting Brexit, the specific language is deeply troubling and shows just how little the Prime Minister cares about the cost of his political point scoring . . . It matters when powerful people say things and it matters what they say . . . Donald Trump was the most powerful man in the world, he railed against the deep state and in doing so he dictated the foremost meaning of that term, around which whole cultures of belief sprang up. It was to these cultures that Boris Johnson spoke from the chamber this week, and when the Prime Minister speaks to you, you feel heard.[32]

Johnson continued to promote the idea that he was a victim of persecution from sinister forces after he left No.10. In the process he challenged the legitimacy of the regulatory system itself and questioned the integrity of those charged with maintaining standards. In June 2023 Johnson stood down as an MP. He did so to pre-empt the House of Commons Committee of Privileges report on whether he had held the House in contempt in answering questions about lockdown gatherings. Johnson stated that the Committee (a majority of the members of which were from his own party) was:

> determined to use the proceedings against me to drive me out of Parliament.
> They have still not produced a shred of evidence that I knowingly or recklessly misled the Commons . . . I did not lie, and I believe that in their hearts, the Committee know it. But

---

30 718 Parl.Deb. H.C. (18 July 2022), col. 732.
31 Morgan Jones, 'Boris Johnson's readiness to mention deep state conspiracy theories will have a dangerous ripple effect', *I*, 20 July 2022, accessed 3 April 2023, https://inews.co.uk/opinion/boris-johnson-deep-state-conspiracy-theories-ripple-effect-1752148.
32 Morgan Jones, 'Boris Johnson's readiness to mention deep state conspiracy theories will have a dangerous ripple effect', *I*, 20 July 2022, accessed 3 April 2023, https://inews.co.uk/opinion/boris-johnson-deep-state-conspiracy-theories-ripple-effect-1752148.

they have wilfully chosen to ignore the truth . . . Their purpose from the beginning has been to find me guilty, regardless of the facts. This is the very definition of a kangaroo court . . . I am not alone in thinking that there is a witch hunt under way, to take revenge for Brexit and ultimately to reverse the 2016 referendum result.

In this scenario, his 'removal' was

the necessary first step, and I believe there has been a concerted attempt to bring it about . . . The Privileges Committee is there to protect the privileges of Parliament. That is a very important job. They should not be using their powers – which have only been very recently designed – to mount what is plainly a political hit job on someone they oppose . . . I am bewildered and appalled that I can be forced out, anti-democratically, by a committee chaired and managed, by [Labour MP] Harriet Harman, with such egregious bias.[33]

In discussions of individual leaders and democratic disruption as applied to the UK since 2016, Johnson is foremost. But others merit inclusion. Theresa May had displayed hostility towards established norms prior to her ascent to the premiership. Serving as Home Secretary from 2010–2016, she was criticised for open animosity towards, and engaging in misrepresentation of, the Human Rights Act.[34] Some of her statements and actions in this vein as Prime Minister gave rise to concerns, including within her own party. In June 2017, before becoming May's Chief of Staff, Gavin Barwell held an initial discussion with her. He expressed discomfort with aspects of her approach including: 'the vans telling illegal immigrants that they should go home or face arrest'. May responded that '[t]hey weren't her idea . . . they'd been approved while she was away and she'd put a stop to them.' Barwell also objected to 'that line in your conference speech that if you are a citizen of the world, you are a citizen of nowhere.' May said that: '[s]he was frustrated that people had taken that phrase out of context'. Barwell responded that 'the line', therefore, 'was badly worded, because people who hadn't read the whole speech would think she had been attacking people who thought of themselves as good global citizens'.[35]

The phrase had certainly made a negative impact. Attending the October 2016 Conservative Party conference in Birmingham at which May made the comment, Lionel Barber wrote in his diary: 'Theresa May delivers a hardline defence of Brexit and an assault on cosmopolitan elites: "If you believe you are a citizen of the world, you're a citizen of nowhere. You don't understand what the very word

---

33 'Resignation statement in full as Boris Johnson steps down', *BBC News*, 8 June 2023, accessed 15 June 2023, https://www.bbc.co.uk/news/uk-politics-65863336.

34 The Secret Barrister, *Fake Law: The Truth About Justice in an Age of Lies* (London: Picador, 2021), chap. 5.

35 Gavin Barwell, *Chief of Staff: An insider's account of Downing Street's most turbulent years* (London: Atlantic Books, 2022), 42.

'citizenship' means." What on earth will Mark Carney, our Canadian head of the Bank of England, make of this?'[36] Travelling on to Brussels, Barber remarked 'Eurocrats are shocked by the anti-business, Britain first rhetoric from the Tory conference. Everyone has picked up the "citizens of nowhere" line. Whatever happened to English pragmatism?'[37]

Another leader who requires discussion is Nigel Farage. He was twice closely associated with populist-leaning, self-styled outsider parties. The first that he led, UKIP, had helped instigate Brexit, including through exerting pressure on the Conservatives, and encouraging Cameron to adopt the commitment he made in January 2013 to a referendum on EU membership, should the Conservatives win an overall Commons majority at the next General Election. Cameron, in whose downfall Farage was therefore a player, includes a description of Farage in his memoir, referring to his:

> many contradictions. A man who preaches anti-politics, but who has himself been a politician for twenty years. A critic of corporate interests and banking who has made his money as a commodities trader in the City. A working-class warrior who went to private school. Someone who bemoaned European immigration, but was married to a German, and lambasted an EU gravy train he'd been riding for years.

Behind the contradictions, Cameron concludes that 'I know the type very well. A Conservative who thought "Enoch was right" about Europe and immigration, who admired Margaret Thatcher for her strength in turning the country around', while failing to take into account her 'commitment to our membership of the EU and to making a success of multiracial Britain.' Cameron goes on:

> What Farage lacked in working class credentials he made up for in charisma and an instinctive understanding of his audience. He was also willing to show an unpleasant side. His dog whistles – more like foghorns on occasion – on TB or HIV sufferers coming into the country seemed designed to stir up anger rather than to solve a problem.[38]

Standing down from his UKIP role shortly after the referendum, Farage nevertheless remained incapable of avoiding attention, for instance for his association with Trump.[39] Farage's next project was to help develop the Brexit Party. Launched early in 2019, he provided impetus, becoming leader in March. The Brexit Party, as

---

36 Lionel Barber, *The Powerful and the Damned: life behind the headlines in the financial times* (London: Penguin, 2020), diary entry for 4–5 October 2016, 327.
37 Lionel Barber, *The Powerful and the Damned: life behind the headlines in the financial times* (London: Penguin, 2020), diary entry for 10 October 2016, 327.
38 David Cameron, *For the Record* (London: William Collins, 2019), 512.
39 Edward Helmore and Martin Pengelly, 'Nigel Farage discusses "freedom and winning" in meeting with Trump', *Guardian*, 13 November 2016, accessed 3 April 2023, https://www.theguardian.com/politics/2016/nov/12/nigel-farage-arrives-in-new-york-to-meet-president-elect.

we will see, also developed a range of policies beyond its core objective of lobbying for the firmest possible Brexit, with a strong populist flavour. To proceed from public announcement of its existence to coming first in a UK-wide election (to the European Parliament in May 2019) in less than six months was a feat without precedent. In doing so, it helped bring about an end to the May premiership and install Johnson in No.10, a significant event for the democratic system as well as for the Brexit process.[40] While running candidates at the 2019 General Election, in recognition of the hardened Conservative posture on Brexit, the Brexit Party leadership chose not to contest seats won by the Conservatives in 2017. It is difficult to discern precisely what difference Farage made as an individual. How far was he skilled at driving success, or was he simply adept at choosing the moment to embark upon – and end – ventures? Whatever the respective weighting of these qualities, neither UKIP nor the Brexit Party (which then changed its name in 2021 to Reform UK) performed as well once he ceased to be its leader. Certainly, some working at high level in politics saw him – through methods of a populist quality – as able to achieve results.[41]

Another manifestation of disruptive leadership during this period came from Jeremy Corbyn. Associated with the hard left of the Labour Party, two crucial distinguishing features of his tenure at its head were his lack of support from his own MPs, and his ability to mobilise members, activists and affiliates beyond Parliament.[42] In the first round of the 2015 leadership contest, he narrowly passed the minimum number of nominations required from Labour MPs (35) partly by securing support from people who were not aligned with him, but who wanted to ensure an open contest (presumably anticipating that he would ultimately lose). But at the second and final stage, the mass vote, the results of which were announced in September 2015, he received slightly over 250,000 votes, nearly 60 percent of the total cast. The second placed candidate, Andy Burnham, secured just over 80,000, or 19 percent. The Parliamentary Labour Party therefore had to accept a leader which only about 10 per cent of its membership had been willing to nominate, some of them without actually wanting him to win. As discussed previously, though technically supporting remain in 2016, Corbyn was known for his long record of opposition to the EU. Following the referendum, dissatisfaction

---

40 May announced her plan to resign on 24 May 2019, after voting had taken place in the European elections, but before the results – which were correctly expected to be bad for the Conservatives – were announced. Heather Stewart, 'Theresa May announces she will resign on 7 June', *Guardian*, 24 May 2019, accessed 9 May 2023, https://www.theguardian.com/politics/2019/may/24/theresa-may-steps-down-resigns-tory-leader-conservative-brexit.
41 See e.g.: Kate Fall, *The Gatekeeper* (London: HQ, 2020), 258.
42 Peter Dorey and Andrew Denham, '"The longest suicide vote in history": the Labour Party leadership election of 2015', *British Politics* 11 (2016), 259–282.

with his leadership among MPs intensified and there were mass resignations from his Shadow Cabinet. After losing a vote of no-confidence in his leadership by 172 to 40 MPs on 28 June 2016 (five days after the referendum), Corbyn opted to remain in post rather than resign. A challenge to his leadership then followed. But, however unpopular he was among Labour MPs, he maintained a powerful following beyond Westminster, with the support of Momentum, an activist grouping, and a personality cult reflected in a range of merchandise which included mugs, T-shirts and a book of poetry dedicated to the leader.[43] Once again, Corbyn comfortably won the second stage vote. The result announced in September 2016 saw him defeat Owen Smith MP by about 313,000 votes (approximately 62 percent) to 193,000 (38 percent).

Predictably, despite overcoming this challenge, Corbyn's period in the post continued to be one of turmoil, with a surprisingly strong performance at the 2017 General Election, but ending following a large defeat in 2019. At the second of these two contests, the 2019 General Election, each of the two main parties was led by an individual whose tenure had populist characteristics: Johnson for the Conservatives, and Corbyn for Labour. In this sense, the political and electoral system had failed to offer voters a realistic alternative to such a person as Prime Minister (in as far as elections are about who should be the premier). Corbyn left in the wake of the Labour defeat. Johnson for a time seemed in a strong position. Yet by July 2022, the process leading to his removal was set in motion. A return for Corbyn was difficult to conceive of and by spring 2023 he appeared to have no future in Labour. In March, the National Executive Committee of the party prohibited him from running as a Labour candidate at the next General Election; and he had been removed from the parliamentary party since 2020.[44] In June 2023 Johnson stood down as an MP; and that he had a future at high level in the Conservative Party seemed doubtful (though he and some of his supporters may have entertained hopes). But did the ending of their tenures entail a clean break with populism?

Through her rise to and brief tenure in the premiership, Liz Truss demonstrated some notably disruptive characteristics of her own. She secured the succession to Johnson with a leadership campaign that had support from media outlets noted for their backing for Johnson and his approach.[45] Truss did not come first

---

43 Emine Saner, 'Momentum merchandise: what to buy the Corbynista in your life', *Guardian*, 26 September 2016, accessed 1 May 2023, https://www.theguardian.com/politics/shortcuts/2016/sep/26/momentum-merchandise-pro-corbyn-tshirts-poems-mugs

44 Sam Francis, 'Jeremy Corbyn banned from standing as candidate for Labour party', *BBC News*, 28 March 2023, accessed 30 April 2023, https://www.bbc.co.uk/news/uk-politics-65102128.

45 Jim Waterson, 'Rightwing papers backpedal after helping Liz Truss reach No 10', *Guardian*, 20 October 2022, accessed 30 April 2023 https://www.theguardian.com/media/2022/oct/20/rightwing-papers-backpedal-after-helping-liz-truss-reach-no-10.

in any of the stages of voting for the leadership by the Conservative parliamentary party; but attained victory through winning the vote of members in the country. For Truss the mandate from the membership seemed to override all other considerations. In pursuit of her policy objectives, she transgressed norms – for instance, upon taking office, in removing the Permanent Secretary to the Treasury, Tom Scholar, from post. Her use of populist-type imagery was notable in the following passage from the speech she gave to the Conservative Party Conference in October 2022:

> We need an economically sound and secure United Kingdom.
> And that will mean challenging those who try to stop growth.
> I will not allow the anti-growth coalition to hold us back.
> Labour, the Lib Dems and the SNP . . . The militant unions, the vested interests dressed up as think-tanks . . . The talking heads, the Brexit deniers and Extinction Rebellion . . . The fact is they prefer protesting to doing.
> They prefer talking on Twitter to taking tough decisions.
> They taxi from North London townhouses to the BBC studio to dismiss anyone challenging the status quo.
> From broadcast to podcast, they peddle the same old answers.
> It's always more taxes, more regulation and more meddling.
> Wrong, wrong, wrong . . . They don't understand the British people.
> They don't understand aspiration.
> They are prepared to leave our towns and cities facing decline.
> My friends, does this anti-growth coalition have any idea who pays their wages?
> It's the people who make things in factories across our country.
> It's the people who get up at the crack of dawn to go to work.
> It's the commuters who get trains into towns and cities across our country.
> I'm thinking of the white van drivers, the hairdressers, the plumbers, the accountants, the IT workers and millions of others up and down the UK.
> The anti-growth coalition just doesn't get it.
> This is because they don't face the same challenges as normal working people.
> These enemies of enterprise don't know the frustration you feel to see your road blocked by protesters, or the trains off due to a strike.
> In fact, their friends on the hard Left tend to be the ones behind the disruption.
> The anti-growth coalition think the people who stick themselves to trains, roads and buildings are heroes.
> I say the real heroes are those who go to work, take responsibility and aspire to a better life for themselves and their family.
> And I am on their side.[46]

---

46 Prime Minister's Speech to Conservative Party Conference 2022, 5 October 2022, accessed 10 March 2023, https://www.conservatives.com/news/2022/prime-minister-liz-truss-s-speech-to-conservative-party-conference-2022.

Upon replacing Truss, Sunak – though attempting to present himself in some senses as a restorer of good practice – soon caused controversy by reappointing Suella Braverman as Home Secretary, despite her having resigned less than a week previously after violating rules pertaining to the handling of official documents.[47] Sunak, moreover, had – along with Johnson – been found in 2022 to have committed a criminal act in 2020 in violating social distancing laws, by attending a party when Covid restrictions were in place. As Prime Minister, he managed to violate the law once again. A publicity film distributed by his own team showed him travelling in a car without wearing a seatbelt, leading to his being fined. Sunak's personal finances were another subject of scrutiny.[48] In 2022, it had emerged that he had held a US Green Card while serving as an MP and also for a time when he was Chancellor of the Exchequer. Though he was found not to have broken any specific rules, public disclosure of the arrangement generated consternation.[49] This issue connected to another characteristic of Sunak: his immense personal and family wealth, what was a sufficient level of transparency about its details, and whether it was appropriate for someone of such affluence to be Prime Minister.[50]

In the post-Corbyn era, Starmer sought in many ways to distance himself from his predecessor and the most controversial aspects of his tenure. But his desire to escape the Corbyn-Johnson experience in some respects trapped him. As noted above, under Starmer, Labour adopted a posture on Brexit that seemed at least partly motivated by the desire to secure recovery in constituencies lost at the 2019 General Election. Accompanying his Brexit stance were various statements regarding matters such as borders and workers from overseas. On 6 November 2022, for instance, Starmer told BBC Scotland that:

---

47 Rajeev Syal, 'Outcry over Suella Braverman's return as home secretary', *Guardian*, 25 October 2022, accessed 30 April 2023 https://www.theguardian.com/politics/2022/oct/25/outcry-suella-braverman-return-home-secretary.

48 'Rishi Sunak fined for not wearing seatbelt in back of car', *BBC News*, 21 January 2023, accessed 30 April 2023, https://www.bbc.co.uk/news/uk-politics-64353054.

49 Joe Sommerlad, 'What controversies has Rishi Sunak been involved in?', *Independent*, 25 October 2022, accessed 30 April 2023, https://www.independent.co.uk/news/uk/politics/rishi-sunak-controversies-partygate-tax-b2209390.html.

50 Rupert Neate, 'Does Rishi Sunak's £730m fortune make him too rich to be PM?', *Guardian*, 22 October 2022, accessed 30 April 2023, https://www.theguardian.com/politics/2022/oct/22/rishi-sunak-rich-730m-fortune-prime-minister#:~:text=Sunak%20and%20his%20wife%2C%20Akshata, III%20and%20Camilla%2C%20Queen%20Consort; Rupert Neate and Rowena Mason, 'Five key questions Rishi Sunak and Akshata Murty have yet to answer', *Guardian*, 9 April 2022, accessed 18 June 2023, https://www.theguardian.com/politics/2022/apr/09/five-key-questions-rishi-sunak-and-akshata-murty-have-yet-to-answer.

> We don't want open borders. Freedom of movement has gone and it's not coming back. So that means fair rules, firm rules, a points-based system.
>
> What I would like to see is the numbers go down in some areas. I think we're recruiting too many people from overseas into, for example, the health service.
>
> But on the other hand, if we need high-skilled people in innovation in tech to set up factories etc, then I would encourage that.[51]

The reference to 'recruiting too many people from overseas into . . . the health service' proved particularly controversial. In response to the interview, the SNP politician and then-Health Secretary in the Scottish Government, Humza Yousaf, tweeted: 'Labour's anti-immigration rhetoric increasingly concerning as well as short-sighted.' An SNP MP, Stewart McDonald, tweeted an objection to 'grubby dog-whistling for votes'.[52] Later in the same month, Starmer spoke to the Confederation of British Industry conference, claiming there was a need to end an 'immigration dependency' in the economy and linking immigration to 'low pay and cheap labour'. He said:

> We won't ignore the need for workers to come to this country . . . But I want to be clear here – with my Labour Government, any movement in our points-based migration system – whether via the skilled worker route, or the shortage occupations list – will come alongside new conditions for business . . . our common goal must be to help the British economy off its immigration dependency to start investing more in training workers who are already here.
>
> Migration is part of our national story – always has been, always will be and the Labour Party will never diminish the contribution it makes to our economy, to public services, to your businesses and our communities.
>
> But let me tell you – the days when low pay and cheap labour are part of the British way on growth must end.[53]

We have seen how Johnson frequently expressed himself in ways that were criticised as unacceptable. Among his most notorious such interventions was his attempt misleadingly to link Starmer to the failure to prosecute a notorious sex offender, discussed above. Starmer had complained that the false allegation was

---

51 'Keir Starmer: Immigration not quick fix to NHS problems', *BBC News*, 6 November 2022, accessed 15 March 2023, https://www.bbc.co.uk/news/uk-scotland-63526167.

52 Adam Robertson, 'Keir Starmer panned for saying UK recruits too many overseas workers into NHS', *The National*, 6 November 2022, accessed 3 April 2023, https://www.thenational.scot/news/23104735.keir-starmer-panned-saying-uk-recruits-many-overseas-workers-nhs/.

53 Keir Starmer speech to the Confederation of British Industry Conference 2022, 22 November 2022, accessed 15 March 2023, https://labour.org.uk/press/keir-starmer-speech-to-the-confederation-of-british-industry-conference-2022/.

linked to fascist conspiracy theories and harassment of him.[54] In April 2023, when launching a campaign of personalised attack adverts against Sunak, Labour generated a similar type of controversy, with dissent within the Labour Party itself, and beyond it.[55] Starmer chose publicly to avow the initiative. When he appeared on Sky News on 30 April, the journalist Sophy Ridge asked him about one advert in particular. She noted that 'far-right groups have weaponised sexual abuse committed by Asian grooming gangs – a very small minority of Asians'. Ridge went on, '[y]our attack ad accuses the first ever British Asian Prime Minister of not thinking child sex abusers should go to prison. Is it racist?' Starmer insisted that it was not.[56]

So much for the leaders. What of their parties? Tendencies within both Labour and the Conservatives could serve to encourage efforts either to seek to accommodate, or more actively to advocate, positions of a populist tinge. For instance, within Labour, some figures attached great significance to the idea of reconnecting with lost supporters. Prioritisation of this goal could lead to policies such as the immigration controls advocated by Starmer. Some provenance for his approach can be found in the work of Maurice Glasman. A Labour member of the House of Lords, Glasman was a relatively fringe figure within the party, with a track record of promoting controversial positions such as opposition to the free movement of people within the EU.[57] But, by the early 2020s, Labour had, in practice, drawn closer to him. Setting out his historical analysis, Glasman wrote in 2022 of a 'new liberal political settlement enacted by Thatcher and consecrated by Blair'. It had 'produced a transnational consensus and a trans-partisan political elite.' It consisted of a division of power. 'Conservatives had adopted liberal economics. They controlled the sphere of the economy. The liberal left controlled culture. Its class power lay in its role as the arbiter of cultural taste and the interpreter of national interests, and in its control of the institutions of media, learning and culture.'[58]

---

54 Matthew Weaver, 'Starmer blames PM's Savile slur for inciting mob that accosted him', *Guardian*, 10 February 2022, accessed 30 April 2023, https://www.theguardian.com/uk-news/2022/feb/10/keir-starmer-blames-pm-boris-johnson-savile-slur-inciting-mob.
55 Alexandra Rogers, 'Labour tweets second attack ad against Rishi Sunak despite "gutter politics" row', *Sky News*, 7 April 2023, accessed 30 April 2023, https://news.sky.com/story/labour-tweets-second-attack-ad-against-rishi-sunak-despite-gutter-politics-row-12851979.
56 Andy Hayes, 'Attack ad "not racist": Starmer defends claim Sunak does not want child abusers jailed', *Sky News*, 30 April 2023, accessed 30 April 2023, https://news.sky.com/story/attack-ad not racist-starmer-defends-claim-sunak-does-not-want-child-abusers-jailed-12869340.
57 Julian Coman, 'Maurice Glasman, architect of "Blue Labour": "Labour needs to be itself again"', *Guardian*, 25 September 2022, accessed 1 May 2023, https://www.theguardian.com/books/2022/sep/25/maurice-glasman-blue-labour-book-interview.
58 Maurice Glasman, *Blue Labour: The Politics of the Common Good* (Cambridge: Polity, 2022), 27.

Such language and imagery was of a populist hue. Continuing in this vein, Glasman described how 'globalization over the past forty years' had 'sought to overturn the assumptions of the post-war settlement by subordinating democracy to treaty law, agreed between states but outside of the control of parliaments to amend. Free trade is conflated with free movement and this then leads to the formation of a market society, which disintegrates, as its only bonds are self-interest and contract. This might be called the liquidation of solidarity.'[59] We have seen in the previous chapter how, in the period from 2016 onwards, and particularly after the 2019 General Election and the enactment of Brexit in 2020, senior figures within Labour – such as Nandy, Miliband and Starmer – developed a desire to accommodate Brexit and those who supported it among their target voters. In the process they came to endorse outlooks similar to that set out by Glasman, according to which Brexit was an expression of dissatisfaction with the economic and political system and its supposedly disruptive, impoverishing and disempowering tendencies. Such a movement, they felt, could be reconciled with Labour values.

Within the Conservative Party, accompanying opposition to EU membership, other ideas relevant to the themes identified in the literature review were already well established by 2016. For instance, there was hostility towards arrangements for the protection of human rights, in particular under the Human Rights Act 1998 which incorporates the European Convention on Human Rights (a treaty which came into force in 1953). Dominic Raab held various Cabinet posts in the period from 2016, including that of Secretary of State for Justice and Lord Chancellor. In 2009 he had published a book entitled *The Assault on Liberty: What Went Wrong with Rights*. In it, he held that:

> The British idea of liberty, developed over eight hundred years, is now caught between conflicting tides, cast adrift from its natural moorings. It has been both corroded and conflated. It has been corroded by the government's direct assault on our fundamental freedoms, including freedom of speech, the presumption of innocence and freedom from arbitrary police detention . . . At the same time, and in parallel, the British tradition of liberty has been conflated as swathes of other comparatively minor grievances, claims and interests have been shoe-horned into the ever-elastic language of inalienable, unimpeachable and judicially enforceable rights.

This 'dramatic expansion of rights', Raab held, was 'not the result of public debate, nor has it been endorsed by our democratically elected representatives. On the contrary, it has emerged by stealth, pioneered by judges in Strasbourg – and more recently the UK – at the expense of any meaningful British democratic con-

---

59 Maurice Glasman, *Blue Labour: The Politics of the Common Good* (Cambridge: Polity, 2022), 18.

trol.'[60] He concluded that 'what we need is a Bill of Rights, to galvanise a national debate on the constitutional direction Britain is taking and reach out across and beyond party political divides.'[61] Within government, Raab continued to promote and seek to implement this outlook.[62]

Another significant presence within the Conservative Party was Lord (David) Frost, a former diplomat who became chief negotiator with the EU under Johnson, and who resigned from the government late in 2021. In a 2022 pamphlet, Frost referred to his previously stated view that 'Brexit was surely above all a revolt against a system – against an "authorised version" of European politics, against a system in which there was only one way to do politics and only one policy choice to be made'. He regretted that this 'revolt' had 'just suffered a setback.' The Johnson administration had failed 'to capitalise on the mood for change and its reversion to establishment policy-making norms on taxation, on net zero, and on regulation meant that a huge amount of momentum for change was lost.' Frost held that '[m]any across that establishment see an opportunity to put an end to so-called "populism" (for want of a better word) and to return to cautious, pragmatic, steady-as-she-goes politics and economics.'[63] In place of this approach, he advocated a programme that would eschew 'the artificial polarity between the "market" – "right wing" economics and economic globalisation – and "society" – "left wing" statism and solidarity – but recognise instead that running a successful country involves elements of both.'[64] The specifics of the agenda he set out included 'effective immigration control'; 'a renewed emphasis on law and order'; promoting pride in 'our culture, values, and history'; '[s]tanding up for the unity of the country'; and 'overriding the Northern Ireland Protocol'.[65]

The publisher of the Frost pamphlet was Policy Exchange, a think tank known for engaging in a number of areas relevant to this book. For instance, it produced

---

60 Dominic Raab, *The Assault on Liberty: What Went Wrong with Rights* (London: Fourth Estate, 2009), xvi–xix.

61 Dominic Raab, *The Assault on Liberty: What Went Wrong with Rights* (London: Fourth Estate, 2009), 215.

62 Michael Cross and Monidipa Fouzder, 'Raab unveils his "modern bill of rights" plan', *The Law Society Gazette*, 14 December 2021, accessed 1 May 2023 https://www.lawgazette.co.uk/law/raab-unveils-his-modern-bill-of-rights-plan/5110944.article.

63 Rt Hon Lord Frost of Allenton CMG, *Holy Illusions: Reality based politics and sustaining the Brexit revolt* (London: PolicyExchange, 2022), 6.

64 Rt Hon Lord Frost of Allenton CMG, *Holy Illusions: Reality based politics and sustaining the Brexit revolt* (London: PolicyExchange, 2022), 19.

65 Rt Hon Lord Frost of Allenton CMG, *Holy Illusions: Reality based politics and sustaining the Brexit revolt* (London: Policy Exchange, 2022), 19–20.

reports referring to supposed excessive exercises of judicial power;[66] containing examination of the so-called 'culture war';[67] and advancing the claim that there was a need for some kind of radical overhaul of the Civil Service.[68] Policy Exchange was one of a number of such groups that received increased scrutiny from 2016 onwards. Concerned observers focused on such organisations' declared and undeclared agendas; the level of influence they attained in the media, the Conservative Party, and the UK government; their sources of funding and their supposed lack of transparency; and whether they served the interests of certain international interest groups.[69] Another entity included in discussion of this type was the *Spiked* website. *Spiked* regularly covered various themes considered in this work, including content of a culture war-related nature. The website and those associated with it contributed to the general intellectual environment from which various Conservative initiatives emerged. We have seen how writers connected to *Spiked* such as Brendan O'Neill and Mick Hume promoted populist-leaning ideas. Munira Mirza, formerly a *Spiked* author, was able to exert a more direct influence, as director of the No.10 Policy Unit under Johnson from 2019–2022.[70] As one commentator, the academic Evan Smith, put it in June 2020: '[p]reviously dismissed as a fringe group on the outer limits of political discourse, more recently Spiked has become an influential force in shifting the Overton window to the right in the UK.'[71]

The origins of *Spiked* have attracted interest. They lay in the Revolutionary Communist Party (RCP), a Trotskyist group that emerged from the late 1970s, and which had come to an end by 1997. There was significant continuity of personnel between the RCP journal, once known as *Living Marxism*, but renamed *LM* in 1992, and which ceased publication in 2000, and *Spiked*, which launched in 2001.

---

66 See e.g.: John Finnis, *The unconstitutionality of the Supreme Court's prorogation judgment* (London: Policy Exchange, 2019).

67 See e.g.: Alexander Gray (ed.), *History Matters Project Compendium*, 12th edition (London: Policy Exchange, 2022).

68 See e.g.: Benjamin Barnard, *Government Reimagined: a handbook for reform* (London: Policy Exchange, 2021).

69 See e.g.: Adam Bychawski, 'US climate deniers pump millions into Tory-linked think tanks', *Open Democracy*, 16 June 2022, accessed 1 May 2023, https://www.opendemocracy.net/en/dark-money-investigations/think-tanks-adam-smith-policy-exchange-legatum-iea-taxpayers-alliance-climate-denial/; George Monbiot, 'Right wing think tanks run this government. But first, they had to capture the BBC', *Guardian*, 5 October 2022, accessed 1 May 2023, https://www.theguardian.com/commentisfree/2022/oct/05/rightwing-thinktanks-government-bbc-news-programmes.

70 See: 'Articles by Munira Mirza', *Spiked*, accessed 1 May 2023, https://www.spiked-online.com/author/munira-mirza/.

71 Evan Smith, 'How a fringe sect from the 1980s influenced No 10's attitude to racism', *Guardian*, 23 June 2020, last accessed 1 May 2023, https://www.theguardian.com/commentisfree/2020/jun/23/fringe-1980s-communist-faction-no-10-attitude-racism-munira-mirza.

Smith notes 'the trajectory of its cohort from the far left to the hard right', and the 'culture war' stances they came to adopt.[72] Describing the process by which this loose conglomeration left behind the desire to supplant capitalism, the journalist Nick Cohen writes of the RCP that '[w]hen it failed to end imperialism and capitalism, it ditched revolutionary politics but kept the absolute contempt for liberalism, labourism and human rights.'[73]

The suggestion of continuity as well as change is significant. Populist-inclined ideas of the post-2016 period appear in some ways congruent with the rhetoric of Lenin; which perhaps – via the network connected to *Spiked* – wielded indirect influence upon patterns of thought and practice in the UK at this time. We can illustrate this point by considering *The State and Revolution*, the fullest account of his theories that Lenin produced. In this work, he advocated the displacement of various established institutions, the personnel of which he regarded as comprising beneficiaries of and vehicles for hierarchical oppression of the mass of the population. They would be replaced by instruments of immediate democratic control. Lenin targeted bodies including executive bureaucracies (in other words, civil services) and parliaments. He referred to accounts of how, following the removal of the Tsarist regime, the 'bureaucratic apparatus' had 'stayed essentially as of old . . . functioning in the old way and quite "freely" sabotaging the revolutionary reforms!'.[74] Desiring the removal of restrictive 'bureaucracy and red tape',[75] Lenin called for 'complete electivity of all officials without exception; their subjection to recall *at any time*; [and] the reduction of their salaries to the level of an ordinary "workman's wages"'.[76] The objective was 'to *smash* the old bureaucratic machine at once and to begin immediately to construct a new one that facilitates the gradual eradication of all bureaucracy';[77] and to 'reduce state officials to the role of simple executors of our instructions'.[78] Lenin also described replacing:

---

72 Evan Smith, 'How a fringe sect from the 1980s influenced No 10's attitude to racism', *Guardian*, 23 June 2020, accessed 1 May 2023 https://www.theguardian.com/commentisfree/2020/jun/23/fringe-1980s-communist-faction-no-10-attitude-racism-munira-mirza.

73 Nick Cohen, 'The far-left origins of No 10s desperate attack on all things "woke"', *Guardian*, 20 June 2020, accessed 1 May 2023, https://www.theguardian.com/commentisfree/2020/jun/20/the-far-left-origins-of-no-10s-desperate-attack-on-all-things-woke-.

74 V. I. Lenin, *The State and Revolution* (London: Penguin, 1992, first published 1918), 43.

75 V. I. Lenin, *The State and Revolution* (London: Penguin, 1992, first published 1918), 43.

76 V. I. Lenin, *The State and Revolution* (London: Penguin, 1992, first published 1918), 40.

77 V. I. Lenin, *The State and Revolution* (London: Penguin, 1992, first published 1918), 43.

78 V. I. Lenin, *The State and Revolution* (London: Penguin, 1992, first published 1918), 45.

the venal and rotten parliamentarianism of bourgeois society with institutions in which freedom of opinion and discussion do not degenerate into deception, for the parliamentarians themselves have to work, have to execute their own laws, have to test their results in real life and to answer directly to their electors. Representative institutions remain, but parliamentarianism *does not exist* here as a special system, as the division of labour between the legislative and the executive, as a privileged position for the deputies.[79]

These newly-democratised functions would be performed for the whole state from a single point of authority, and not dissipated through federal divisions of power.[80]

A number of former associates of the RCP surfaced in prominent positions in the Brexit Party in 2019.[81] Without wishing to overstate the overt Leninist influence, it is reasonable to note a degree of similarity between the tone and content of the Bolshevik passage cited above and of the Brexit Party programme – and indeed of the Conservatives at this point. When we seek to consider developing challenges to democracy, there is merit in using a perspective that extends beyond more standard reference points. The Brexit Party *Contract with the People*, published in late November 2019 in advance of the forthcoming General Election, included a section headed 'A Political Revolution'. It proclaimed that '[t]he way the political Establishment has conspired to frustrate democracy over Brexit has highlighted the need for fundamental political reform. The Brexit Party can deliver real democratic change because we are not part of the Westminster status quo.' To this end, it committed itself to a series of reforms, among which were to '[a]bolish the unelected House of Lords'; and to '[m]ake MPs who switch parties subject to recall petitions'. The party pledged to '[r]eform the Supreme Court', arguing that 'judges who play a role in politics must be subject to political scrutiny.' It would guarantee 'political balance' in the judiciary 'by broadening participation in the Selection Commission or conduct interviews by Parliamentary Committee.' A further Brexit Party policy was to '[m]ake the Civil Service more accountable to the public – we would require civil servants to sign an oath to act with political neutrality.' It would also '[p]hase out the BBC licence fee' and '[r]equire Universities to incorporate an obligation to protect legal free speech.' A final item in this list was to '[i]ntroduce Citizens' Initiatives to allow people to call referendums'.[82]

---

79 V. I. Lenin, *The State and Revolution* (London: Penguin, 1992, first published 1918), 43.

80 V. I. Lenin, *The State and Revolution* (London: Penguin, 1992, first published 1918), 47.

81 Nick Cohen, 'The far-left origins of No 10s desperate attack on all things "woke"', *Guardian*, 20 June 2020, accessed 1 May 2023, https://www.theguardian.com/commentisfree/2020/jun/20/the-far-left-origins-of-no-10s-desperate-attack-on-all-things-woke-.

82 The Brexit Party, *Contract with the People* (London: The Brexit Party, 2019), 4, accessed 19 March 2023 https://www.thebrexitparty.org/wp-content/uploads/2019/11/Contract-With-The-People.pdf.

Around the same time, the 2019 Conservative Party General Election manifesto appeared. With Johnson in the leadership, firm leavers were ascendant within the party, and accompanying their enthusiasm for departure from the EU was a broader policy package. Like the Brexit Party, the Conservatives were critical of an elite resistant to the popular will, and held that reforms were needed. While the specific proposals differed, the tone was similar. In a section headed 'Protect our democracy' it complained of: '[t]he failure of Parliament to deliver Brexit – the way so many MPs have devoted themselves to thwarting the democratic decision of the British people in the 2016 referendum'. This conduct had, the manifesto held, 'opened up a destabilising and potentially extremely damaging rift between politicians and people.' It proposed measures including abolishing the Fixed-term Parliaments Act 2011; equalising the size of parliamentary constituencies, although retaining the 'First Past the Post' voting system; introducing voter identification; making it 'easier for British expats to vote', but keeping the minimum voting age at 18, rather than lowering it. The Conservatives would 'champion freedom of expression and tolerance, both in the UK and overseas.' They would 're-peal section 40 of the Crime and Courts Act 2014, which seeks to coerce the press'; and would not 'proceed with the second stage of the Leveson Inquiry' into the conduct of the press. After they secured Brexit, the Conservatives would:

> look at the broader aspects of our constitution: the relationship between the Government, Parliament and the courts; the functioning of the Royal Prerogative; the role of the House of Lords; and access to justice for ordinary people. The ability of our security services to defend us against terrorism and organised crime is critical. We will update the Human Rights Act and administrative law to ensure that there is a proper balance between the rights of individuals, our vital national security and effective government. We will ensure that judicial review is available to protect the rights of the individuals against an overbearing state, while ensuring that it is not abused to conduct politics by another means or to create needless delays.[83]

Using the framing suggested by the literature review in this book, this programme can be seen as democratically disruptive in nature. Between them, these proposals might be interpreted as suggesting various propensities, including to concentrate authority in the executive at the expense of Parliament and the courts; to weaken judicially enforceable rights protection; to cultivate allies in the media; to pursue 'culture wars'; and to seek to facilitate further election success for the Conservative Party in future. The need to fulfil the requirements of the people

---

[83] Conservative and Unionist Party, *Get Brexit Done: Unleash Britain's Potential* (London: Conservative and Unionist Party, 2019), 47–48, accessed 11 March 2023, https://assets-global.website-files.com/5da42e2cae7ebd3f8bde353c/5dda924905da587992a064ba_Conservative%202019%20Manifesto.pdf.

was offered as a justification for the programme. As we will see, agendas of this type have outlasted the Johnson leadership, in areas such as refugee policy. Those at the forefront included associates of the pro-Brexit European Research Group (ERG), such as Suella Braverman, once again demonstrating how departure from the EU has fed into other issues. By 2023, there were signs that the ERG might be a declining force. But there had also been a proliferation of internal Conservative factions. They included, inside Parliament, the Common Sense Group and the Northern Research Group.[84] Outside Parliament, January 2023 saw the launch of the Conservative Democratic Organisation, a grassroots campaign in which Johnson allies played a leading role.[85] In May 2023, the National Conservatism Conference (NatCon), an initiative originating in the United States, was held in London. The general message emerging from the event, in which two Cabinet members – Suella Braverman and Michael Gove – participated, was that the Sunak government was not sufficiently radical in its approach.[86] Between them these entities and interventions contributed to a general climate of ideological and political ferment, and the challenging of established norms.

Aside from their policy positions, behaviour within parties and how it was dealt with requires consideration. During the period 2016–2022, antisemitism within Labour and the handling of it by the party authorities generated much attention. In 2018 and 2019, there were more than 20 resignations from the Labour Party by councillors, Peers and MPs, referring to this issue when explaining their motives.[87] In May 2019, following complaints by the Campaign Against Antisemitism and Jewish Labour Movement, the Equality and Human Rights Commission began an investigation, reporting in October 2020. It found:

> serious failings in leadership and an inadequate process for handling antisemitism complaints across the Labour Party, and . . . multiple failures in the systems it uses to resolve them. We have concluded that there were unlawful acts of harassment and discrimination for which the Labour Party is responsible.

---

84 For a discussion of some of these groupings see: Peter Walker, 'What are the different Conservative factions?', *Guardian*, 8 January 2022, accessed 18 June 2023, https://www.theguardian.com/politics/2022/jan/08/what-are-the-different-conservative-factions.

85 Sam Francis, 'The Boris Johnson backers with a plan to save the Tory party', *BBC News*, 15 February 2023, accessed 18 June 2023, https://www.bbc.co.uk/news/uk-politics-64263243.

86 Chris Mason, 'Vocal Tory right give Rishi Sunak a headache', *BBC News*, 15 May 2023, accessed 18 June 2023, https://www.bbc.co.uk/news/uk-politics-65595954.

87 Equality and Human Rights Commission, *Investigation into Anti-Semitism in the Labour Party* (London: Equality and Human Rights Commission, 2020), 17, accessed 11 March 2023 https://www.equalityhumanrights.com/sites/default/files/investigation-into-antisemitism-in-the-labour-party.pdf.

> While there have been some recent improvements in how the Labour Party deals with anti-semitism complaints, our analysis points to a culture within the Party which, at best, did not do enough to prevent antisemitism and, at worst, could be seen to accept it.

Despite previous investigations, Labour had 'failed to implement the recommendations made in these reports fully, or to take effective measures to stop antisemitic conduct from taking place.' This inaction was indicative of 'a culture that is at odds with the Labour Party's commitment to zero tolerance of antisemitism . . . Although some improvements have been made to the process for dealing with antisemitism complaints, it is hard not to conclude that antisemitism within the Labour Party could have been tackled more effectively if the leadership had chosen to do so.'[88] Starmer had become leader by the time of the publication of the report. By February 2023, the Commission found that there had been appropriate changes implemented, stating that it was 'content with the actions taken and has concluded its work with the Party.'[89]

Institutions, Principles and Rules

A further aspect of democratic deterioration identified in the literature is the undermining of institutions, along with the bypassing and weakening of the norms and standards connected to them. There is evidence of such tendencies in the UK during the period under consideration. By 2023, they had combined to draw international attention. Transparency International, an anti-corruption agency, produces an annual *Corruption Perceptions Index* (CPI). Drawing on data from a variety of sources, it gives countries a rank and a score. The lower the ranking number and higher the score, the less corrupt a given state is perceived as being. Transparency International UK (TIUK) reported in January 2023 that, compared with the 2021 CPI, in 2022 the UK had fallen from 11 to 18 in the rankings; and its score had dropped from 78 to 73. Both the drop in score and rank were the largest the UK had experienced in a single year in the period for which comparable data were available (from 2012); and were the lowest for both in absolute terms. The UK score had peaked at 82 in 2017, and had fallen every year

88 Equality and Human Rights Commission, *Investigation into Anti-Semitism in the Labour Party* (London: Equality and Human Rights Commission, 2020), 6, accessed 11 March 2023, https://www. equalityhumanrights.com/sites/default/files/investigation-into-antisemitism-in-the-labour-party. pdf.
89 Equality and Human Rights Commission, 'Equality watchdog concludes monitoring of Labour Party action plan', 15 February 2023, accessed 11 March 2023, https://www.equalityhumanrights. com/en/our-work/news/equality-watchdog-concludes-monitoring-labour-party-action-plan.

thereafter apart from in 2021. The best rank, of 7, was achieved in 2014, 2015, and 2016; and the UK had never been better than 11 since 2018.[90]

A number of factors, UKTI noted, might have influenced this reputational deterioration. They included the ongoing emergence of information about the use of a 'VIP lane' during the pandemic. It entailed providing businesses that had political contacts with expedited treatment when offering to supply the government with personal protective equipment (PPE). This practice, TIUK had previously found, seemed to favour enterprises with Conservative Party links. A further issue referred to by UKTI was the use of a towns fund worth £3.6 billion, purportedly for targeted disbursal to disadvantaged areas. A parliamentary investigation, TIUK noted, had found that decisions about allocation had been made on a political basis.[91] The inquiry in question was carried out by the House of Commons Committee of Public Accounts (or Public Accounts Committee, PAC). It had published its findings on the subject in 2020, stating that it was 'not convinced by the rationales for selecting some towns and not others. The justifications offered by ministers for selecting individual towns are vague and based on sweeping assumptions. In some cases, towns were chosen by ministers despite being identified by officials as the very lowest priority (for example, one town selected ranked 535th out of 541 towns).' Furthermore, PAC noted, the government had 'not been open about the process it followed and it did not disclose the reasoning for selecting or excluding towns. This lack of transparency has fuelled accusations of political bias in the selection process, and has risked the Civil Service's reputation for integrity and impartiality.'[92] Another issue TIUK identified involved the *Ministerial Code*, a non-statutory document issued in the name of the Prime Minister, that sets out for ministers key principles and rules applying to their conduct. There had been, TIUK found, 40 possible breaches of the Code over a period of five years, none of which had been investigated. Finally, TIUK noted how journalists had uncovered a pattern of large donors to the Conservative Party becoming party treasurers for a period, and then receiving membership of the House of Lords.[93]

---

90 'UK plunges to lowest ever position in Corruption Perceptions Index'; *Transparency International UK*, 31 January 2023, accessed 12 March 2023, https://www.transparency.org.uk/uk-corruption-perceptions-index-2022-score-CPI.

91 'UK plunges to lowest ever position in Corruption Perceptions Index'; *Transparency International UK*, 31 January 2023, accessed 12 March 2023 https://www.transparency.org.uk/uk-corruption-perceptions-index-2022-score-CPI.

92 House of Commons Public Accounts Committee, *Selecting towns for the Towns Fund*, Twenty-Fourth Report of Session 2019–2021 (London: House of Commons, 11 November 2020), H.C. 651, 3, accessed 12 March 2023, https://publications.parliament.uk/pa/cm5801/cmselect/cmpubacc/651/651.pdf.

93 'UK plunges to lowest ever position in Corruption Perceptions Index'; *Transparency International UK*, 31 January 2023, accessed 12 March 2023, https://www.transparency.org.uk/uk-corruption-perceptions-index-2022-score-CPI.

It is possible to identify other developments in areas with which TIUK was concerned, that were not specifically mentioned in its statement. For instance, another PAC report published in mid-2022 focused on the award of pandemic-related contacts amounting to close to £777 million by the Department of Health and Social Care to Randox Laboratories Ltd, to provide testing goods and services. The Committee found that 'the Department's poor record-keeping means that we cannot be sure that all these contracts were awarded properly. Even allowing for the exceptional circumstances at the start of the pandemic, basic civil service practices to document contract decision making were not followed.' Furthermore '[t]he Department . . . failed in its duties to be transparent about meetings that its ministers had with Randox. The potential for conflicts of interest was obvious, but the Department neglected to explicitly consider conflicts of interest in its awarding of contracts to Randox.' According to PAC, the first contract Randox received in March 2020 was granted without a competitive process and was not subject to the normal level of scrutiny from senior officials. The exact part played by ministers in the decision was difficult to ascertain – although, PAC noted, no evidence had been found of wrongdoing. In the event, the Committee went on, Randox fell short of expectations in fulfilling this initial contract, yet it was extended, 'again without competition.'[94]

For TIUK, the main focus was on matters such as financial propriety, and their implications for how corruption-free the UK as a state appeared to be. But the issues the organisation raised had wider implications extending across the constitution, and was suggestive of strains being placed upon it. For instance, the *Ministerial Code* document, potential breaches of which were noted by TIUK, deals with many core aspects of how the executive is supposed to function, internally and in its external relations. A crucial passage from the Code, (found in paragraph 1.3) gives an idea of its overall breadth and importance as a text:

> The Ministerial Code should be read against the background of the overarching duty on Ministers to comply with the law and to protect the integrity of public life. They are expected to observe the Seven Principles of Public Life . . . and the following principles of Ministerial conduct:
> a. The principle of collective responsibility applies to all Government Ministers;
> b. Ministers have a duty to Parliament to account, and be held to account, for the policies, decisions and actions of their departments and agencies;

---

94 House of Commons Committee of Public Accounts, *Government's contracts with Randox Laboratories Ltd*, Seventeenth Report of Session 2022–2023 (London: House of Commons, 27 July 2022), H.C. 28, 3, accessed 12 March 2023, https://committees.parliament.uk/publications/23257/documents/169721/default/.

c.   It is of paramount importance that Ministers give accurate and truthful information to Parliament, correcting any inadvertent error at the earliest opportunity. Ministers who knowingly mislead Parliament will be expected to offer their resignation to the Prime Minister;

d.   Ministers should be as open as possible with Parliament and the public, refusing to provide information only when disclosure would not be in the public interest, which should be decided in accordance with the relevant statutes and the Freedom of Information Act 2000;

e.   Ministers should similarly require civil servants who give evidence before Parliamentary Committees on their behalf and under their direction to be as helpful as possible in providing accurate, truthful and full information in accordance with the duties and responsibilities of civil servants as set out in the Civil Service Code;

f.   Ministers must ensure that no conflict arises, or appears to arise, between their public duties and their private interests;

g.   Ministers should not accept any gift or hospitality which might, or might reasonably appear to, compromise their judgement or place them under an improper obligation;

h.   Ministers in the House of Commons must keep separate their roles as Minister and constituency Member;

i.   Ministers must not use government resources for party political purposes; and

j.   Ministers must uphold the political impartiality of the Civil Service and not ask civil servants to act in any way which would conflict with the Civil Service Code as set out in the Constitutional Reform and Governance Act 2010.[95]

By considering various themes in this paragraph in turn, it is possible to identify areas in which institutions, rules and principles which form part of the democratic system have come under pressure. The author has addressed some of these issues in a previous work written with a co-author, Peter Hennessy.[96] Here the content is updated with fresh and in some cases more recent examples, to illustrate the points.

Collective Responsibility

Within the UK executive, by tradition the ultimate decision-making authority is a committee: the Cabinet. Made up of a main body and series of sub-entities, it comprises senior ministers within the government, with the Prime Minister in the chair. In reality, power processes within government do not necessarily operate entirely through such neatly defined structures. However, Cabinet has value as a

---

95 Cabinet Office, *Ministerial Code* (London: Cabinet Office, 22 December 2022), para. 1.3, accessed 4 April 2023, https://www.gov.uk/government/publications/ministerial-code/ministerial-code.

96 Andrew Blick and Peter Hennessy, *The Bonfire of the Decencies: Repairing and Restoring the British Constitution* (London: Haus, 2022), 91–94.

means by which decisions can be discussed from different departmental and political perspectives, and form part of a coherent programme around which all government members are bound. To undermine it is to call into question the ability of an administration to develop effective, interlinked policies which are intelligible to the outside world, and for which it can be held democratically to account. If Cabinet is to work in the way it is supposed to, its members and other ministers much adhere to a principle known as collective responsibility.[97] An executive-issued text, *The Cabinet Manual*, describes collective responsibility in the following terms:

> Cabinet and Cabinet committees take decisions which are binding on members of the Government. Cabinet and Cabinet committees are composed of government ministers, who are then accountable to Parliament for any collective decisions made. Collective responsibility allows ministers to express their views frankly in discussion, in the expectation that they can maintain a united front once a decision has been reached.[98]

The *Ministerial Code* itself offers further elaborations on the meaning of this principle:

> The internal process through which a decision has been made, or the level of Committee by which it was taken should not be disclosed. Neither should the individual views of Ministers or advice provided by civil servants as part of that internal process be disclosed. Decisions reached by the Cabinet or Ministerial Committees are binding on all members of the Government.[99]

Furthermore, the Code states that: '[m]inisters should ensure that their statements are consistent with collective Government policy. Ministers should take special care in referring to subjects which are the responsibility of other Ministers'.[100]

There are certain ways in which the rules suggested in these passages can to some extent be circumvented. A long-established tradition exists of internal government disagreements being reported in the media, seemingly sometimes with

---

97 Andrew Blick and George Jones, *Premiership: the origins, nature and power of the office of the British Prime Minister* (Exeter: Imprint Academic, 2010), chap. 4.

98 Cabinet Office, *The Cabinet Manual: A guide to laws, conventions and rules on the operation of government* (London: Cabinet Office, October 2011), 30, accessed 4 April 2023, https://assets.publishing.service.gov.uk/government/uploads/system/uploads/attachment_data/file/60641/cabinet-manual.pdf.

99 Cabinet Office, *Ministerial Code* (London: Cabinet Office, 22 December 2022), para. 2.3, accessed 4 April 2023, https://www.gov.uk/government/publications/ministerial-code/ministerial-code.

100 Cabinet Office, *Ministerial Code* (London: Cabinet Office, 22 December 2022), para. 2.3, accessed 4 April 2023, https://www.gov.uk/government/publications/ministerial-code/ministerial-code.

the covert encouragement of ministers and people close to them.[101] Ministers can sometimes be permitted expressly to depart from the official position. As we have seen, during the 2016 EU referendum campaign a formal modification of the rule was applied, allowing ministers publicly to differ from the government support for remain. In this sense, it might be held, divergence was allowed for while preserving the underlying principle. Yet Brexit-related controversy made Cabinet solidarity harder to sustain in the longer term, with cracks becoming visible in various ways, over Brexit and other matters.

Ministerial behaviours since 2016 which have been difficult or impossible to reconcile with collective responsibility in general and with the specific principles set out above have included speculation in public about government policy before it was agreed; and expressions (also in public) of regret about a particular decision or the way in which it had been reached. Laxity of this sort on the part of ministers manifested itself during the Conservative Party conference of October 2022, with both Braverman, the Home Secretary, and Penny Mordaunt, Leader of the House of Commons, making public utterances on matters such as taxation policy, the impact of Conservative backbenchers on decisions, and benefits levels, in ways that tested convention. More seriously, on 2 October, Truss had seemed to attempt create a gap between herself and the most important policy decision of her government. When a BBC interviewer asked her if the Cabinet as a whole was aware in advance of the recent (and soon abandoned) policy of abolishing the highest income tax rate, Truss replied: 'No, no we didn't. It was a decision that the chancellor made'. Truss explained '[w]hen budgets are developed, they are developed in a very confidential way. They are very market sensitive. Of course, the cabinet is briefed, but it is never the case on budgets that they are created by the whole cabinet.'[102]

---

101 For a parliamentary investigation of this general subject, see: House of Commons Public Administration Select Committee, *Leaks and Whistleblowing in Whitehall*, Tenth Report of Session 2008–2009, H.C. 83 (London: Stationery Office, 10 August 2009), accessed 2 May 2023, https://publica tions.parliament.uk/pa/cm200809/cmselect/cmpubadm/83/83.pdf.

102 Andrew Blick (ed.), *The Constitution in Review: Fourth Report from the United Kingdom Constitution Monitoring Group, For period 1 August – 31 December 2022*, (London: Constitution Society, March 2023), 34, accessed 1 April 2023, https://consoc.org.uk/wp-content/uploads/2023/03/Constitution-in-Review-4-1.pdf.

Executive-Legislature Relationship

In the UK system, rather than being directly elected, the executive derives its constitutional authority from Parliament, and in particular from the House of Commons, the elected Chamber. Crucial to this principle is the idea of 'confidence'. The precise meaning of this concept is hard to define with precision, but broadly it means that a government must have general consent from the House of Commons – whether assumed or tested in a vote – to its existence. Aspects of this principle are blurred – for instance, the extent to which it focuses on a Prime Minister or a whole administration.[103] But during the period under consideration at times there was scope for more serious doubts about the viability of the entire confidence tenet. During 2019, it came under Brexit-related strain, with first the May and then the Johnson administrations repeatedly losing Commons votes on fundamental issues, yet continuing to exist (at least for a time, in the case of May). The formation of the Truss government raised further questions about this aspect of the relationship between executive and Parliament. As we have seen, when contesting the leadership, Truss was the favoured candidate in none of the five rounds of voting by Conservative MPs, coming third in the first four, and second in the fifth. Rishi Sunak, who came first in every ballot of MPs, beat Truss by 137 to 113 in the last of these rounds. Truss's advantage was among party members outside Parliament, with those who voted favouring her over Sunak by 57 to 43 percent. Consequently, Truss became Prime Minister despite failing to secure majority support at any point even from her own parliamentary cohort, let alone that of the Commons as a whole. The confidence she and/or her government could claim to command might seem attenuated, and may have been a factor in the briefness of her tenure.

The constitutional connection between the UK executive and legislature does not end with the latter providing a basis for the existence of the former. Governments are required to answer to the legislature for their actions, past, ongoing and intended, and are subject to various controls by it. Such processes require cooperation from the government. One manifestation of this compliance is to furnish Parliament with reliable information. During the period under consideration, there were growing concerns about ministers misleading the legislature, intentionally or otherwise. For instance, one investigation the results of which were published in the press in April 2022 claimed that Johnson and ministers in

---

103 Andrew Blick (ed.), *The Constitution in Review: Fourth Report from the United Kingdom Constitution Monitoring Group, For period 1 August – 31 December 2022* (London: Constitution Society, March 2023), 19–20, accessed 1 April 2023, https://consoc.org.uk/wp-content/uploads/2023/03/Constitution-in-Review-4-1.pdf.

his government had, since the December 2019 General Election, 'made at least 27 false statements to parliament . . . .and have failed to correct them.' Of this total, it attributed 17 to Johnson himself; 4 to Matt Hancock when Secretary of State for Health and Social Care; two to Priti Patel as Home Secretary; with Victoria Atkins (Minister for Afghan Resettlement); Suella Braverman (Attorney General); Nadine Dorries (Secretary of State for Culture Media and Sport); and Jacob Rees-Mogg (Leader of the House of Commons) each accounting for one. Inaccuracies covered matters including refugees; crime figures; PPE production capacity; economic growth; heating subsidies; economic inequality; employment figures; and vaccination rates.[104]

The lockdown parties scandal that swamped the Johnson government from late 2021 into spring 2022 involved not only the events themselves, but what Johnson had told Parliament about them when asked, and the veracity or otherwise of his utterances. Following a Commons vote, he was referred on 21 April 2022 to the House of Commons Committee of Privileges. The Committee investigation into (as the Chair, the Labour MP Harriet Harman, put it) 'whether or not Mr Johnson misled the House of Commons, whether or not he committed a contempt of the House and whether or not this was in any way intentional or reckless' continued work after his loss of high office. Taking oral evidence from Johnson on 22 March 2022, in an opening statement, Harman captured the seriousness, from a democratic point of view, of the executive failing to be truthful in its communications with the legislature:

> Misleading the House might sound like a technical issue, but it is a matter of great importance. Our democracy is based on Parliament scrutinising legislation and holding the Government to account for its actions. We proceed on the basis that what we are told by Ministers is accurate. Parliament expects proactive candour and transparency. If what Ministers tell us is not the truth, we can't do our job. Our democracy depends upon trust that what Ministers tell MPs in the House of Commons is the truth, and without that trust, our entire parliamentary democracy is undermined.[105]

In a report startling in its ferocity for a publication of this type, the Privileges Committee ultimately found that Johnson had committed 'repeated contempts' and that he had set out:

> to undermine the parliamentary process, by:
> a) Deliberately misleading the House
> b) Deliberately misleading the Committee

---

104 Lizzie Dearden, 'Every misleading statement Boris Johnson has made to parliament since the general election', *Independent*, 19 April 2022, accessed 5 April 2023 https://www.independent. co.uk/news/uk/politics/boris-johnson-false-statements-list-parliament-b2060797.html.
105 712, Committee of Privileges, H.C. 564, 2.

c) Breaching confidence
d) Impugning the Committee and thereby undermining the democratic process of the House
e) Being complicit in the campaign of abuse and attempted intimidation of the Committee.

In other words, Johnson had behaved improperly towards Parliament, its rules and its mechanisms for upholding its standards. As well as violating norms, he had questioned their very basis. Had Johnson continued as an MP, the Committee would have recommended a 90 day ban, a punishment almost without precedent and which – if implemented – could have led to a recall proceeding. Since he had decided to leave, it held that he should be denied the parliamentary pass that would otherwise have been available to him as an ex-member.[106]

Another way in which Parliament holds the executive to account is by scrutinising and approving, amending or rejecting the legislative proposals of the government. However, some types of law are subject to more parliamentary oversight than others. The passing of Acts of Parliament involves a sequence of procedures, with multiple votes and line-by-line scrutiny in both Houses of Parliament, in plenary and committee. But another form of law – delegated legislation – issued using authorities vested in ministers by Acts of Parliament is not subject to the same degree of oversight. Delegated legislation provides ministers with powers that are more arbitrary and less subject to constraints. On 24 November 2021, two House of Lords committees synchronised the issue of reports raising concerns regarding this subject. The House of Lords Secondary Legislation Scrutiny Committee produced *Government by Diktat: A call to return power to Parliament*, which described its purpose as being: 'to issue a stark warning—that the balance of power between Parliament and government has for some time been shifting away from Parliament, a trend accentuated by the twin challenges of Brexit and the COVID-19 pandemic.' The Committee went on to observe that '[o]ver recent years, bills – which become Acts of Parliament and which are subject to robust scrutiny in their passage through Parliament – have often provided only the broadest outlines of the direction of policy travel, with all the detail that will have a direct impact on individual members of the public left to secondary legislation.' Yet 'the more that is left to secondary legislation, the greater the democratic deficit because, in contrast to primary legislation, there is relatively scant effective parliamentary scrutiny of secondary legislation; it cannot be amended; in some cases, it may become law with-

---

106 House of Commons Committee of Privileges, *Matter referred on 21 April 2022 (conduct of Rt Hon Boris Johnson): Final Report*, Fifth Report of Session 2022–2023 (London: House of Commons, 15 June 2023) HC 564, 7, accessed 15 June 2023, https://committees.parliament.uk/publications/40412/documents/197199/default/.

out any parliamentary debate; and, because the decision to accept or reject is all or nothing, very rarely will the Houses reject it.'[107]

The parallel House of Lords Delegated Powers and Regulatory Reform Committee report, *Democracy Denied? The urgent need to rebalance power between Parliament and the Executive*, stated that it addressed: 'a potentially serious threat to a cornerstone of our constitution – effective parliamentary scrutiny of legislation.'[108] Particular impetus for the tendency it discussed had come from two sources in particular: '[f]ollowing the referendum in June 2016 and the decision of the UK to leave the EU, the legislative landscape was dominated by Brexit-related primary and delegated legislation. Then, in 2020, the legislative response to the pandemic added to the weight of urgent legislation.'[109] Against this background, the Committee identified 'a disturbing trend in the way in which bills are framed with the effect that they often limit or even avoid appropriate legislative scrutiny.' The report recognised 'that the delegation of legislative powers is necessary'. Yet 'far too often primary legislation has been stripped out by skeleton provisions and the inappropriate use of wide delegated powers. This means that it is increasingly difficult for Parliament to understand what legislation will mean in practice and to challenge its potential consequences on people affected by it in their daily lives.'[110] The report concluded: 'The shift of power from Parliament to the executive must stop . . . **The abuse of delegated powers is in effect an abuse of Parliament and an abuse of democracy** [emphasis in original]'.[111]

---

107 House of Lords Secondary Legislation Scrutiny Committee, *Government by Diktat: A call to return power to Parliament*, 20th Report of Session 2021–2022 (London: House of Lords, 24 November 2021), HL 105, 2, accessed 12 March 2023, https://publications.parliament.uk/pa/ld5802/ldselect/ldsecleg/105/105.pdf.

108 House of Lords Delegated Powers and Regulatory Reform Committee, *Democracy Denied? The urgent need to rebalance power between Parliament and the Executive*, 12th Report of Session 2021–2022 (London: House of Lords, 24 November 2021), H.L. 106, 3, accessed 12 March 2023, https://committees.parliament.uk/publications/7960/documents/82286/default/.

109 House of Lords Delegated Powers and Regulatory Reform Committee, *Democracy Denied? The urgent need to rebalance power between Parliament and the Executive*, 12th Report of Session 2021–2022 (London: House of Lords, 24 November 2021), H.L. 106, 22, accessed 12 March 2023, https://committees.parliament.uk/publications/7960/documents/82286/default/.

110 House of Lords Delegated Powers and Regulatory Reform Committee, *Democracy Denied? The urgent need to rebalance power between Parliament and the Executive*, 12th Report of Session 2021–2022 (London: House of Lords, 24 November 2021), H.L. 106, 3, accessed 12 March 2023, https://committees.parliament.uk/publications/7960/documents/82286/default/.

111 House of Lords Delegated Powers and Regulatory Reform Committee, *Democracy Denied? The urgent need to rebalance power between Parliament and the Executive*, 12th Report of Session 2021–2022 (London: House of Lords, 24 November 2021), H.L. 106, 4–5, accessed 12 March 2023, https://committees.parliament.uk/publications/7960/documents/82286/default/.

Civil Service

The *Ministerial Code* notes the importance of the political impartiality of the Civil Service and the need to respect the *Civil Service Code*. Yet within government there were signs of a desire to challenge the Civil Service more than maintain its principles. As already discussed, support for Brexit often overlapped with a tendency to regard the Civil Service as a resistant force, a view expressed by Braverman.[112] Beyond the specific Brexit issue, Whitehall could be a target for populist-leaning programmes for the overhaul of the political system, such as that presented by the Brexit Party in 2019, which advocated binding officials to an oath of political neutrality.[113] From mid-2019 up to the end of 2020, the desire for radical change within the Civil Service had a forceful advocate at No.10, in the form of Dominic Cummings, who was – before their relationship soured – the most senior special adviser to Johnson, in whom the Prime Minister vested extensive delegated authority.

As a special adviser to Michael Gove as Secretary of State for Education (2011–2014), Cummings had demonstrated a tendency to challenge established arrangements. As another former Conservative special adviser, Peter Cardwell, puts it: 'Michael Gove and Dominic Cummings once referred to elements of the civil service and educational establishment as "The Blob". They believed parts of it to be obstructive, sclerotic and resistant to ministerial discretion.'[114] Cummings was found in March 2019 to be in contempt of Parliament for failure to cooperate with an inquiry into misinformation by the House of Commons Digital, Culture, Media and Sport Committee.[115] Cummings was notorious for his abrasive and eccentric behaviour. He was – as previously noted – campaign director of Vote Leave for the 2016 referendum. David Cameron writes of the senior personnel in the campaign to exit the EU (who were not all part of the same organisation) that '[t]hey may have had Gove and Boris, but they were also a cauldron of toxicity, including figures

---

112 Beckie Smith, 'Attorney General's "Remain bias" jibe "damaging to civil service morale"', *Civil Service World*, 4 July 2022, accessed 20 March 2023, https://www.civilserviceworld.com/pro fessions/article/unsubstantiated-criticism-damaging-civil-service-morale-after-attorney-general-slams-remain-bias.

113 The Brexit Party, *Contract with the People* (London: The Brexit Party, 2019), 4, accessed 19 March 2023, https://www.thebrexitparty.org/wp-content/uploads/2019/11/Contract-With-The-People.pdf.

114 Peter Cardwell, *The Secret Life of Special Advisers* (London: Biteback, 2020), 104.

115 Rajeev Syal, 'Dominic Cummings found in contempt of parliament', *Guardian*, 27 March 2023, accessed 2 May 2023, https://www.theguardian.com/politics/2019/mar/27/commons-report-rules-dominic-cummings-in-contempt-of-parliament#:~:text=The%20report%20concluded%20that%20Cummings,house%27s%20order%20of%207%20June.

like Nigel Farage, Dominic Cummings and the businessman Aaron Banks.'[116] In a diary entry for 8 August 2019, with Johnson and Cummings recently installed in No.10, Sasha Swire wrote: 'Up in London, our current Rasputin figure (Cummings) is sending rockets up the arses of anyone in range (spads, ministers, civil servants, the Queen, Dominic Grieve, probably Boris).' Swire went on: 'we all know Cummings is stark raving mad (you just need to look at his blog) but we are hoping that his maverick, radical, lunatic streak is what just, might, possibly, get us over the line.'[117] Leadsom records that:

> I did not take to Dominic Cummings. From his arrival in No. 10, rather than devoting himself to his powerful role in a methodical and collegiate way, he had particular whims, it seemed to me – specific policy issues on which he had strong views. A number of these issues fell under my remit: corporate governance, executive pay, science funding, space technology. And he would go directly to the responsible civil service teams, instructing them to do what he wanted.

As regards '[h]is views on ministers and on the civil service', which were 'on the record', Cummings, Leadsom states, felt that 'most are pretty useless. He could have led profoundly positive reform from his powerful position as the PM's chief adviser. But in my experience, his approach was to bully, not to lead.'[118] One of the numerous controversial episodes in which Cummings was involved, as Cardwell notes, was the dismissal in August 2019 of Sonia Khan, special adviser to Sajid Javid as Chancellor of the Exchequer. Khan's 'phone and pass were taken from her and she was escorted from Downing Street by an armed police officer.'[119] In February 2020, Javid himself resigned because Cummings insisted on the special advisers to the Chancellor that remained in post reporting to him, Cummings, not Javid, an arrangement that Javid considered unacceptable.[120]

However disliked he was, Gove, Johnson and others judged Cummings useful, at least for a time. Whether the benefits he conferred outweighed the difficulties he created for them can be debated. But over a long period of time, they placed him in various positions of responsibility. He was thereby able to pursue his own agendas as well as propel (and perhaps undermine) those who had engaged him. The disruption with which Cummings was associated is exemplified by his willingness while in

---

116 David Cameron, *For the Record* (London: William Collins, 2019), 659.

117 Sasha Swire, *Diary of an MP's Wife: Inside and outside power* (London: Abacus, 2021), diary entry for 8 August 2019, 506.

118 Andrea Leadsom, *Snakes and Ladders: navigating the ups and downs of politics* (London: Biteback, 2022), 246.

119 Peter Cardwell, *The Secret Life of Special Advisers* (London: Biteback, 2020), 104.

120 Matt Hancock with Isobel Oakeshott, *Pandemic Diaries: The inside story of Britain's battle against Covid* (London: Biteback, 2023), diary entry for 13 February 2020, 65.

office to express controversial views on the Civil Service publicly and in a rambling, hard to penetrate, fashion. In a blog published on 2 January 2020, he asserted that 'there are . . . some profound problems at the core of how the British state makes decisions.' To help correct these difficulties, Cummings stated an intention to 'to hire an unusual set of people with different skills and backgrounds to work in Downing Street'. Among the categories of people he sought were '[s]uper-talented weirdos', which he described in the following terms:

> People in SW1 talk a lot about 'diversity' but they rarely mean 'true cognitive diversity'. They are usually babbling about 'gender identity diversity blah blah'. What SW1 needs is not more drivel about 'identity' and 'diversity' from Oxbridge humanities graduates but more *genuine cognitive diversity*.
>
> We need some true wild cards, artists, people who never went to university and fought their way out of an appalling hell hole, weirdos from William Gibson novels like that girl hired by Bigend as a brand 'diviner' who feels sick at the sight of Tommy Hilfiger or that Chinese-Cuban free runner from a crime family hired by the KGB. If you want to figure out what characters around Putin might do, or how international criminal gangs might exploit holes in our border security, you don't want more Oxbridge English graduates who chat about Lacan at dinner parties with TV producers and spread fake news about fake news.
>
> By definition I don't really know what I'm looking for but I want people around No10 to be on the lookout for such people.
>
> We need to figure out how to use such people better without asking them to conform to the horrors of 'Human Resources' (which also obviously need a bonfire).[121]

The period during which Cummings held his No.10 role was one of considerable turbulence at high level in Whitehall, with a number of senior officials abruptly leaving their posts.[122] It should not be assumed that Cummings was the sole reason for this pattern, however. A further such departure occurred some time after his exit, when – as previously noted – Truss, upon becoming Prime Minister in September 2022, removed Scholar as Permanent Secretary to the Treasury. Such a tendency has the potential to create difficulties from a constitutional perspective. There is a longstanding principle of permanent employment: that the tenure of officials in particular roles is not dependent upon particular individuals holding ministerial posts, or the party composition of the government. The UK is an outlier internationally in this regard,

---

121 '"Two hands are a lot" – we're hiring data scientists, project managers, policy experts, assorted weirdos . . .', *Dominic Cummings's Blog*, 2 January 2020, last accessed 15 March 2023, https://dominiccummings.com/2020/01/02/two-hands-are-a-lot-were-hiring-data-scientists-project-managers-policy-experts-assorted-weirdos/.
122 Rajeev Syal, 'Number of UK civil servants leaving Whitehall rises by 9% in a year', *Guardian*, 28 August 2020, accessed 2 May 2023, https://www.theguardian.com/politics/2020/aug/28/number-of-uk-civil-servants-leaving-whitehall-rises-by-9-in-a-year.

with ministers recruiting relatively few aides of their own from outside on a party political basis, and not in formal management roles.[123] There are arguments for and against the UK model. But, if the position of senior officials becomes more precarious – which it seemed to in the period under consideration – then it becomes harder for them and the Civil Service as a whole to provide some of the key functions required of them. They include the ability to offer honest, evidence-based advice; and to support the maintenance of ethical standards. This excerpt from the *Civil Service Code* (a document issued under the 2010 Constitutional Reform and Governance Act) conveys the characteristics and contribution required of officials, and its connection with the basis on which they are employed.

Civil Service Values

As a civil servant, you are appointed on merit on the basis of fair and open competition and are expected to carry out your role with dedication and a commitment to the Civil Service and its core values: integrity, honesty, objectivity and impartiality. In this code:
 – 'integrity' is putting the obligations of public service above your own personal interests
 – 'honesty' is being truthful and open
 – 'objectivity' is basing your advice and decisions on rigorous analysis of the evidence
 – 'impartiality' is acting solely according to the merits of the case and serving equally well governments of different political persuasions[124]

To focus on the second two of the four values, objectivity and impartiality, the Code offers the following explanations:

Objectivity
You must:
 – provide information and advice, including advice to ministers, on the basis of the evidence, and accurately present the options and facts
 – take decisions on the merits of the case
 – take due account of expert and professional advice

You must not:
 – ignore inconvenient facts or relevant considerations when providing advice or making decisions
 – frustrate the implementation of policies once decisions are taken by declining to take, or abstaining from, action which flows from those decisions . . .

---

123 Institute for Public Policy Research, *Accountability and Responsiveness in the Senior Civil Service: Lessons from Overseas* (London: Cabinet Office, June 2013), accessed 2 May 2023, https://www.civilservant.org.uk/library/2013_ippr_Accountability_and_Responsiveness_in_the_SCS.pdf.
124 Civil Service, *The Civil Service code*, 16 March 2015, accessed 6 April 2023, https://www.gov.uk/government/publications/civil-service-code/the-civil-service-code.

Political Impartiality

You must:

- serve the government, whatever its political persuasion, to the best of your ability in a way which maintains political impartiality and is in line with the requirements of this code, no matter what your own political beliefs are
- act in a way which deserves and retains the confidence of ministers, while at the same time ensuring that you will be able to establish the same relationship with those whom you may be required to serve in some future government
- comply with any restrictions that have been laid down on your political activities

You must not:

- act in a way that is determined by party political considerations, or use official resources for party political purposes
- allow your personal political views to determine any advice you give or your actions.[125]

These passages make it clear that civil servants have a balanced role. They are required to provide loyal support to ministers and implement policies once formed. But they also need to maintain a degree of distance from party political matters, and ensure that ministers are aware of the context in which their decisions are made, and the range of options available. If a civil servant appears to have come into a particular role because of direct intervention by a minister, they may be – or at least seem to be – closer to that politician and to the party political environment than is proper in the UK context. It is also reasonable to speculate that officials who feel less than secure in their posts might feel constrained in offering the objective advice to ministers that they are supposed to. More generally, they might find it difficult to resist pressure to act in ways contrary to other aspects of the Code, such as some of the political impartiality requirements. Furthermore, their status as promoters of values such as honesty and integrity could come into doubt. All of these tendencies would be problems for the operation of the UK democratic system.

General Issues

Beyond the principles referred to in paragraph 1.3 of the *Ministerial Code*, observers noted numerous other areas of concern. Some involved matters addressed in paragraph 1.2 of the *Code*, which states that:

---

125 Civil Service, *The Civil Service code*, 16 March 2015, accessed 6 April 2023 https://www.gov.uk/government/publications/civil-service-code/the-civil-service-code.

> Ministers should be professional in all their dealings and treat all those with whom they come into contact with consideration and respect. Working relationships, including with civil servants, ministerial and parliamentary colleagues and parliamentary staff should be proper and appropriate. Harassing, bullying or other inappropriate or discriminating behaviour wherever it takes place is not consistent with the Ministerial Code and will not be tolerated.[126]

During the period under consideration, and more specifically from the Johnson premiership onwards, more than one minister was investigated for allegations that they had failed to live up to this requirement.[127] For example, in November 2020, the Independent Adviser on Ministerial Interests, Alex Allan, found that – in her behaviour towards officials – the Home Secretary, Priti Patel, had violated the *Ministerial Code* stipulations against bullying (even if she had not intended to do so). However, Johnson rejected this finding and chose to retain Patel in post.[128] This episode illustrated a potential weakness in the system. As the *Code* states, 'The Prime Minister is the ultimate judge of the standards of behaviour expected of a Minister and the appropriate consequences of a breach of those standards.'[129] The promotion and maintenance of standards within the UK executive was to a significant extent dependent upon the Prime Minister, and therefore upon the general approach of whoever held the post at a given time. Moreover, should a premier themselves become the subject of concern – as did Johnson – addressing this issue was harder still. Even if a Prime Minister appeared to have some intention of bringing about greater compliance with principles, as Sunak appeared to, they might feel under political pressure to display leniency towards certain individuals. Such tendencies could undermine the overall credibility of constitutional regulation associated with texts such as the *Ministerial Code* and the *Civil Service Code*. Under Johnson, two successive holders of the post of Independent Adviser on Ministerial Interests resigned, and the office was vacant between June and December 2022.[130]

---

126 Cabinet Office, *Ministerial Code* (London: Cabinet Office, 22 December 2022), para. 1.2, accessed 4 April 2023, https://www.gov.uk/government/publications/ministerial-code/ministerial-code.

127 House of Commons Public Administration and Constitutional Affairs Committee, *Propriety of Governance in Light of Greensill*, Fourth Report of Session 2022–2023 (London: House of Commons, 2 December 2022), H.C. 888, 3–4, accessed 12 March 2023, https://committees.parliament.uk/publications/31830/documents/178915/default/.

128 Andrew Blick and Peter Hennessy, *The Bonfire of the Decencies: Repairing and Restoring the British Constitution* (London: Haus, 2022), 91.

129 Cabinet Office, *Ministerial Code* (London: Cabinet Office, 22 December 2022), para. 1.2, accessed 4 April 2023, https://www.gov.uk/government/publications/ministerial-code/ministerial-code.

130 House of Commons Public Administration and Constitutional Affairs Committee, *Propriety of Governance in Light of Greensill*, Fourth Report of Session 2022–2023 (London: House of Com-

Various observers suggested that the weaknesses of a system dependent to a significant extent upon self-regulation by politicians had been exposed. The philosopher A.C. Grayling, writing in 2020, described the traditional view that: 'principles of gentlemanly behaviour . . . prevented governments from exercising through Parliament what were in fact – and which in the UK remain today – absolute powers.' However, Grayling felt that

> this is a very tenuous way of constraining what governments and their ministers can do, unhappily made obvious when the legislature and government offices come to be populated by less honourable and principled people, controlled by party machines whose influence over representatives, exercised by promises and threats relating to the representatives' careers, is great . . . events of recent years (signal examples are the election of Donald Trump to the Presidency of the US and Brexit in the UK) ring alarm bells as symptoms of failure in a system which has too long relied overmuch on self-imposed restraint and personal principles.[131]

The Courts

A background obligation noted by the *Ministerial Code* is to comply with the law. Such a statement should not strictly be necessary. However, in 2022, Johnson, Sunak and numerous officials were found to have broken lockdown law by attending gatherings at Downing Street in 2020–2021 (the event for which the then Prime Minister and Chancellor of the Exchequer were found to have transgressed was a birthday celebration for Johnson that took place in the Cabinet room on 19 June 2020).[132] More than a hundred fixed penalty notices were issued for attendance at illegal gatherings. This episode illustrates a further aspect of the regulation of government and those working within it. When softer methods of compliance, such as the promulgation of texts like the *Ministerial Code*, fail, sometimes the law is needed. While not involved in ruling on the Downing Street gatherings, the judiciary is an important source of protection for constitutional principles. As we have seen, it was called upon to protect the role of Parliament against executive encroachment in the two Miller cases, on which the Supreme Court issued judgments in 2017 and 2019. But, as also previously noted, the Brexit experience encouraged the Conservative Party

---

mons, 2 December 2022), H.C. 888, 3–4, accessed 12 March 2023, https://committees.parliament.uk/publications/31830/documents/178915/default/.

131 A.C. Grayling, *The Good State: On the Principles of Democracy* (London: Oneworld, 2020), e-book locs. 195–203.

132 'Partygate: A timeline of lockdown parties', *BBC News*, 21 March 2022, accessed 6 April 2023, https://www.bbc.co.uk/news/uk-politics-59952395.

(along with more marginal groups) to take an increasingly critical attitude towards legal professionals. The Johnson government (as suggested in the 2019 Conservative General Election manifesto, discussed above) appeared to show an interest in imposing legal restrictions on the courts. At the time of writing, a project of this type has yet fully to materialise. However, it is possible that other, less formal, means were employed to achieve a more compliant judiciary.

Reviewing the experience since 2016, the All-Party Parliamentary Group on Democracy and the Constitution found in a 2022 report that: '[r]ecent years have seen the judiciary accused, by both politicians and the media, of "interfering in politics".' The Group noted that evidence for this accusation had not been found. Yet 'the behaviour of the executive towards the judiciary may be considered constitutionally problematic'. Ministers had 'generally acted in a manner that may be considered improper or unhelpful given their constitutional role.' Their transgressions included 'making public statements which misrepresent judicial decisions, launching ad-hominem attacks on judges who decide against them, responding to adverse decisions with threats to "reform" the judiciary (including to bring it under political control), and conflating "decisions with political consequences" with "political decisions", thereby giving the misleading impression that judges are stepping outside their constitutional bounds.' Such conduct could 'in extremis, be constitutionally improper because it erodes public confidence in the judiciary and implies that ministers are better able to decide on matters of law than judges.' There was a danger that judges would 'be subject to a context of soft pressure, in which the constant threat of political reform hangs over them if they decide against the executive.' The Group noted that '[s]everal commentators have suggested that this may influence judicial decisions'.[133]

The People

In a democratic system, governmental authority derives ultimately from the people. Moreover, even challengers to the system identified in the literature review in this work claim authority from the people through the lens of populism. The subject which this book addresses, therefore, necessitates a consideration of the public and its role, behaviour and attitudes. The advances made by some of the politicians, ideas and programmes discussed in this work rest to some extent on a mixture of active support from

---

133 All-Party Parliamentary Group on Democracy and the Constitution, *An Independent Judiciary – Challenges Since 2016* (London: Institute for Constitutional and Democratic Research, 8 June 2022), 7–9, accessed 12 March 2023, https://static1.squarespace.com/static/6033d6547502c200670fd98c/t/62a05b38f1b9b809f61853ef/1654676281940/SOPI+Report+FINAL.pdf.

some of the public or lack of resistance from others; but also upon the fact that those opposed to such movements have failed to configure in a way that fully prevents those advances. The securing of approximately 17.4 million votes in favour of leave was crucial to instigating Brexit, while the outcome of the 2019 General Election was critical not only to the implementation of departure, but also to the enabling of the Conservatives under Johnson and their wider agenda.

Overall majorities need not necessarily be required. In neither 2016 nor 2019 did more than 50 percent of those able to vote support the victorious side. At the referendum, while most of those who took part supported leave, they only constituted 37 percent of those who could have voted. In the 2019 General Election, the Conservatives achieved 43.6 percent of total votes cast – a comparatively strong performance, but well short of half even of those taking part, on a turnout of 67.3 percent. Yet the way in which votes divided between other parties (for example, Labour 32.1 percent; Liberal Democrats 11.6 percent), and where those votes were cast, worked to the advantage of the Conservatives. This outcome suggests an observation regarding the Single Member Plurality ('First-Past-the-Post') system, through which the membership of the House of Commons is determined. It has been held by its advocates as rewarding parties for avoiding extremism, and thereby as being a stabilising influence.[134] But on this occasion at least it appeared to have the opposite effect.

In the past, pessimists about the resilience of the UK constitution have held that it is vulnerable to a seizure by a mainstream party that has itself come under the control of an extremist internal faction.[135] The period considered here in some respects saw this scenario become reality – and also extended upon it. In 2019 the main opposition party, Labour, had its own issues. They included, as noted above, a leader in tension with his own parliamentary cohort; and occurrences of antisemitism which the party had not properly addressed. In other words, for many voters concerned about tendencies within the Conservatives and Labour, the electoral system offered no realistic alternative in their own constituency. Moreover, since – in accordance with a pattern known as 'Duverger's law' – Single Member Plurality broadly tends to support the existence of two main par-

134 For a discussion of this issue, see: David Klemperer, *The Electoral System and British Politics* (London: Constitution Society, 2019), especially 20–21, accessed 3 May 2023, https://consoc.org.uk/wp-content/uploads/2019/04/David-Klemperer-The-Electoral-System-and-British-Politics.pdf.
135 Andrew Blick, *Stretching the Constitution: the Brexit shock in historic perspective* (Oxford: Hart/Bloomsbury, 2019), 248–251.

ties, the contest as a whole excluded other meaningful contenders (who can at most hope to hold the balance of power if there is no overall winner).[136]

This discussion of the electoral system underlines the importance of the means by which the relationship between the people and the constitutional system are mediated. Having secured a comfortable parliamentary majority in 2019, the Conservative government went on to introduce a number of controversial measures that impacted upon its relationship with and accountability to the public. Two aspects of the Elections Act 2022 were widely criticised. First, it introduced voter identification requirements in Great Britain, the necessity of which was challenged, and which – it was feared – might have a disproportionate negative impact upon turnout among certain marginalised social groups. In this sense, some of its opponents regarded it as a voter suppression measure, intended to enhance Conservative electoral prospects through reducing participation among those less likely to support the party should they take part.[137] There was some evidence that at the May 2023 local elections held in England under this new system, a disproportionately large number of people from ethnic minorities were turned away from voting for lacking the necessary documentation.[138] Second, giving further cause for concern about tampering with the system, the Elections Act also reduced the autonomy of the Electoral Commission, the body charged with ensuring good practice in elections and in associated areas such as party finance. The Act had the effect of reducing the power of the Commission, and making it more subject to ministerial influence.[139]

Between elections, one of the ways in which members of the public can participate politically is through taking part in protests. The Police, Crime, Sentencing and Courts Act 2022 introduced new police powers to restrict the ability to engage in protest. It generated widespread concern for being excessive and endangering legitimate political dissent, a crucial component of democracy. Similar complaints were raised regarding the Public Order Act 2023; and the Strikes (Minimum Service

---

136 David Klemperer, *The Electoral System and British Politics* (London: Constitution Society, 2019), especially 12–13, accessed 3 May 2023, https://consoc.org.uk/wp-content/uploads/2019/04/David-Klemperer-The-Electoral-System-and-British-Politics.pdf.

137 See e.g.: Alina Rocha Menocal, 'The Elections Bill is about undermining democracy, not shoring it up', *Open Democracy*, 18 April 2022, accessed 3 May 2023, https://www.opendemocracy.net/en/uk-elections-bill-tory-government-democracy/.

138 Rowena Mason, 'Local election observers say 1.2% of voters turned way for lacking ID', *Guardian*, 13 May 2023, accessed 18 June 2023, https://www.theguardian.com/politics/2023/may/13/local-election-observers-say-12-of-voters-turned-away-for-lacking-id.

139 See e.g.: Alina Rocha Menocal, 'The Elections Bill is about undermining democracy, not shoring it up', *Open Democracy*, 18 April 2022, accessed 3 May 2023, https://www.opendemocracy.net/en/uk-elections-bill-tory-government-democracy/.

Levels) Act 2023 was controversial also.[140] Alongside particular measures effecting the freedom of the public, the Conservative government showed an ongoing interest in the possibility of replacing the Human Rights Act 1998, a statute that incorporates the European Convention on Human Rights into the domestic legal order.[141] The envisaged replacement would, critics held, serve to weaken the overall protections that could be obtained via the courts.[142]

Sometimes measures that prompted objections for their democratic implications seemed to be motivated at least partially by a desire to mobilise support among members of the public. As discussed previously, Brexit seemed to reveal and make more salient sharp divisions in popular opinion over social issues, which the Conservative Party might regard as an electoral opportunity, and Labour as a threat. This tendency is well illustrated by the approach taken to the issue of refugees. The Conservatives proposed courses of action that some regarded as based on a false premise, in principle wrong, and abusive of rights. Yet in response, Labour seemed reluctant to emphasise criticism of this nature, perhaps fearing that to do so was to risk being depicted as failing to recognise and be willing to act upon popular concern. It focused instead on the claim that Conservative policy would fail to deliver on its stated objectives. The dynamic, then, was for the Conservatives to pursue a particular approach which Labour opposed but failed fundamentally to challenge. That this tendency survived the passing of the Johnson era is confirmed by a consideration of the period from October 2022 onwards.

Suella Braverman, the Home Secretary, spoke to the Conservative Party conference on 4 October 2022 on the subject of refugees who arrived after crossing the Channel on small vessels, a source of consternation for some of the media and politicians such as herself. She said that: 'we have got to stop the boats crossing the Channel. This has gone on for too long.' Her plan involved measures including a plan to deport refugees to Rwanda and efforts 'to get asylum-seekers out of hotels – currently costing the British taxpayer £5 million per day.' Braverman also insisted that 'we cannot allow a foreign court to undermine the sovereignty of our borders. A few months ago, the European Court of Human Rights in Strasbourg did just that. By a closed process, with an unnamed judge and without any representation by the UK, a European court overrode our Supreme Court. As a

---

140 Natasha Walker, '"They've taken away my freedom": the truth about the UK state's crackdown on protestors', *Guardian*, 5 February 2023, accessed 3 May 2023, https://www.theguardian.com/world/2023/feb/05/protest-laws-state-police-crackdown-uk-activists-prison.

141 For sustained attempts to undermine the Human Rights Act, see: The Secret Barrister, *Fake Law: The Truth About Justice in an Age of Lies* (London: Picador, 2021), 131.

142 Kartik Raj, 'The UK Government's Bill of Wrongs', *Human Rights Watch*, 22 June 2022, accessed 3 May 2023, https://www.hrw.org/news/2022/06/22/uk-governments-bill-wrongs.

result, our first flight to Rwanda was grounded.' Linking the subject back to Brexit, Braverman proclaimed: '[w]e need to take back control.' There were also internal legal issues, she held. Claiming that the UK had 'a proud history of offering sanctuary to those in need', she nonetheless held that 'the law simply isn't working.' She pledged 'to bring forward legislation to make it clear that the only route to the United Kingdom is through a safe and legal route.' Amplifying the populist content of her speech, Braverman then warned of 'many forces working against us. The Labour Party will try to stop this. The Lib Dems will go bananas. The *Guardian* will have a meltdown. As for the lawyers. Don't get me started on the lawyers. And I'm a recovering lawyer.' Yet, '[d]espite the obstacles, I won't give up on you and I won't give up on the British people. The time for words is over. Now is the time for action. Time to put the will of the hard-working patriotic majority at the heart of all we do'.[143] The following day, speaking at another conference event, Braverman told the audience: 'I would love to have a front page of *The Telegraph* with a plane taking off to Rwanda, that's my dream, it's my obsession'.[144]

The promised legislative initiative eventually came. Introducing the Illegal Migration Bill to the Commons on 7 March 2023, Braverman made the unsubstantiated claim that:

> there are 100 million people around the world who could qualify for protection under our current laws. Let us be clear: they are coming here. We have seen a 500% increase in small boat crossings in two years. This is the crucial point of this Bill. They will not stop coming here until the world knows that if you enter Britain illegally, you will be detained and swiftly removed—back to your country if it is safe, or to a safe third country, such as Rwanda.[145]

The Labour MP and Shadow Home Secretary, Yvette Cooper, responded in a way that was suggested the Labour leadership felt vulnerable on this issue, and wanted to avoid allowing itself to be depicted as valuing liberal principles over border security. Cooper opened by stating that:

> A record 45,000 people crossed the channel on dangerous small boats last year, up from just 280 four years ago. In that short time, the Government have allowed criminal gangs to take hold along the channel and along our border. At the same time, convictions of people smugglers have halved; Home Office asylum decisions have collapsed, down 40%; the backlog and costly, inappropriate hotel use have soared; removals of unsuccessful asylum seekers are

143 Suella Braverman, '2022 speech to Conference Party conference', 4 October 2022, accessed 12 March 2023, https://www.ukpol.co.uk/suella-braverman-2022-speech-to-conservative-party-conference/.
144 Lizzie Dearden, 'Suella Braverman say it is her "dream" and "obsession" to see a flight take asylum seekers to Rwanda', *Independent*, 5 October 2022, accessed 12 March 2023, https://www.independent.co.uk/news/uk/politics/suella-braverman-rwanda-dream-obsession-b2195296.html.
145 729 Parl.Deb. H.C. (7 March 2023), col. 152.

down 80% on the last Labour Government; and legal family reunion visas for refugees are down 40%. That is deeply damaging chaos, and there is no point in Ministers trying to blame anyone else for it. They have been in power for 13 years. The asylum system is broken, and they broke it.[146]

Speaking for the Scottish National Party, Stuart C. McDonald MP stressed the humanitarian approach that the Labour frontbench seemingly felt unable to, by commencing with the following passage:

The SNP stands proudly behind the refugee convention and the European convention on human rights. We believe that all who seek asylum and refugee status deserve a fair hearing and we are 100% behind the clear statement from the United Nations High Commissioner for Refugees that there is no such thing as an illegal asylum seeker.

McDonald went on to complain of 'dreary dog-whistle rhetoric'.[147] When taking his turn to speak, Lee Anderson MP, the Vice-Chair of the Conservative Party, claimed that '[w]hen asked by a reporter if foreign rapists and murderers should be deported to the country they came from, the lawyer of the Opposition replied that it depends. Well, I say get rid. Can the Home Secretary confirm that the Bill will indeed get rid of foreign rapists and murderers?'[148] Diana Johnson, a Labour MP and Chair of the Home Affairs Committee, then challenged the premise of the policy, recalling that:

In the Home Affairs Committee report on channel crossings, which was published last summer, we found that small boats have not overwhelmed the asylum system as the Home Secretary is claiming. The backlog has been allowed to grow since 2013, and is now at over 160,000.[149]

Through its initiatives, the Conservative government appeared both to court popular support and set public traps for Labour. Apparently seeking to avoid them, the Labour frontbench chose to criticise policy but within the general framework – that the boats were a serious problem that needed urgently to be dealt with – advanced by the Conservatives. It chose not to emphasise rights and international legality; or to question the idea of arrivals in small vessels as the central challenge. In this sense, there was a populist dynamic at work. One of the two main parties party was pursuing such an approach, which the other was reluctant to resist, and in which it to some extent acquiesced.

The nature of the communications environment was seemingly important to the Labour Party's approach. Discourse is vital to the functioning of a political system.

---

146 729 Parl.Deb. H.C. (7 March 2023), col. 153.
147 729 Parl.Deb. H.C. (7 March 2023), col. 156.
148 729 Parl.Deb. H.C. (7 March 2023), col. 156.
149 729 Parl.Deb. H.C. (7 March 2023), col. 157.

Publicly transmitted messages help shape the way in which issues are understood, and the way in which people behave. The media have a central role in determining and operating this framework. As we have seen, promoters of populist-infused narratives, in the UK and elsewhere, tend to present elites including broadcasters and newspapers as configured in opposition to the attainment of their objectives.[150] But such a viewpoint in the UK context overlooks the provision of vociferous support for Brexit, Johnson, and much of the Conservative platform as discussed in this work, from newspapers such as the *Daily Mail* and the *Daily Telegraph*. Certainly, other titles, such as the tabloid *Mirror* and broadsheet *Guardian*, offered a different perspective.[151] But to imply some kind of media conspiracy against Brexit and other connected agendas would be misleading. One idea the *Mail* promoted was that the courts were meddling inappropriately in political matters. The 'Enemies of the People' headline of 2016, discussed in the previous chapter, was a notable expression of this stance. In full, it read: 'Enemies of the People: Fury over "out of touch" judges who have "declared war on democracy" by defying 17.4m Brexit voters and who could trigger constitutional crisis'.[152] There was overlap not only of ideas but of people and behaviours between the press and the Conservative government. The author of the article that appeared underneath these words, James Slack, then Political Editor at the *Daily Mail*, subsequently moved to No.10, working under Theresa May and then Boris Johnson between 2017 and 2021. Slack then returned to journalism, becoming Deputy Editor-in-Chief at the *Sun*.[153] His leaving event, which took place on 16 April 2021, the day before the funeral of Prince Philip, was one of those held during lockdown restrictions at Downing Street that later generated controversy.[154] When details of this event emerged in January 2022, the *Guardian* reported that the

---

150 Mark Francois, *Spartan Victory: the inside story of the battle for Brexit by The Rt Hon Mark Francois MP* (privately published, 2021), 153.

151 For press positions on Brexit, see: 'UK newspapers' positions on Brexit', *University of Oxford*, 23 May 2016, accessed 3 May 2023, https://www.ox.ac.uk/news/2016-05-23-uk-newspapers-positions-brexit.

152 James Slack, 'Enemies of the People: Fury over "out of touch" judges who have "declared war on democracy" by defying 17.4m Brexit voters and who could trigger constitutional crisis', 3 November 2016, *Mail Online*, accessed 3 May 2023, https://www.dailymail.co.uk/news/article-3903436/Enemies-people-Fury-touch-judges-defied-17-4m-Brexit-voters-trigger-constitutional-crisis.html.

153 Jim Waterson, 'James Slack: the Sun deputy editor in latest No 10 party scandal', *Guardian*, 14 January 2022, accessed 3 May 2023, https://www.theguardian.com/media/2022/jan/14/james-slack-the-sun-deputy-editor-in-latest-no-10-party-scandal.

154 Peter Walker, 'PM's former aide apologises for Downing Street party held in his honour', 14 January 2022, accessed 3 May 2023, https://www.theguardian.com/politics/2022/jan/14/pms-ex-press-official-james-slack-apologises-for-downing-street-party-held-in-his-honour.

news prompted 'scrutiny of the Sun's own coverage of the unfolding Downing Street party scandals' as well as raising 'the awkward question of why they had not broken the news of this No 10 event, given they employ a witness who was present.'[155]

Broadcasters such as the BBC are subject to impartiality requirements that newspapers are not.[156] Nonetheless, as described above, the BBC was a target for those who presented themselves as challenging entrenched elites. It also came under government pressure in different ways. During the Cummings ascendancy, there was a boycott of the Radio 4 *Today* programme. As Matt Hancock put it in a diary entry for 9 January 2020: 'Dominic Cummings, Boris's chief adviser, sees the *Today* programme as an anti-Tory resistance bunker packed with Islington Remoaners and doesn't think we should dignify it with our presence.'[157] On 16 January 2022, Nadine Dorries, Secretary of State for Digital, Culture, Media and Sport tweeted that the upcoming announcement of a BBC licence fee 'will be the last' – calling into question the funding basis of the Corporation. Dorries soon drew back on this position.[158] But for the minister whose portfolio covered the BBC, issuing public statements about it of this nature was less than supportive of the institution. One particular episode involving Johnson and the BBC demonstrated how the integrity of a public body could come under threat, not only from the placing of an individual with party political connections in a senior role within that body (which had precedent in the case of the BBC[159]), but also almost as a by-product of the tendency of a (former) Prime Minister and people associated with him to be associated with questionable activities.

Richard Sharp was appointed Chair of the BBC Board in February 2021. The previous month, Sharp had – after being identified by the government as its favoured candidate for the position – given pre-appointment written and oral evidence to the House of Commons Digital, Culture, Media and Sport Committee. The Committee had published a report expressing support for Sharp. Nearly two years

---

155 Jim Waterson, 'James Slack: the Sun deputy editor in latest No 10 party scandal', *Guardian*, 14 January 2022, accessed 3 May 2023, https://www.theguardian.com/media/2022/jan/14/james-slack-the-sun-deputy-editor-in-latest-no-10-party-scandal.

156 See: 'Editorial Guidelines', Section 4, 'Impartiality – Introduction', *BBC*, accessed 3 May 2023, https://www.bbc.co.uk/editorialguidelines/guidelines/impartiality.

157 Matt Hancock with Isobel Oakeshott, *Pandemic Diaries: The inside story of Britain's battle against Covid* (London: Biteback, 2023), diary entry for 9 January 2020, 15.

158 Jim Waterson, 'BBC funding "up for discussion", says Nadine Dorries, as licence fee frozen', *Guardian*, 17 January 2022, accessed 3 May 2023, https://www.theguardian.com/media/2022/jan/17/no-final-decision-made-on-bbc-licence-fee-says-nadine-dorries.

159 Andrew Rawnsley, 'After the fall of Richard Sharp, the next BBC chair must not be a political appointment', *Observer*, 30 April 2023, accessed 3 May 2023, https://www.theguardian.com/commentisfree/2023/apr/30/bbc-chair-role-independence-cronyism-richard-sharp-exit.

later, a media story appeared that was relevant to this process. According to it, Sharp had, in 2020 – after applying to be Chair, but before his hearing with the Committee, and before taking on the post – played a part in discussions about the securing of a loan for the then-Prime Minister, Johnson, of up to £800,000. Sharp had not revealed this information as part of the interview or to the Committee. The Committee opened an investigation into the matter (as, in parallel, did the Commissioner for Public Appointments and the BBC).[160] The Committee concluded in March 2023 that:

> Richard Sharp's decisions, firstly to become involved in the facilitation of a loan to the then Prime Minister while at the same time applying for a job that was in that same person's gift, and then to fail to disclose this material relationship, were significant errors of judgement, which undermine confidence in the public appointments process and could deter qualified individuals from applying for such posts. Mr Sharp's failure to disclose his actions to the panel and the Committee, although he believed this to be completely proper, constitute a breach of the standards expected of individuals applying for such public appointments.[161]

Sharp eventually resigned from his post in April 2023, after further critical findings from a report on behalf of the Commissioner for Public Appointments.[162] It found that his failure 'to disclose potential perceived conflicts of interest to the Panel' interviewing for the role created 'a potential perceived conflict of interest.' There was 'a risk of a perception that Mr Sharp was recommended for appointment because he assisted', albeit to a 'very limited extent . . . the former Prime Minister in a private financial matter, and/or that he influenced the former Prime Minister to recommend him by informing him of his application before he submitted it. There may well have been a risk of a perception that Mr Sharp would not be independent from the former Prime Minister, if appointed.'[163]

---

160 House of Commons Digital, Culture, Media and Sport Committee, *Appointment of Richard Sharp as Chair of the BBC*, Eighth Report of Session 2022–2023, (London: House of Commons, 12 February 2023), H.C. 1147, 3–4; 8–9; 14, accessed 12 March 2023, https://committees.parliament. uk/publications/33962/documents/186346/default/.

161 House of Commons Digital, Culture, Media and Sport Committee, *Appointment of Richard Sharp as Chair of the BBC*, Eighth Report of Session 2022–2023, (London: House of Commons, 12 February 2023), H.C. 1147, 14–15, accessed 12 March 2023, https://committees.parliament.uk/pub lications/33962/documents/186346/default/.

162 Andrew Rawnsley, 'After the fall of Richard Sharp, the next BBC chair must not be a political appointment', *Observer*, 30 April 2023, accessed 3 May 2023, https://www.theguardian.com/com mentisfree/2023/apr/30/bbc-chair-role-independence-cronyism-richard-sharp-exit.

163 Commissioner for Public Appointments, 'Decision Notice: The Appointment of the Chair of the Board of the British Broadcasting Corporation (BBC) 2020/2021', 2023, accessed 3 May 2023, https://publicappointmentscommissioner.independent.gov.uk/wp-content/uploads/2023/04/2023-

Beyond the broadcast media, the Internet and its democratic implications became a matter of first-order concern among political commentators during this period. Scrutiny of practices during the 2016 referendum campaign contributed to an international debate on this subject. Beyond the particular issue of the Brexit vote, some accounts suggested that the Internet was impacting upon the political landscape in ways threatened the system itself. They included the promotion of extremism, the dissemination of false information, and the use by hostile actors, including states and non-state entities, to exploit vulnerable individuals and undermine democratic societies. As the House of Lords Select Committee on Democracy and Digital Technologies found in 2020: '[d]emocracy is an enduring feature of British society, but it can be eroded unless it is upheld and protected by citizens, civil society, companies and elected representatives . . . We must resist the emergence of undemocratic practices and institutions and strengthen public trust and confidence in democratic processes.' The committee found that digital:

> technologies are reshaping not only our private lives but also our public life and our democracy. People now have a printing press, a broadcast station and a place of assembly in their pockets . . . People who would not have previously engaged in the everyday discussion of democracy are now taking an active part. This increased participation, although it has empowered many, has, paradoxically, shifted power toward a very small group of new gatekeepers; the individuals who determine the ways in which the technology platforms operate. These individuals can, purposefully or not, change whose voice is heard. It has also introduced new opportunities for individuals and organisations with malign intentions to manipulate the flow of political debate.[164]

One negative aspect of the Internet as a tool for political communication formed part of an inquiry conducted by the Committee on Standards in Public Life. Its resulting report, published in 2017 and entitled *Intimidation in Public Life*, found that:

> [i]ntimidation in public life presents a threat to the very nature of representative democracy in the UK . . . While intimidation in public life is nothing new, the scale and intensity of intimidation is now shaping public life in ways which are a serious issue.
>
> Social media companies have been too slow in taking action on online intimidation to protect their users. The political parties have failed to show leadership in calling out intimidatory behaviour and changing the tone of political debate. Police authorities have shown

---

04-28-OCPA-DECISION-NOTICE-IN-RELATION-TO-THE-APPOINTMENT-OF-CHAIR-OF-THE-BBC-BOARD -MR-RICHARD-SHARP.pdf.

164 House of Lords Select Committee on Democracy and Digital Technologies, *Digital Technology and the Resurrection of Trust*, Report of Session 2019–2021 (London: House of Lords, 29 June 2020), 9, accessed 15 March 2023, https://committees.parliament.uk/publications/1634/documents/17731/default/.

inconsistency in supporting those facing illegal intimidatory activities, and electoral law is out of date on this issue.[165]

As this finding demonstrated, patterns of public behaviour have important implications for the viability of democracy. All the foregoing discussion about the means by which people can be influenced and their inputs mediated should not create the impression that they are merely the recipients of politics. The public can make a difference. Voting in referendums and elections is an obvious way in which they do so, albeit subject to the complexities discussed above. A further way in which people beyond the elite had a substantial impact was in determining who should be the leaders of political parties. In the period since 2016, the Conservative and Labour parties each had two contests which were resolved by mass votes. Both of the Conservative votes favoured a candidate who was more populist-inclined than their opponent (Johnson in 2019; Truss in 2022), and with Truss, the one who had received less support from MPs. In the case of Labour in 2016, the effect of the vote was to reinforce the position of a leader who MPs had sought to oust.

People voting in party elections are far from a representative sample of the general population. But what were the views of that wider public? Their susceptibility or otherwise to the agendas discussed here, and the extent and nature of their support for democracy or other systems are critical to the robustness of the system itself. Discerning clear answers is not easy, but there is evidence that should be considered. For instance, polling conducted for the Hansard Society late in 2018 showed 54 percent of respondents in Great Britain agreeing with the proposition that 'Britain needs a strong leader willing to break the rules', with 23 percent disagreeing. However, there was more hesitancy about an empowered executive when they were asked to choose between the following two statements:

> It would be a risk to give the government more power to deal directly with many of the country's problems

> Many of the country's problems could be dealt with more effectively if the government didn't have to worry so much about votes in Parliament

50 percent favoured the former; 42 percent the latter. Voters were also asked to select one of the following options:

---

165 Committee on Standards in Public Life, *Intimidation in Public Life* (London: Committee on Standards in Public Life, December 2017), Cm 9543, 13, accessed 12 March 2023, https://assets.pub lishing.service.gov.uk/government/uploads/system/uploads/attachment_data/file/666927/6.3637_ CO_v6_061217_Web3.1__2_.pdf.

At a time like the present, we should stick with political parties and leaders who have been in power before

We should consider electing parties or leaders with radical ideas for change who haven't been in power before

47 percent chose the first; 43 percent the second.[166] There was evidence here, then, of majorities or substantial minorities being willing to support options that might be democratically troubling. Opinion research carried out for the Constitution Unit, University College London, in July 2021 probed on a wider range of issues in this area among UK respondents. It found the court system was the most trusted part of the political system (of a list of four) to 'act in the best interests of people in the UK'; followed by the Civil Service; the UK Parliament; and last the Prime Minister. This outcome suggested an inclination towards institutions supportive of the rule of law, and away from more populist constitutional models. When presented with the following two statements:

Healthy democracy requires that politicians always act within the rules

Healthy democracy means getting things done, even if that sometimes requires politicians to break the rules

75 percent favoured the former; 6 percent the latter, with 10 percent agreeing to both equally (9 percent did not know). This result suggested strong acceptance of the idea that democratic mandates were subject to consistent limitations. There was less consensus on where the constraints should come from. Respondents were offered the following two propositions:

Judges have an important role in ensuring that elected politicians operate within the rules

Elected politicians must themselves be responsible for ensuring that they act within the rules

33 percent agreed with the first; 28 percent the second (30 percent both equally; 9 percent did not know).

There was some support for majoritarianism, although again it was not decisive. A choice was offered between the following:

In a democracy, it is more important to follow the will of the majority

In a democracy, it is more important to protect the rights of minorities

---

166 Hansard Society, *Audit of Political Engagement 16: The 2019 Report* (London: Hansard Society, 2019), 17–18.

The split was 30 percent for the former; 19 percent the latter; 41 percent both equally; 10 percent did not know.[167] Further relevant data appeared in April 2023 as part of the World Values Survey. It found that the percentage of respondents in the UK who saw democracy as 'a very or fairly good way of governing' had risen from 76 percent in 1999 to 92 percent in 2018, and stood at 90 percent in 2022.[168] In 2022, 90 percent of people in the UK said that 'a democratic political system' was 'a very or fairly good way of governing the country.'[169] Between 2005 and 2022, the percentage of people who felt it was 'important for them to live in a country that is governed democratically' rose slightly, from 77 percent to 81 percent.[170] There was some evidence that younger people were less likely to value living in a democratically governed country.[171] It should be noted that, of all the countries in which this question was asked, only in Russia was there less than majority support for this proposition (where it was exactly half). The figure for the UK was similar to that in Australia, France, Canada and Spain (80; 79; 78; and 85 percent respectively). Other comparable states, such as Germany, Norway and Greece, produced higher scores (93; 93; and 92 percent respectively).[172] While people in the UK and elsewhere were likely to approve of democracy, what, precisely, they meant by it was less clear.

There was minority support for what appear to be firmly undemocratic positions, with 12 percent of UK respondents supporting 'army rule'; and 24 percent agreeing with having a 'strong leader who doesn't have to bother with parliament and elections'. Both figures had remained at similar levels since 1998. Support for

---

167 Alan Renwick, Ben Lauderdale, Meg Russell and James Cleaver, *What Kind of Democracy Do People Want? Results of a Survey of the UK Population* (London: Constitution Unit, January 2022), 3, 6, accessed 12 March 2023, https://www.ucl.ac.uk/constitution-unit/sites/constitution_unit/files/report_1_final_digital.pdf.

168 The UK in the World Values Survey, *Democracy in theory and practice: how UK attitudes compare internationally*, April 2023, 4, accessed 7 April 2023, https://www.kcl.ac.uk/policy-institute/assets/democracy-in-theory-and-practice.pdf.

169 The UK in the World Values Survey, *Democracy in theory and practice: how UK attitudes compare internationally*, April 2023, 6, accessed 7 April 2023, https://www.kcl.ac.uk/policy-institute/assets/democracy-in-theory-and-practice.pdf.

170 The UK in the World Values Survey, *Democracy in theory and practice: how UK attitudes compare internationally*, April 2023, 7, accessed 7 April 2023, https://www.kcl.ac.uk/policy-institute/assets/democracy-in-theory-and-practice.pdf.

171 The UK in the World Values Survey, *Democracy in theory and practice: how UK attitudes compare internationally*, April 2023, 8, accessed 7 April 2023, https://www.kcl.ac.uk/policy-institute/assets/democracy-in-theory-and-practice.pdf.

172 The UK in the World Values Survey, *Democracy in theory and practice: how UK attitudes compare internationally*, April 2023, 9, accessed 7 April 2023, https://www.kcl.ac.uk/policy-institute/assets/democracy-in-theory-and-practice.pdf.

'experts rather than government' making decisions had reached 61 percent – compared with 41 percent in 1999.[173] Vesting confidence in experts might be seen either as undemocratic, or as opposing populist mistrust of this group. On the subject of political change, 76 percent supported gradual reform to achieve improvements (largely stable since the early 1980s); 11 percent favoured 'revolutionary action' (an increase from 4 percent in 1981); and 10 percent agreed with the proposition that 'society must be valiantly defended against subversive forces' (down from 22 percent in 1981).[174]

Theresa May's statement announcing resignation in Downing Street, 24 May 2019[175]
Excerpts with commentary

Excerpts

Ever since I first stepped through the door behind me as Prime Minister, I have striven to make the United Kingdom a country that works not just for a privileged few, but for everyone.
And to honour the result of the EU referendum.
Back in 2016, we gave the British people a choice.
Against all predictions, the British people voted to leave the European Union.
I feel as certain today as I did three years ago that in a democracy, if you give people a choice you have a duty to implement what they decide.
I have done my best to do that.
I negotiated the terms of our exit and a new relationship with our closest neighbours that protects jobs, our security and our Union.
I have done everything I can to convince MPs to back that deal.
Sadly, I have not been able to do so.
I tried three times.
I believe it was right to persevere, even when the odds against success seemed high.
But it is now clear to me that it is in the best interests of the country for a new Prime Minister to lead that effort . . .
It will be for my successor to seek a way forward that honours the result of the referendum.
To succeed, he or she will have to find consensus in Parliament where I have not.
Such a consensus can only be reached if those on all sides of the debate are willing to compromise.
. . .

---

173 The UK in the World Values Survey, *Democracy in theory and practice: how UK attitudes compare internationally*, April 2023, 21, accessed 7 April 2023, https://www.kcl.ac.uk/policy-institute/assets/democracy-in-theory-and-practice.pdf.

174 The UK in the World Values Survey, *Democracy in theory and practice: how UK attitudes compare internationally*, April 2023, 30, accessed 7 April 2023, https://www.kcl.ac.uk/policy-institute/assets/democracy-in-theory-and-practice.pdf.

175 Theresa May, 'Prime Minister's statement in Downing Street: 24 May 2019', *gov.uk*, accessed 7 May 2023, https://www.gov.uk/government/speeches/prime-ministers-statement-in-downing-street-24-may-2019.

(continued)

As we strive to find the compromises we need in our politics – whether to deliver Brexit, or to restore devolved government in Northern Ireland – we must remember what brought us here. Because the referendum was not just a call to leave the EU but for profound change in our country. A call to make the United Kingdom a country that truly works for everyone. I am proud of the progress we have made over the last three years . . .

My focus has been on ensuring that the good jobs of the future will be created in communities across the whole country, not just in London and the South East, through our Modern Industrial Strategy.

Commentary

In this speech, May presents the referendum result as creating a democratic obligation. She stresses the need to find 'consensus'. It was not achieved within the existing Parliament, and in a wider sense was perhaps unobtainable over Brexit.

Theresa May's statement following loss of overall majority at 2017 General Election, 9 June 2017[176]
Excerpts with commentary

Excerpts

I have just been to see Her Majesty the Queen, and I will now form a government – a government that can provide certainty and lead Britain forward at this critical time for our country.

This government will guide the country through the crucial Brexit talks that begin in just 10 days, and deliver on the will of the British people by taking the United Kingdom out of the European Union . . . .

What the country needs more than ever is certainty, and having secured the largest number of votes and the greatest number of seats in the general election, it is clear that only the Conservative & Unionist Party has the legitimacy and ability to provide that certainty by commanding a majority in the House of Commons.

As we do, we will continue to work with our friends and allies in the Democratic Unionist Party in particular. Our 2 parties have enjoyed a strong relationship over many years, and this gives me the confidence to believe that we will be able to work together in the interests of the whole United Kingdom.

This will allow us to come together as a country and channel our energies towards a successful Brexit deal that works for everyone in this country – securing a new partnership with the EU which guarantees our long-term prosperity.

---

176 Theresa May, 'PM statement: General election 2017', *gov.uk*, accessed 7 May 2023, https://www.gov.uk/government/speeches/pm-statement-general-election-2017.

(continued)

That's what people voted for last June.
That's what we will deliver.
Now let's get to work.

Commentary

May seeks to present winning the most votes and seats as a source of legitimacy to govern; but acknowledges the need for support from the Democratic Unionist Party (DUP). While stressing the need for unity, the Brexit issue, the new parliamentary arithmetic, and the reliance on the DUP will make it harder to achieve. It refers to 'what people voted for last June'.

Theresa May's statement on becoming Prime Minister, 13 July 2016[177]
Excerpts with commentary

Excerpts

I have just been to Buckingham Palace, where Her Majesty The Queen has asked me to form a new government, and I accepted.

. . . .

not everybody knows this, but the full title of my party is the Conservative and Unionist Party, and that word 'unionist' is very important to me.
It means we believe in the Union: the precious, precious bond between England, Scotland, Wales and Northern Ireland. But it means something else that is just as important; it means we believe in a union not just between the nations of the United Kingdom but between all of our citizens, every one of us, whoever we are and wherever we're from.

. . .

We are living through an important moment in our country's history. Following the referendum, we face a time of great national change.
And I know because we're Great Britain, that we will rise to the challenge. As we leave the European Union, we will forge a bold new positive role for ourselves in the world, and we will make Britain a country that works not for a privileged few, but for every one of us.
That will be the mission of the government I lead, and together we will build a better Britain.

Commentary

This statement suggests underestimation of the difficulties that Brexit would entail, including for the Union to which it pledges commitment. Use of the title 'Great Britain' seemingly unwittingly excludes Northern Ireland, in contradiction of the Unionist content.

---

177 Theresa May, 'Statement from the new Prime Minister Theresa May', *gov.uk*, accessed 7 May 2023, https://www.gov.uk/government/speeches/statement-from-the-new-prime-minister-theresa-may.

Chapter Five
2022: A Year in Democracy

(Based on reports by United Kingdom Constitution Monitoring Group, with research from Dr. Dexter Govan and Alex Walker)

January

17 January:	Government is defeated on fourteen amendments to the Police, Crime, Sentencing and Courts Bill, the most in a day since the House of Lords was reformed in 1999.
19 January:	Joint Committee on Human Rights publishes legislative scrutiny report on the Nationality and Borders Bill, concluding the Bill would make a number of changes to the UK's asylum system that are not compatible with the UK's international rights commitments.
20 January:	Chair of the Public Administration and Constitutional Affairs Committee William Wragg suggests that if MPs are being improperly intimidated by government whips, they should report it to the police.
24 January:	Lord Agnew resigns as a Treasury minister, citing the government's handling of fraudulent Covid business loans.
25 January:	Metropolitan Police announces that it will be investigating potentially unlawful gatherings held in Downing Street during the coronavirus pandemic.
31 January:	Second Permanent Secretary in the Cabinet Office Sue Gray publishes interim report on gatherings in Downing Street during the coronavirus pandemic, concluding there were 'failures of leadership and judgement'; in response, the Prime Minister announces that a new Prime Minister's department will be created and the special adviser and Civil Service codes reviewed.

February

2 February:	Democratic Unionist Party minister Edwin Poots orders officials to stop conducting checks at the Irish Sea border; a UK government spokesperson says the operation of checks 'is a matter for the Northern Ireland Executive'.
3 February:	DUP Northern Ireland First Minister Paul Givan announces his resignation from the power-sharing Executive of Northern Ireland.
4/5 February:	Reports emerge that Business Secretary Kwasi Kwarteng intervened to block the appointment of Jonathan Michie to the role of executive chair of the Economic and Social Research Council because of his perceived political leanings. Steve Barclay is appointed Downing Street Chief of Staff whilst remaining Chancellor of the Duchy of Lancaster and a Member of Parliament.
9 February:	The Court of Appeal dismisses an appeal by the Welsh Counsel General against a refusal of leave to seek judicial review of interpretation of provisions in the UK Internal Market Act which might serve to constrain the Senedd's legislative competence.
21 February:	Commissioners of the Electoral Commission send a letter to the government objecting to the measures in the Elections Bill that seek to change the Commission's oversight arrangements, saying that the measures are 'inconsistent with the role that an independent electoral commission plays in a healthy democracy'.

https://doi.org/10.1515/9783110735925-005

(continued)

March

11 March:	The High Court holds that the Metropolitan Police repeatedly violated the freedom of speech and freedom of assembly of the four organisers of the Sarah Everard vigil and had unlawfully prevented them from organising the vigil. This is a landmark judgment for the right to protest.
14 March:	The Northern Ireland Protocol of the EU Withdrawal Agreement is found to be lawful by Court of Appeal in an appeal of the case brought by the head of the Traditional Unionist Voice Jim Allister and other Unionists.
17 March:	Online Safety Bill has its first reading in the House of Commons.
	Reports emerge that the government has dropped plans to cap MPs' earnings from second jobs, saying such a restriction would be 'impractical'.
23 March:	First meeting takes place of the Inter-Ministerial Standing Committee established under the new arrangements for managing intergovernmental relations. Chaired by the Secretary of State for Levelling Up, Housing and Communities (and Minister for IGR), the agenda includes items on Ukraine; UK legislation and the Sewel Convention; the Levelling Up White Paper; and a stocktake of implementation of the IGR Review.
24 March:	Dissolution and Calling of Parliament Act 2022 receives Royal Assent.

April

4 April:	A provision in the Nationality and Borders Bill allowing removal of citizenship without notice is removed from the Bill by Lords amendment and the Bill is returned to the Commons.
6 April:	A provision in the Elections Bill requiring photographic identification at polling stations is amended by the House of Lords to expand the types of accepted identification to include non-photographic forms of identification.
12 April:	The Prime Minister, Boris Johnson, and the Chancellor of the Exchequer, Rishi Sunak, receive Fixed Penalty Notices from the Metropolitan Police for breaching lockdown restrictions during the coronavirus pandemic. It is the first time that people holding these offices have been found to have committed criminal offences.
13 April:	Justice minister Lord Wolfson resigns in response to the Downing Street parties scandal.
	Joint Committee on Human Rights publishes a report on the government's plans to replace the Human Rights Act 1998 with a Bill of Rights, opposing the plan as presented.
14 April:	Government announces plans to fly certain asylum seekers to Rwanda, where their claims will be processed.
27 April:	Lord Geidt finds that Chancellor of the Exchequer did not breach the Ministerial Code in relation to possible conflicts of interest.
28 April:	After extensive 'ping pong' between the House of Lords and the House of Commons, several controversial pieces of constitutional legislation receive Royal Assent and pass into law with only minimal concessions on points of constitutional controversy.

(continued)

	The Elections Act 2022 receives Royal Assent.
	The Nationality and Borders Act 2022 receives Royal Assent.
	The Police, Crime, Sentencing and Courts Act 2022 receives Royal Assent.
	The Judicial Review and Courts Act 2022 receives Royal Assent.
29 April:	The Administrative Court finds that it is not contrary to the Public Records Act 1958 or the Freedom of Information Act 2000 for ministers to use encrypted or self-deleting messaging platforms to communicate regarding government business

May	
7 May:	Following Northern Ireland Assembly elections, Sinn Féin allocated 27 seats, to become the largest party in the Northern Ireland Assembly for the first time.
10 May:	The UK government outlines its legislative agenda for the next parliamentary session in the Queen's Speech; including several bills with likely constitutional implications, such as the 'Brexit Freedoms Bill', Bill of Rights, Levelling Up Bill and Public Order Bill.
13 May:	DUP refuses to nominate a speaker to the Northern Ireland Assembly meaning that it cannot function, despite the provisions of the Northern Ireland (Ministers, Elections and Petitions of Concern) Act 2022.
	Reports emerge that the Prime Minister intends to reduce size of the Civil Service by up to 91,000 posts, with the aim of returning to 2016 staffing levels within three years.
	Government publishes its response to the House of Commons' humble address motion seeking publication of documents relating to the appointment of Lord Lebedev, but the response omits internal correspondence between the Cabinet Office, the Prime Minister's office and the House of Lords Appointment Commission on the basis it would not be in the public interest.
17 May:	Foreign Secretary Liz Truss announces in the House of Commons that the UK will introduce domestic legislation to disapply aspects of the NI Protocol, but insists that the government's intention is still to reach a negotiated settlement with the European Union.
31 May:	Independent Adviser on Ministers' Interests, Lord Geidt, publishes his annual report in which he says that the Prime Minister receiving a Fixed Penalty Notice has raised legitimate questions about whether he breached the *Ministerial Code*, and criticising the fact that the Prime Minister has not explained his conduct in relation to the *Code*.

June	
1 June:	The Chair of the Committee on Standards in Public Life, Lord Evans, publishes an article criticising the government's lack of ambition with regards to enhancements of the *Ministerial Code*.
6 June:	A vote of no confidence held on Boris Johnson's leadership of the Conservative Party after the requisite number of letters are sent to the Chair of the 1922 Committee, Sir Graham Brady. Boris Johnson wins by 211 votes to 148.

(continued)

8 June:	The Scottish government publishes aspects of its legal advice on a second independence referendum after being ordered to do so by the Scottish Information Commissioner, although advice on the central issue of whether a referendum would be within the legislative competence of the Scottish Parliament is withheld. A case is lodged with the High Court by various charities and action groups, ahead of the first deportation flight to Rwanda.
9 June:	A general injunction on Rwanda flight refused by the High Court. High Court also refuses to issue a general pause on removing refugees.
14 June:	The Supreme Court rules that the flight to Rwanda can take off; permission to appeal the decision of the Court of Appeal was refused. The Court of Appeal itself had upheld the High Court's decision to refuse an injunction prohibiting an asylum seeker from being deported on the first flight.
	Despite criticisms including from Justin Welby, Archbishop of Canterbury and reportedly from the then-Prince of Wales, Charles, the Prime Minister defends the Rwanda plans, declaring that they will go ahead, and the first asylum seekers will be deported that day. However, at 19.30, the European Court of Human Rights (ECtHR) grants an injunction to stop one of the asylum seekers from being deported; this allows the lawyers representing the remaining passengers to apply for last minute injunctions from the ECtHR. Consequently, the flight does not take off.
15 June:	Lord Geidt resigns as the Prime Minister's ethics adviser.
22 June:	The government announces a plan to ignore ECHR rulings and deport asylum seekers to Rwanda. This includes a new Bill of Rights Bill.
24 June:	The Conservatives are defeated in two by-elections. Labour wins Wakefield on a 12.7 percent swing. Tiverton and Honiton falls to the Liberal Democrats on a 30 percent swing.
	Conservative Party chairman Oliver Dowden resigns, citing the by-election and mentioning distress and disappointment at recent events.
28 June:	Nicola Sturgeon announces that she will be seeking a second independence referendum.
	Metropolitan Police placed into special measures; this follows failures over Sarah Everard vigil and Stephen Port murders.
30 June:	Chris Pincher, Conservative Deputy Chief Whip, resigns over claims of personal misconduct.

July

5 July:	Rumours surface that Conservative backbenchers are coordinating fresh letters for a vote of no confidence in the Prime Minister despite a leadership contest not being technically possible until next year. The Health Secretary, Sajid Javid, resigns, citing the need of the people of the UK for integrity from the government.
	The Chancellor of the Exchequer, Rishi Sunak, resigns at the same time, citing fundamental difference of approach with the Prime Minister and the need for maintenance of ethical standards. A series of ministerial resignations follow.

(continued)

	Steve Barclay is appointed Health Secretary and Nadhim Zahawi is appointed Chancellor of the Exchequer.
	It is revealed that the Prime Minister was aware in 2019 of a complaint made about Chris Pincher.
6 July:	More MPs go public with letters of no-confidence in Boris Johnson. Javid gives a damning resignation speech in the Commons, claiming that the Prime Minister should not be asking others in government to purvey inaccuracies over parties and over knowledge of the allegations against Pincher.
	A string of resignations follows, including five ministerial departures announced in one letter. Resigning ministers include former Johnson loyalists.
	Suella Braverman calls for the Prime Minister to resign. Braverman announces her intention to remain as Attorney General and to run for leader of the Conservative Party at the next leadership election.
	Delegation of ministers, including Michael Gove, tell the Prime Minister to resign. Michael Gove is consequently dismissed from government by Johnson.
7 July:	Ministerial resignations continue; amongst those to resign are the secretaries of state for Wales and Northern Ireland.
	Nadim Zahawi, the newly appointed Chancellor of the Exchequer, releases an official letter calling for Boris Johnson to resign. This is a constitutionally unconventional move, following in the footsteps of Braverman, who called for Johnson's resignation despite remaining in government.
	After a record-breaking 28 ministerial resignations since 5 July, Boris Johnson announces that there will be a new Conservative leader. He states that he will remain Prime Minister until the Conservative Party leader is chosen.
	An entire cabinet reshuffle is announced.
	Tom Tugendhat announces his bid for leadership of the Conservative Party.
8 July:	Rishi Sunak announces that he will be standing for leadership of the Conservative Party. Former Equalities Minister, Kemi Badenoch, also declares that she will enter the leadership race.
9 July:	Jeremy Hunt, Nadhim Zahawi and Grant Shapps each declare that they will be running for leadership of the Conservative Party. No. 10 rebuts speculation that Boris Johnson might attempt to stand in a leadership contest.
10 July:	Liz Truss, Penny Mordaunt, Sajid Javid and Rehman Chishti each declare their bids for leadership of the Conservative Party. There are now 11 candidates who have declared their interest.
11 July:	The Conservative Party's new 1922 Committee is appointed. It is announced that nominations for the Conservative leadership race will open and close on 12 July. New, specific rules are set for the leadership race. To enter the first round candidates will need to obtain 20 nominations from MPs. Candidates will require 30 nominations for the second round. The first ballot is announced for 13 July. It is announced that that result of the leadership contest will be made public on 5 September.

(continued)

12 July:	Chishti withdraws from the leadership race, after failing to win the support of any other Conservative MPs; he subsequently endorses Tugendhat. Grant Shapps withdraws from the race and endorses Rishi Sunak. Sajid Javid also withdraws from the leadership contest and declares his endorsement of Liz Truss. There are now eight candidates that proceed to the first round of the Conservative leadership contest.
13 July:	No. 10 announces that Boris Johnson will formally tender his resignation to the Queen on 6 September, the day after the conclusion of the leadership contest. The results of the first ballot of the leadership contest are announced. The leading candidates are Rishi Sunak (88) and Penny Mordaunt (67). Jeremy Hunt (18) and Nadhim Zahawi (25) fail to meet the threshold, leaving a total of six candidates for the next round.
14 July:	The results of the second ballot for the Conservative Party leadership are announced: Suella Braverman is eliminated. Rishi Sunak (101) and Penny Mordaunt (83) are the leading candidates.
17 July:	ITV hosts a leadership debate with the remaining five candidates standing for leadership of the Conservative Party. Tugendhat publicly criticises Boris Johnson's handling of the Downing Street parties affair.
18 July:	The results of the third Conservative leadership ballot are announced. Rishi Sunak is the frontrunner with 115 votes, with Penny Mordaunt coming in second with 82 votes. Tugendhat is eliminated from the contest.
19 July:	The results of the fourth Conservative leadership ballot are announced. Kemi Badenoch is eliminated from the race, having received 59 votes. The remaining three candidates are Rishi Sunak (118), Penny Mordaunt (92) and Liz Truss (86).
20 July:	In the House of Commons, Boris Johnson takes his final Prime Minister's Questions. The Conservative Party announces that members will be able to change their votes between August and September. Voting can be conducted by post or online, but only the last vote will count.
21 July:	MPs vote for the final two candidates for the Conservative Party leader: Rishi Sunak leads with 137 votes. By contrast, Liz Truss wins 113 votes. Penny Mordaunt is eliminated from the contest, having received 105 votes. Mordaunt endorses Truss. A public inquiry into the UK government's handling of the COVID-19 pandemic is launched; the chair, Baroness Hallett, promises a robust investigation that will cover whether more could have been done.
22 July:	The European Commission launches four new infringement proceedings against the UK for not complying with significant parts of the Northern Ireland Protocol.
August	
1 August:	The postal ballot for the leadership of the Conservative Party opens.
2 August:	The postal ballot for the leadership of the Conservative Party is delayed after a security warning is issued by GCHQ.
3 August:	After the Northern Ireland Assembly is recalled by the Social Democratic and Labour Party, the Democratic Unionist Party block the election of a speaker. Consequently, no executive can be formed.

(continued)

12 August:	Conservative leadership candidate Liz Truss makes critical comments about the culture of the Civil Service, while rival Rishi Sunak proposes job cuts to fund energy support payments.
15 August:	New Cabinet Office policy allows speakers who have a history of criticising the government to be banned from learning and development events.
25 August:	Senior civil servant Neil Gibson takes control of Northern Ireland finances under section 59 of the Northern Ireland Act 1998.

September
5 September:	Liz Truss wins the Conservative Party leadership election.
6 September:	Boris Johnson resigns as Prime Minister.
	Liz Truss is installed as Prime Minister and announces her new Cabinet.
7 September:	The UK government announces that the new Bill of Rights Bill has been shelved and will not progress through Parliament.
8 September:	The Permanent Secretary to the Treasury, Tom Scholar, is removed with immediate effect by new Chancellor of the Exchequer, Kwasi Kwarteng.
8 September:	The death of Queen Elizabeth II is announced. King Charles III becomes Monarch.
10 September:	The Accession Council meets and formally proclaims Charles III king.
	Charles III takes the Oath relating to the Security of the Church of Scotland.
11 September:	Senior MPs take the Oath of Allegiance to the new King.
12 September:	King Charles III addresses the Westminster Parliament before traveling to Scotland to meet with First Minister Nicola Sturgeon.
13 September:	King Charles III visits Northern Ireland and meets Stormont political parties including Sinn Fein.
19 September:	The funeral of Queen Elizabeth II takes place.
22 September:	Speaker of the House of Commons, Lindsay Hoyle, criticises Jacob Rees Mogg for informing the media of government plans in advance of informing the House.
	The Retained EU Law (Revocation and Reform) Bill is introduced to Parliament.
23 September:	Chancellor of the Exchequer, Kwasi Kwarteng, announces a fiscal package which has not been scrutinised by either Parliament or the Office for Budget Responsibility.
26 September:	Labour Party members vote in favour of proportional representation for general elections at their annual conference.
26 September:	It is revealed that the Cabinet Office ethics team signed off on payment arrangements, subsequently reversed, for Prime Minister Liz Truss's chief of staff, that differed from the normal means of paying people in such posts.

October
11 October:	Prime Minister Liz Truss announces that responsibility for Union policy and devolution will return to the Cabinet Office.
	The First Minister of Wales, Mark Drakeford, confirms to the Senedd that Prime Minister Liz Truss has yet to contact him. A similar situation exists in regard to Scotland, where the Prime Minister has yet to contact First Minister Nicola Sturgeon.

(continued)

14 October:	Boris Johnson's political honours list is announced, creating 13 new Conservative peers.
15 October:	In response to political pressure following the exceptionally poor market reception for 23 September's fiscal package, Prime Minister Liz Truss announces Kwasi Kwarteng has been replaced as Chancellor of the Exchequer by Jeremy Hunt.
17 October:	New Chancellor Jeremy Hunt announces that almost all changes announced in the fiscal package are to be reversed.
19 October:	Suella Braverman is forced to resign as Home Secretary after it is revealed she sent confidential documents via a personal email account.
20 October:	Following continued significant political pressure in the wake of the fiscal package, Liz Truss announces her departure as Prime Minister once a successor as leader of the Conservative Party is chosen.
24 October:	Boris Johnson announces he will not put his name forward as a candidate for Leader of the Conservative Party despite, he claims, having secured support from a number of MPs sufficient to pass the threshold of 100 set by Graham Brady MP and the 1922 Committee. Rishi Sunak becomes the only Conservative MP to pass this nomination threshold and is duly elected Leader of the Conservative Party. Rishi Sunak becomes Prime Minister.
25 October:	Rishi Sunak announces his new cabinet with Suella Braverman reappointed as Home Secretary following her resignation six days previously.

November

8 November:	Gavin Williamson resigns as Minister of State without Portfolio following complaints about his conduct.
16 November:	Dominic Raab answers questions in Parliament over two allegations of bullying.
20 November:	The Leader of the Opposition, Keir Starmer, pledges to abolish the House of Lords, appearing to mean that it will be replaced with a differently composed second chamber.
21 November:	Suspended former Conservative MP David Warburton is found to have breached the Code of Conduct for Members by failing to declare a £150,000 loan from a Russian-born businessman.
23 November:	The UK Supreme Court rules unanimously that it had jurisdiction to decide the Lord Advocate's reference and unanimously that the Scottish Parliament does not have the right to legislate for an independence referendum. It also holds that the international law right of self-determination does not confer on the people of Scotland the right to become independent.
25 November:	The inquiry into allegations of bullying against Dominic Raab MP is expanded and Prime Minister Rishi Sunak appoints employment barrister Adam Tolley KC to investigate the matter (there is no Independent Adviser on Ministers' Interests in post yet, following the resignation of Lord Geidt from the post in June 2022).

(continued)

December

2 December: The Public Administration and Constitutional Affairs Committee publishes its *Propriety of Governance* report. This includes criticism of the reappointment of Suella Braverman as Home Secretary.

5 December: Labour's Commission on the UK's Future, led by former Prime Minister Gordon Brown, releases its report *A New Britain*. The report proposes a raft of constitutional reforms for adoption by the Labour Party ahead of the next general election.

7 December: A fifth unsuccessful attempt is made to recall Stormont, with the Democratic Unionist Party again preventing the recall.

   The Prime Minister expresses shock over claims made about the activities of Conservative Peer Michelle Mone in relation to the award of pandemic related contracts.

12 December: Secondary legislation is published ahead of the introduction of compulsory Voter ID at elections in 2023.

15 December: The High Court rules that Edwin Poots acted unlawfully in seeking to halt post-Brexit goods checks in Northern Ireland.

   The Prime Minister's spokesman confirms five additional complaints have been made by civil servants about Dominic Raab's behaviour as a minister.

19 December: The High Court rules that the government's agreement to send asylum seekers to Rwanda is lawful in general, though individual cases can remain subject to review.

22 December: Laurie Magnus is named as the Prime Minister's new Ethics Adviser. He is the first person to occupy the post since Lord Geidt's resignation in June 2022.

   The High Court rules the government's EU resettlement plan is not lawful.

22 December: Rishi Sunak issues a new edition of the Ministerial Code.

Chapter Six
Critical Review: The Historical Perspective

This book has considered literature produced since 2016 on the difficulties faced by democracy internationally. It has identified manifestations of such problems in the UK during the same period. Brexit has been an important factor; alongside broader tendencies. The approach taken is useful because it enables the analysis of a wider set of issues in the context of a particular state. Yet it has limitations: for instance, it is constrained in that it is focused on a specific time span. The author has chosen this method because of the detailed consideration it allows. But a broader historic perspective can enhance understanding. To take this wider view is not necessarily to contradict conclusions otherwise reached. Indeed, as we will see, it can nuance or possibly reinforce them. But it can ground them in a firmer evidential and analytical base.

This historical review begins with Brexit. The nature of the relationship with the continent of which the UK is a part has been a source of tension throughout the history of the UK as a state. Debates about how far and on what basis it should entangle itself in the business of its region have played an ongoing and prominent role in UK politics; and indeed in the politics of its precursors. Such tensions have played a central role in events of the highest importance, including for the political system itself. For instance, a key catalyst of the various upheavals experienced by the British Isles in the seventeenth century was disagreement about the appropriate response to conflict and tension on the continental mainland. In the wake of the Second World War, after long development as an idea, the contemporary European integration project began to develop as a practical reality. It soon became, and has continued to be, a vexing issue for the UK, engaging various first-order concerns for the UK. How did European integration align with the historically global perspective of the now-declining Empire; and the close relationship more recently established with the US? Might it provide the UK with a new means of wielding external influence? Was it culturally, intellectually and constitutionally compatible with UK traditions? Was it a natural and important expression of the European identity of the UK? Was it an economically beneficial option? What did it mean politically? What would be the cost of being outside? The idea of UK exceptionalism was important to such discussions in the UK. They had the potential to create divisions between parties as well as within them; and perhaps between the political elite and the wider population (as suggested at those times when opinion polling showed relatively high levels as being opposed to membership, and by the 2016 referendum result).

https://doi.org/10.1515/9783110735925-006

From the early 1970s through to the following decade, the Labour Party experienced serious internal conflicts fuelled by the issue of participation in European integration. In this context, opposition within Labour often (though not always) came from the Left of the party, which regarded European integration as a capitalist project that would inhibit pursuit of a more radical socialist agenda: a forerunner to the Lexit perspective. At the time, Europe was more disruptive for Labour than for the Conservatives. But the Conservative Party has also seen sustained resistance to the project. Motives for this scepticism could include attachment to the UK's global role, the desire to protect certain sectors of the economy, and concerns about threats to sovereignty. By the early 1990s, encouraged in part by the former leader and Prime Minister, Margaret Thatcher, Euroscepticism, as it came to be known, was becoming a more dynamic force within the Conservatives, while it had subsided within Labour. Divisions over this issue helped define the Conservative Party over the next three decades. Europe has been a significant concern for other parties, who have also displayed a propensity to alter their stance on the subject. During the 1970s, for example, the Scottish National Party exhibited anti-integrationist tendencies. By the 2020s, objections to Brexit were central to its drive for independence.

Hesitant about a number of early initiatives such as the European Coal and Steel Community of 1952, the UK was not a participant in the European Economic Community at the time of its launch in 1957. But perceived political and economic failings in the UK encouraged the Conservative Prime Minister, Harold Macmillan, to change course and begin seeking membership in 1961. This initial application was rejected; as was a second in 1967. The UK finally acceded to the European Communities in 1973, but it proved reluctant fully to embrace membership, often seeking (and securing) opt-outs and exceptions, ranging from the budget rebate to remaining outside the single currency; it also held two referendums on whether to continue membership or to leave, in 1975 and 2016. But despite a lack of enthusiasm for the project, the UK shift towards what became the EU during 1961–1973, sustained for more than four decades, was a change of immense consequence. It was important because of the implications both for the external posture of the UK and for its internal policy, law and constitutional arrangements. The further reversal of approach that occurred from 2016 has been of similar significance.

The UK that left the EU was different to the UK that had entered the European Communities. For instance, in the interim, the UK had introduced legislative devolution to Wales and Scotland for the first time; and restored it to Northern Ireland. The system of governance for the latter territory was part of a peace agreement which rested on Northern Ireland being open to the Republic of Ireland and Great Britain – made possible by the Republic and UK being members of the EU. The UK economy had become increasingly incorporated into the

European Single Market, the development of which it had encouraged. Crucial to this entity were four freedoms: for the movement of capital, goods, services, and people, within the EU. The UK was intertwined with the EU in other fields: for instance, scientific research, cultural projects, and development programmes. It participated in its political institutions, including the European Parliament, with UK parties joining pan-EU groupings. The UK, along with the other member states, shared in EU law. That the process of severance from this enveloping entity, followed by the experience of being outside it, should prompt such turbulence as it did, is as understandable as the notion that Brexit could remove controversy from the matter of UK relations with its continent is dubious. As an issue, Europe has proved persistent in its capacity to divide. It can realistically be expected to continue to do so.

Brexit itself provided a perverse illustration of the extent to which the UK was politically embedded within the EU. It might be seen as a manifestation of wider Eurosceptic tendencies within the EU – though the only such expression to date to have led to renunciation of membership by an entire Member State. Furthermore, the mechanism by which departure was triggered was itself in part an import from elsewhere in the continent. The holding of referendums on European issues was widespread among prospective and actual Member States. Though opponents of participation were principal drivers of the votes held in the UK on continued membership in 1975 and 2016, through encouraging the use of this device they contributed to a Europeanisation of UK politics. Yet while continental politics was in this sense a powerful influence on UK constitutional practices, as a proposed instrument in the UK referendums have a history that predates the European integration project. The possibility of holding popular votes of this type first came on to the agenda in the UK in the later nineteenth century as a means of settling issues of particular importance which might be hard to settle by other means. Potential subjects included the idea of 'home rule' for Ireland (a precursor to devolution). A further suggested application concerned a policy suggestion that caused considerable controversy among Conservatives and Unionists in the first third of the twentieth century: that of protectionism, as advocated by Joseph Chamberlain. It was in many ways a precursor to the European integration issue, though ultimately not one on which a popular vote was ever held.

The UK finally began using referendums on major issues from 1973 onwards, commencing with a vote in Northern Ireland over whether it should continue to be part of the UK, followed in 1975 by the first UK-wide vote, on membership of the European Communities. Before 2016, referendums had shown the potential to foment political disruption, although not to the same degree as the Brexit vote has achieved. For instance, in 1979, a vote on Scottish devolution yielded a 'yes' outcome, but without meeting the required threshold of 40 per cent of registered voters supporting the proposition. In response to this result, in the House of Commons, the Scottish National Party tabled a no-confidence motion in the minority Labour government. Taken on by the Conservative Party, the motion ended in defeat for Labour, forcing a dissolution of Parliament, and a General Election, resulting in Margaret Thatcher leading the Conservatives back into government.

The referendum had previously been advocated partly as a means of separating major decisions from day-to-day politics and resolving matters without disturbing the representative system. Long before 2016, though, this device had shown it was capable of triggering turbulence in the political system. However, the vote of 2016 had disruptive characteristics that made it unique. What set it apart was the way in which it combined a series of factors. First, it involved members of the public voting (by a narrow margin in percentage terms) for a course of action to which the government (along with majorities in both Houses of Parliament) was opposed. Secondly, though the result was not legally binding, successive administrations treated it as creating an obligation. Thirdly, they did so despite the lack of clarity as to its precise meaning, and notwithstanding that many within those same governments (and among their parliamentary bases) had opposed leaving the EU at the time of the referendum.

The referendum and the result it produced were essential to Brexit taking place (though in themselves not sufficient, since its implementation required further action, for instance by the executive and legislature). But how disruptive, placed in historical perspective, was the turmoil they helped facilitate? In the wake of the vote, there was considerable party political and electoral tumult. The 2019 General Election saw some notable shifts in patterns of seat distribution, connected to the Brexit issue. There may be reason to doubt the durability of these trends, but even if they fail to sustain in the future they made a dramatic impact at the time, helping to secure the Johnson premiership and to fertilise its subsequent democratic disruptions, as well as ensuring the implementation of Brexit in the specific form it took. Despite the ability of parties such as UKIP and the Brexit Party to make a significant impact, there has not yet been a realignment in the system of the type that manifested itself at the 1918 General Election, when Labour eclipsed the Liberals as the principal opposition to the Conservatives. Nonetheless, within the two main parties, there were consequential shifts. Radical anti-EU forces achieved ascendancy within the Conservatives, banishing or to a significant extent subduing other influences. The public conversion of the Labour leadership to supposed firm commitment to Brexit was also significant, and was connected to the adoption of further positions that are significant from the perspective of this work.

Beyond the immediate Brexit issue, there are many parallels helpful to an analysis of democratic challenges faced by the UK since 2016. Populist or extremist-type leaders, parties and groupings have made an impact at various points in political history. In the first decade of the twentieth century, for instance, the British Brothers' League campaigned against inward migration, obtaining a following in the East London area in particular, using slogans including 'British Homes for British Workers'. At this time the focus was on Jewish people arriving from Eastern Europe. A legislative response to the concern came in the form of the *Aliens Act 1905*, which created a '[p]ower to prevent the landing of undesirable immigrants'.[1] The UK has seen also political parties associated with wider international movements of an authoritarian character, such as the Communist Part of Great Britain (formed in 1921) and the British Union of Fascists, active during the 1930s. Individual politicians have gained a degree of public prominence and even influence. Enoch Powell, initially a Conservative, generated a popular following through the anti-immigration stance he first widely publicised in a speech in 1968.[2] Tony Benn became the leader of a radical left faction within the Labour Party in the 1970s and 1980s which rested to a large extent on activist members and brought him into tension with many within the parliamentary party. (Both politicians became notable opponents of UK participation in European integration, campaigning to leave at the 1975 referendum). Powell and Benn came from within the two main parties of the post-1918 period (though Powell left the Conservatives in 1974). Yet neither managed to capture the leadership. From this perspective, the period from 2016 stands out. For a politician of populist flavour to attain the leadership of either the Conservatives or Labour was a new departure; for individuals of this type to achieve ascendancy within both of the two parties in the same time period (with one becoming Prime Minister) was even more remarkable.

In some respects, there is precedent for the approaches pursued by the Conservatives during the period considered in this work. The emergence of a mass electorate from the nineteenth century onwards might have posed a challenge to the viability of a party associated with traditional values and more privileged social groups. Yet the Conservatives managed to retain electoral competitiveness into the twenty-first century, proving to be the most successful party over the period. It performed this feat partly by campaigning on issues that could unite a cross-class coalition of voters, dividing and drawing support away from opponents. In this sense,

---

1 Aliens Act 1905, s.1. For a discussion of the British Brothers' League in historic perspective, see: David Rosenberg, 'Ukip is nothing new: the British Brothers' League immigration fears in 1901', *Guardian*, 4 March 2015, accessed 16 April 2023, https://www.theguardian.com/uk-news/2015/mar/04/ukip-nigel-farage-immigrants-british-brothers-league.
2 Andy Richards, 'Enoch Powell: What was the "Rivers of Blood" speech? Full text here', *BirminghamLive*, 30 March 2015, accessed 18 June 2023, https://www.birminghammail.co.uk/news/mid lands-news/enoch-powell-what-rivers-blood-8945556.

what might be termed the 'culture wars' approach, which had populist aspects to it, was part of a well-established Conservative pattern. But there were also characteristic differences from earlier programmes of this type. Benjamin Disraeli, Conservative Prime Minister in 1868 and again from 1874–1880, honed a technique of rallying support around established entities and institutions, such as the monarchy, the Church of England, the legal system, the House of Lords, and the Empire; and presented the existing system as under threat from radical, alien ideas and movements. He also offered the working classes improved quality of life through measures for the enforcement of higher standards in areas such as housing and sanitation. In the later period assessed in this work, the Conservative Party continued to seek to mobilise voters of different social grades against the supposed dangers coming from groups such as the liberal intelligentsia. But the tone it maintained was one of criticism of or outright hostility towards, rather than support for, institutions such as the EU, the BBC, the courts, the Civil Service, and Parliament. It is curious that in *The Victorians: Twelve Titans Who Forged Britain*, a book first published in 2019, Jacob Rees-Mogg praised Disraeli for his approach set out in 'his two great speeches of 1872, one in the Manchester Free Trade Hall and the other in the Crystal Palace', in which he pledged 'to maintain the institutions of Britain, to elevate "the condition of the people" and to uphold Empire'.[3] Rees-Mogg, a leading and firm advocate of Brexit among Conservative parliamentarians, was a prominent critic of institutions such as the Civil Service, the Bank of England and the Supreme Court; and promoted a radical deregulation agenda. In this respect, he epitomised both the differences and similarities between the Disraeli prescription for the Conservative Party and that which came to the forefront in the post-2016 era.

Apparently motivated by a desire to reverse the successful Conservative voter mobilisation in constituencies it had previously held at the 2019 General Election, Labour in the 2020s likewise sought to present itself as intent upon controlling the flow of people into the country from outside. It also seemingly drew back from challenging the premise of Conservative initiatives on refugees. Labour already had a prior record of fearing it had somehow become estranged from traditional support bases over such matters; and of responding through initiatives regarding the movement of people from outside the UK that consciously sought to distance it from supposedly elitist, liberal, metropolitan priorities. During the 2015 General Election campaign, on 28 April, the *Guardian* reported that – in a speech due to take place that day – the Labour leader, Ed Miliband, would discuss immigration, saying that: 'We will deal with people's concerns because we have listened, we have learned

---

3 Jacob Rees-Mogg, *The Victorians: Twelve Titans Who Forged Britain* (London: Penguin, 2020), 142–143.

and we have changed.' The article noted that he had a '10-point plan' which encompassed 'recruiting an extra 1,000 borders staff, paid for by a small charge on non-visa visitors to the UK, and stopping those who have committed serious crimes coming to Britain and deporting those who commit them after they arrive.' He would also pledge to introduce 'full exit checks so border staff can count people in and out of the country.' Ending the 'indefinite detention of people in the asylum and immigration system', Miliband would also 'promise to impose a cap on workers from outside the EU and a tightening of the rules requiring large firms hiring workers from outside to offer apprenticeships in the UK.' The Labour leader would commit himself to introducing 'the single toughest clampdown on benefits for EU citizens', and he 'proposed' a ban on people claiming benefits for at least two years, and a ban on sending child benefit to families living abroad.'[4]

Miliband also wanted to stress that 'as the son of two refugees myself, I will never do anything to denigrate or demean the contribution people who have come to this country have made.' However, his approach was a source of unease within Labour. The article described how 'a tea mug with the slogan "control immigration" produced by Labour to go alongside one of its five pledges has caused controversy, with many party members including . . . shadow cabinet figures saying they would not buy one.'[5] The adoption of such a tone, its potential to generate controversy and seemingly discomfort for the very politician who had chosen it, had antecedents. In the previous decade, speaking to the Trade Union Congress on 10 September 2007, the Labour Prime Minister, Gordon Brown, of whom Miliband was a protégé, announced his intention to 'respond to globalisation by creating more jobs for British men and women and young people throughout our economy . . . If we make the right decisions, we can advance even further and faster to full employment than ever before, with a British job on offer for every British worker'.[6] At the Labour conference two weeks later, Brown continued in

4 'Labour has changed on immigration, says Ed Miliband', *Guardian*, 28 April 2015, accessed 15 March 2023, https://www.theguardian.com/uk-news/2015/apr/28/labour-changed-immigration-ed-miliband-promise.

5 'Labour has changed on immigration, says Ed Miliband', *Guardian*, 28 April 2015, accessed 15 March 2023, https://www.theguardian.com/uk-news/2015/apr/28/labour-changed-immigration-ed-miliband-promise.

6 Vincent Keter, *Government policy on 'British jobs for British workers'* (London: House of Commons Library, 2009), 2, accessed 15 March 2023, https://researchbriefings.files.parliament.uk/documents/SN04501/SN04501.pdf.

this vein, setting out a 'vision' of 'Britain leading the global economy . . . drawing on the talents of all to create British jobs for British workers.'[7]

Sensing an opportunity in this stance, the Conservative Leader of the Opposition, David Cameron, in a House of Commons debate of 6 November that year, referred to: 'the slogan that the Prime Minister wheels out every week: British jobs for British workers. Yes, if only he could see how embarrassed his Labour MPs are, how they shudder when he utters those words.' Cameron went on to criticise the proposal from a practical perspective, before remarking that: 'I did a bit more research to find out where he got his slogans from: he borrowed one off the National Front; he borrowed another off the British National party. Where was his moral compass when he was doing that?'[8]

Labour, then, has long perceived itself as vulnerable in this area and attempted to respond accordingly. The idea that the views of voters have been ignored on this issue or their opinions stigmatised is therefore inaccurate. It is probably more accurate to conclude that Labour (and other parties) have been willing to defer to such attitudes rather than challenge them. There is another sense in which the Labour approach is part of a pattern that had manifested itself long before 2016. The proposition that the previously more stable lives of sections of the population have become subject to disruption has long lineage. In accounts discussed in this book, such as those of Nandy and Glasman, it is held that at some point in the last few decades – perhaps by around the early 1980s – certain groups and ideas became ascendant, exposing society to disruptive global economic forces. But this attitude has also existed in supposedly more secure earlier periods.

Probably without intending to, Nadine Dorries offers support for this observation. In her fictional work set in mid-twentieth century Liverpool and Ireland, the *Four Streets* trilogy, Dorries describes 'the order of life on the four streets. All day long house-wives complained about their lot but they got on with it. Through a depression, war, illness and poverty . . . No one ever thought it would alter. Their way of life was constant and familiar, as it had been as long as anyone could remember . . . Neighbours in Liverpool had taken the place of family in Ireland and the community was emotionally self-supporting.' However, 'this was the fifties . . . Times were about to change and the future hung heavy in the air.'[9] The reference to Ireland is significant. People arriving from elsewhere has been a sustained feature of UK society, long predating the accession of post-Communist states into the EU. The sense of disruption is

---

7 Vincent Keter, *Government policy on 'British jobs for British workers'* (London: House of Commons Library, 2009), 2, accessed 15 March 2023, https://researchbriefings.files.parliament.uk/documents/SN04501/SN04501.pdf.

8 467 Parl.Deb H.C. (6 November 2007), col. 22.

9 Nadine Dorries, *The Four Streets Saga* (London: Head of Zeus, 2017), 4.

frequent, perhaps even continuous. Interpretations built on the idea that destabilisation is only relatively recent, and that a more grounded life once existed, that might even be restored, are, therefore, questionable. Indeed, we can go back far further and to an observer of different political persuasion to confirm this point. Friedrich Engels gave an account of the disruptive impact of economic and industrial development upon the lives and livelihoods of workers in Manchester in his 1845 work *The Condition of the Working Class in England.* The presence of Irish labour was treated as a notable factor.[10] In this sense, Labour by the early 2020s was repeating earlier general diagnoses, and responses to them.

To move to a further focus of this book – the issue of lack of probity and departures from constitutional norms in government – there is again much background to consider. David Lloyd George, Prime Minister at the head of a coalition government from 1916–1922, acquired a reputation for dubious practices, including corruption in the conferral of honours – a system that persistently lends itself to abuse, perceived and actual. Examples of questionable contributions to political debate came in 1945 when both the Conservative and Labour leaderships, who had worked together in the wartime coalition from the beginning of the decade, both made statements implying possible parallels between the other party and the Nazis. A Prime Minister who is probably best remembered for an association with duplicitous behaviour, in relation to the Suez conflict of 1956, is Anthony Eden. After this episode, and its disastrous failure, he left office the following year, on grounds of ill health. But there is no comparable example of a premier whose exit was so clearly linked to misconduct as that of Boris Johnson in 2022 (though other factors, such as evidence he had become a political liability, were involved).

The removal of a Prime Minister – ultimately forced by his own party colleagues – in such circumstances might be seen as indicator (or perhaps source) of political instability. Such a perception is possibly strengthened by the fact that that a further three premiers left office during the period under consideration (Cameron in 2016; May in 2019; Truss in 2022). Such a frequency of attrition was exceptional. The four previous exits (Brown in 2010; Blair in 2007; Major in 1997; Thatcher in 1990) took place over a span of 20 years rather than six. From a different point of view, the ousting of a Prime Minister might be seen as a sign of constitutional health: the ability of the system to test and scrutinise premiers, and if they prove lacking in some way, force them out. This book has sought – and found a profusion of – problems. But an equally valid exercise would be to iden-

---

10 Friedrich Engels, *The Condition of the Working Class in England* (London: Penguin, 2009). Chapter 4 is entitled 'Irish Immigration'.

tify successes. Even when faced with the difficult circumstances of Brexit, democracy has survived; and – despite the elevation of an individual such as Johnson – has managed to correct itself. Bleak assessments of the prospects for the system can be found in many previous periods. Yet, as in those earlier times, it has persisted. Perhaps it is the continual seeking out of and drawing attention to problems that has helped ensure this durability. Nonetheless, complacency should always be avoided.

Essay question

What are the implications of political developments in the United Kingdom since 2016 for the debate about prime ministerial power?

The debate about prime ministerial power in the UK is as old as the office itself. The person generally regarded as being the first Prime Minister, Robert Walpole, was criticised for being too powerful, while he insisted that he did not have the authority attributed to him. The discussion has continued in more recent times. Some have held that the Prime Minister is dominant within government, and perhaps increasingly so, even to the point of becoming, in effect, a president. They point to a number of advantages possessed by the Prime Minister. They include being chair of Cabinet, setting its agenda and summarising its meetings, and being responsible for establishing and choosing the members of its sub-committees. Premiers have the power to hire and fire ministers and allocate portfolios. It is also held that their responsibility for the Civil Service provides them with institutional influence, and that they can draw on specialised support staff, including political appointments, to take part in policy formation and implementation, and communications. Prime ministers have special responsibilities in areas such as emergency responses and the work of the intelligence and security agencies. They issue ethical and constitutional guidance contained in documents such as the *Ministerial Code*, and make decisions about their enforcement. Prime ministers have the personal authority that arises from being the most prominent member of the government, the leader of the party that is dominant within the House of Commons, and a focus for media attention. They alone are able to request dissolutions of Parliament, triggering general elections. They represent the UK on the world stage.

Other commentators have stressed the limitations upon prime ministerial power. They note that Cabinet is a collective body, reaching decisions through discussion, and the Prime Minister cannot expect simply to issue it with instructions that its members will accept. In choosing ministers, prime ministers must balance a range of political considerations, and take into account how suitable someone may be for a particular role. Choosing their own close allies is not always a realistic option. There are limits to how far they can involve themselves in policy. Other Cabinet members might resist intervention in their portfolios, and prime ministers and their staff do not between them have the capacity to engage in detail in every aspect of government, each part of which is the work of a full-sized department. Emergencies and related matters can be a distraction as well as an opportunity for premiers to assert themselves. Being the figurehead of a government can make them a target, for politicians on their own and opposing sides, and for the media. Their personal authority is dependent to some extent on their perceived performance as leaders, which can vary; and also the way in which they choose to operate. Parliament and party can be difficult to manage, and may at times challenge them and their governments. They are subject to various changing external factors that can limit them, such as legal decisions, economic trends, and international events beyond their control. Most prime ministers leave office earlier than they would like. They can lose general elections; or – perhaps if their own party judges them to have become an electoral liability – they can potentially be removed by their own colleagues.

Consideration of the period since 2016 provides much material relevant to this debate. During the period, there were multiple changes of Prime Minister: from David Cameron to Theresa May in 2016; from May to Boris Johnson in 2019; from Johnson to Liz Truss in 2022 and – also in 2022 – from Truss to Rishi Sunak. This pattern confirms that prime ministers are vulnerable to removal from office. In this period the turnover was quicker than usual, suggesting that they were weaker than in some earlier periods. Significantly, in none of these cases was the Prime Minister ousted by a General Election defeat, but because they felt – or were made to conclude – that they could no longer carry on in office. Cameron judged that he was not the right Prime Minister to oversee Brexit; while May, Johnson and Truss all faced immense pressure to leave from within the Conservative Party. In government throughout the period, the Conservatives, both inside and outside Parliament, had become increasingly difficult to manage.

Prime ministers' hands could seem tied by a variety of other sources of influence. As Prime Minister, May struggled to control members of her own Cabinet, including Johnson. Through his controversial behaviour, Johnson himself eventually prompted members of his government and party into a revolt against him. During his premiership, Sunak's controversial decision to reappoint Suella Braverman as Home Secretary seems to have been driven by certain forces within his own parliamentary party who were Braverman supporters.

Another entity that appeared to grow in its ability to restrict prime ministers during the period was the judiciary. Two prime ministers – Truss in 2017 and Johnson in 2019 – lost landmark legal cases related to Brexit in the Supreme

Court. And though it left the EU during this period, UK prime ministers still had to contend with it as a power base. The views of the US were also significant to how it conducted the Brexit process, perhaps discouraging prime ministers from taking a harder line over Northern Ireland in particular. International financial markets were also significant. Their reaction to the fiscal package Truss introduced upon taking office in 2022 ultimately led to her removal as Prime Minister.

For most of this period, prime ministers no longer possessed a power they had previously possessed – to request, on their own initiative, a dissolution of Parliament and bring about a General Election. Under the Fixed-term Parliaments Act of 2011, they now had to obtain approval from Parliament (by a two-thirds Commons majority) if they wanted to hold an election in advance of the five-year limit. For a time in the autumn of 2019, Johnson was unable to secure House of Commons support for his Brexit policy, but could not get agreement to a General Election either. When he finally managed to trigger an election, he won with a comfortable majority in December. He was then able, in 2022, to repeal the Fixed-term Parliaments Act and restore the ability of the Prime Minister to request dissolutions without involving Parliament. But being able to hold a General Election was not necessarily a source of prime ministerial power. When Theresa May secured parliamentary agreement to an early election in April 2017, the result in June saw the Conservatives lose their overall majority, undermining May's standing within party, Parliament and country.

General elections are one means by which the public can impact upon prime ministers. Another is through referendums. The 'leave' vote in the EU referendum of 23 June 2016 had complex consequences. It brought about an end to the premiership of Cameron; and the political imperative it created to leave the EU, and then deal with the consequences of having done so, was a strain for all the prime ministers who came after Cameron. It brought down May in 2019. But at times, prime ministers could claim that they were the primary vehicles for the referendum result, and that they should therefore be deferred to, for instance by colleagues in government and by Parliament. The Johnson slogan 'Get Brexit Done' conveyed the sense that his agenda for putting the referendum result into effect must prevail, and seemed to make an important political impact.

The emergency role of prime ministers came to the fore for Johnson during the pandemic. This episode was an immense challenge for him, and at times his performance was a subject of criticism. But Johnson was also able to achieve a boost for the popular appeal of his government when the vaccine was made available from late 2020 onwards. The pandemic saw immense exercises of prime ministerial power, for instance introducing lockdown measures applying to the whole population. But this experience revealed another limitation that now applies to prime ministers: they do not have the same role in the devolved territories of Wales, Scotland and Northern Ireland – each of which pursued its own approaches to the pandemic – as they do in England.

Despite all the limitations, the period from 2016 saw significant exercises of prime ministerial power. May seems to have taken a leading role in the conduct of the Brexit negotiations. Johnson successfully forced through a Brexit deal and took the UK out of the EU. In September 2019, he also expelled multiple Conservative MPs from the party who were not willing to support his approach; and vested immense power in his political staff, in particular his most senior adviser, Dominic Cummings. Johnson placed his imprint on the Civil Service, with numerous senior officials leaving their posts. Truss, during her short premiership, engaged in remarkable exercises of prime ministerial authority related to the introduction of a fiscal package. For instance, she removed the Permanent Secretary to the Treasury; and introduced major fiscal changes without full scrutiny from Parliament and the Office for Budget Responsibility. Finally, Sunak took a lead in reaching a deal on Northern Ireland with the EU, and achieved parliamentary support for it.

But as the fate of four of the five prime ministers who held office during this period demonstrates, while they could exercise power, it did not last forever. If they were seen to have made mistakes or if circumstances changed, they lost their authority and their position could come under threat. All had to contend with background challenges such as Brexit, the pandemic and war in Ukraine, bringing them into contact with tendencies beyond their immediate control. Meanwhile they were subject to domestic scrutiny. While some newspapers might offer support, they could not evade oversight completely. Moreover, there are now numerous codes against which their behaviour can be judged, and – if necessary – condemned. There are, however, practical limits on their effectiveness.

Chapter Seven
Tract

Democratic Instability in the United Kingdom: Context, Cause and Cure

Ongoing convulsions in the political and constitutional system of the UK have made it a subject of international attention of an unfortunate kind. The act of leaving the European Union (EU), and the controversies and political battles associated with it, helped generate a reputation for volatility. Other events – including the multiple scandals of the Boris Johnson premiership and the rapid implosion of the Liz Truss administration – reenforced this perception. As well as coming increasingly to be marked out for its instability, the UK now exhibits its own manifestations of certain worrying international tendencies. Over the last decade or more, analysis of the prospects for democracy in the world has taken on a strengthening mood of pessimism. Patterns of development from the 1970s onwards had previously encouraged a view that this system of government was enjoying an ascendancy that was hard to resist let alone reverse. They included transitions away from dictatorship in Greece, Portugal and Spain; the collapse of Soviet-led Communism; and developments in Asia, for instance in the Republic of Korea (i.e.: South Korea) and Indonesia. It is understandable that many observers were tempted to regard this so-called 'third historic wave' of democratisation as a decisive period of triumph.

As the twenty-first century progressed, such notions came to appear excessively optimistic. Some authoritarian states it was hoped would democratise remained resolute in their imperviousness to political reform. Most notable within this category was China. In others, though they had changed regimes, gains proved to be shallow. Russia fits within such a group. Certain post-Communist states, such as Hungary, were admitted to the EU on the basis that they had achieved a lasting transition to democracy, an assumption that now appears false. Furthermore, supposedly mature, stable democracies, have become less secure than might previously have seemed plausible. Members of this final group include the United States and France, both of which have faced threats from political leaders and movements that represent challenges to the liberal democratic order, that have come close to, or have actually achieved, high office; and which continue to pose serious threats. Furthermore, states and movements that are ambivalent or hostile towards democratic principles do more than simply exercise problematic influence within their domestic environments. They are also assertive externally, sometimes working together (in as far as their nature allows for such cooperation). Such activity can take in rhetorical interventions, surreptitious operations of various kinds, and overt military action.

https://doi.org/10.1515/9783110735925-007

Developments in the UK, especially since 2016, mean that it can reasonably be placed within the category of established democracies that face challenges. The UK thus provides evidence of and contributes to a troublesome international tendency. The UK – and the Conservative government which has operated (under different premiers) throughout the period in question – has displayed characteristics associated with tendencies such as democratic backsliding, and what is known as 'populism'. Some of them have deep roots in UK political and social history, but others are more novel or have at least acquired greater intensity lately. They include:

- The population of a country of about 65 million people indefinitely losing the expansive European citizenship rights that they would otherwise have possessed, on the basis of approximately 17.4 million people voting to leave the EU;
- The advent, in Brexit, of a polarising episode. It has prompted the dissemination of misleading information in political discourse; disrupted more traditional patterns of party-political interaction; and revealed and accentuated a variety of divisions over assorted issues. Connected to such cleavages, the Conservative Party has sought to promote and benefit from what might be regarded as culture war issues in areas such as refugee policy;
- In relation to the above, concerned about alienating some of its support base, Labour has come to present itself as accepting of Brexit, and even of embracing it as an opportunity. It has also seemed reluctant fully to oppose the Conservatives on other divisive issues such as asylum policy, and the party has employed some controversial rhetoric in such areas.
- The promotion from a number of sources of populist-type theses in which the people – defined in an exclusive sense – are engaged in a struggle with manipulative elites. The latter category can include institutions such as the Civil Service, the legal profession, experts (however defined), Parliament, and the BBC. Adherence to such views has permeated entities including the Brexit Party and the Conservatives;
- The ascendancy at various points of populist traits and forces within both Labour and the Conservatives. Members and affiliates voting in leadership elections in both parties being willing to favour candidates leaning towards such positions. Politicians displaying populist characteristics – such as Boris Johnson, Jeremy Corbyn, Nigel Farage and Liz Truss – have come to occupy leadership positions within parties;
- A willingness among sufficient numbers of members of the public to vote in elections or in a referendum in ways that encourage populist or backsliding outcomes. Absolute majorities are not necessarily needed for such purposes.
- The occurrence – in the form of the 2016 European Union (EU) referendum – of an exercise in direct democracy which has challenged more established representative principles. Proponents of Brexit and related political causes

often claim a special legitimacy derived from the popular will that enables them to override other restraints. Implementation of the 2016 'leave' result has created a wide variety of constitutional challenges, uncertainties, and instabilities;

- Active support in some sections of the media for populist-leaning agendas; and public criticism and undermining of the BBC, including from within government. During the period, concern rose about the Internet having negative implications for democracy, including through its being a source of false information and being used for the purpose of threats and intimidation.
- Less than satisfactory approaches to the territorial constitution of the UK, including disregard for the status of the devolved systems, and destabilisation of the Northern Ireland peace process;
- Objectionable handling by the UK executive of its relationship with the legislature, with, for instance, misleading statements made by ministers. A heavy reliance on delegated legislation, a means by which ministers can make law while minimising or circumventing parliamentary oversight. In 2019, an attempt – ruled unlawful – to frustrate Parliament in the performance of its democratic functions through prorogation;
- Questionable behaviour with respect to international treaty commitments, including the Northern Ireland Protocol of the EU Withdrawal Agreement;
- Undermining – through government actions and legislative measures – of human rights, including a questioning of the international and domestic mechanisms by which they are supported;
- Open disdain among sections of the media and some politicians for legal professionals and the judicial processes by which the rule of law is upheld, possibly entailing the intimidation of the courts;
- Compromising of freedom to engage in public protest, including through the Police, Crime, Sentencing and Courts Act 2022, and further measures;
- A reduction in the autonomy of the Electoral Commission, and the introduction to Great Britain – without a convincing need to do so – of a requirement for voter identification that might have the effect of reducing participation by already marginalised groups;
- The dissemination of misleading information by government in areas such as the presentation of official statistics on the economy and crime, and over the conduct of participants in the government; and behaviour contributing to a deterioration in the quality of public political discourse.
- Disregard for norms and standards of conduct that are essential to the proper functioning of the constitution, and the mechanisms by which they are upheld. Examples of behaviour of this type include decisions made by Johnson over ministerial appointments and discipline, and his questionable approach

to the *Ministerial Code*, a rulebook for members of the government. Successors to Johnson have failed fully to eradicate such problems;

– Illegal actions by the then-Chancellor of the Exchequer Rishi Sunak and the then-Prime Minister Boris Johnson, as well as officials, who broke the law by participating in gatherings while pandemic restrictions were in force;

– Worrying departures from regular practice in the disbursal of public money, as revealed by investigations into the award of pandemic-related contracts;

– The undermining of impartial public institutions, including the Civil Service and the BBC;

– The exposure of vulnerabilities in the UK constitution, such as the dependence upon self-regulation by those in positions of power; and the lack of firm constitutional restraints upon the UK Parliament, and by extension upon a government that is able to carry the legislature with it. These qualities create potential for abuse. The disproportionate voting system used for elections to the House of Commons can also serve to magnify difficulties; and

– In exhibiting the various tendencies discussed above, following in wider international patterns in states including the US and parts of Europe. It is not possible entirely to exclude the possibility that the UK has been subject to foreign interference. Moreover, recent political instability in the UK, and the withdrawal of a member state from the EU, might well have been welcome to some authoritarian powers. Brexit has involved in some respects a degree of antagonism with the EU, and with some of its member states, despite their being longstanding allies of the UK.

This list – which is extensive but not exhaustive – demonstrates a range of difficulties, establishing clearly that the UK should be considered as part of an international trend towards democratic deterioration, to which it has added its own distinctive variant. They partly involve social developments, for instance in the nature of the media and in public attitudes. But party political aspects are important also. A number of the factors discussed might principally have seemed characteristic of the Johnson premiership and his personal style of leadership. Yet some of them were becoming apparent before he took over from Theresa May in 2019. May – who, after all, chose to appoint Johnson to a senior position in her Cabinet – adopted various populist-type approaches. Among them were her apparent condemnation of internationalist principles, and her depiction of the result of the 2016 referendum as binding, in a particular way which it was the function of the UK executive to discern, and which should not be questioned.

Neither of the two successors to Johnson at No.10 fully dispelled the concerns that intensified during the Johnson period. The bypassing of constitutional norms was a defining feature of the Truss premiership, and made a key contribution to its costly and swift collapse. Truss violated established principles through such actions as the removal of the Permanent Secretary to the Treasury and the evasion of proper scrutiny of the fiscal initiatives of her government. This episode demonstrates how democratic deterioration, as well as being a problem in itself, can contribute to further deleterious outcomes. Both the ousting of a senior official and the bypassing of oversight of financial policy were executed in pursuit of a course of action that proved to be disastrous. Indeed the market response to this package was presumably aggravated by the government's curious behaviour, serving to heighten unease among traders over the path being taken by the UK.

Upon succeeding Truss, Rishi Sunak (who, as we have seen, had – like Johnson – committed a criminal act during lockdown) soon became embroiled in controversy which raised further concerns about the maintenance of standards. Seemingly as a consequence of at least implicit understandings that helped secure him the premiership, he appointed Suella Braverman to the post of Home Secretary. Less than a week previously, Braverman – who supported Sunak in his bid for Conservative leadership – had resigned as Home Secretary under Truss, having violated official protocols in the handling of confidential documents. Adding to doubts about her suitability for this senior role, Braverman, moreover, has displayed disdain towards various other norms, including those pertaining to the treatment of refugees. Other dubious tendencies under Sunak have included a continuation of the habit of making misleading public statements,[1] and the aggressive pursuit of the exclusion, removal and deterrence of refugees.

Much of the focus of discussion regarding democratic deterioration in the contemporary UK has focused, understandably, on the Conservative Party and the UK government which it has formed, alone or in collation, continuously since 2010. It is now reasonable to consider the possibility that, after the next General Election – due by early 2025 at the absolute latest – a different party, Labour, will come to power. For this reason it is worth scrutinising the recent history of the Labour Party. The leadership of Jeremy Corbyn, which commenced in 2015, raised various concerns regarding the challenging of established democratic norms, for instance, in the way in which his position at the head of the party – endorsed by those voting in mass leadership elections – placed him in a position of pronounced tension with his parliamentary party, the overwhelming bulk of which was firmly opposed to him.

---

1 Patrick Daly, 'Sunak used incorrect asylum backlog figures in Parliament, stats tsar finds', *Independent*, 25 March 2023, accessed 4 May 2023, https://www.independent.co.uk/news/uk/robert-chote-prime-minister-labour-home-office-uk-statistics-authority-b2307958.html.

This particular conflict was overcome when Keir Starmer, with broad Labour support both from within and beyond Parliament, succeeded Corbyn. Starmer was known for his pro-EU inclinations, and when campaigning for the leadership early in 2020 stated his commitment to freedom of movement. But Starmer became increasingly accepting of Brexit to the point that the official Labour position appeared to be to present Brexit as offering opportunities that Labour can succeed in grasping where the Conservatives have failed, as well as in some way removing barriers Brexit has created. The motives for this alignment appear to include a desire to leave behind the prolonged turmoil of the Brexit era; a view that it is now necessary to accept the referendum, perhaps combined with the 2019 General Election, as settling the matter; and – perhaps most importantly – a belief that taking this position is necessary to the regaining of constituencies which had voted leave in 2016 and were lost in 2019.

Labour's commitment to Brexit hardened even as evidence of the harm inflicted by it became increasingly hard to deny, and as public opinion turned against it. Brexit damage has affected many areas – the international reputation of the UK, the quality of domestic politics, to the functioning of the territorial constitution. Much attention has focused on the economic aspects. One authoritative source of analysis is the Office for Budget Responsibility, a body which provides public forecasts and analysis to the government. It models the impact of Brexit using new data relating to real developments as it becomes available. As of April 2023, it estimated that, under the post-Brexit Trade and Cooperation Agreement, productivity would in the long run be 4 percent lower than it would have been had the UK remained within the EU. Imports and exports would be 15 percent lower; and new trade agreements with countries outside the EU would make no significant difference.[2] These figures are difficult to reconcile with a positive view of Brexit, something the public appears increasingly to have moved away from.

Among the many ways of measuring popular attitudes on Brexit, YouGov regularly asked people from 2016 onwards whether the vote to exit the EU was right or wrong. Up to mid-2017, more people agreed with the decision than opposed it. Thereafter, almost every poll has produced majorities disagreeing with the leave vote. By November 2022 the lead of people thinking it was a mistake over those who did not had reached its highest, at 24 percent.[3] Ongoing polling commis-

---

2 For an official assessment, see: Office for Budget Responsibility, Brexit analysis, 17 April 2023, accessed 4 May 2023, https://obr.uk/forecasts-in-depth/the-economy-forecast/brexit-analysis/ #assumptions.

3 Peter Raven, 'One in five who voted for Brexit now think it was the wrong decision', *YouGov*, 14 November 2022, accessed 4 May 2023, https://yougov.co.uk/topics/politics/articles-reports/2022/ 11/17/one-five-who-voted-brexit-now-think-it-was-wrong-d.

sioned by UK in a Changing Europe during 2022 found that, in February, 49 percent would vote in a referendum to rejoin the EU, while by December the figure had risen to 56 percent.[4] These data should not be read as meaning that there is overwhelming demand for an immediate effort to rejoin. But they do show a substantial body of opinion that Brexit has proved to be an error.

In embracing one populist-type project, however, Labour has come to associate itself with other, associated, aspects of democratic malaise. For instance, there are signs of the party leadership being reluctant firmly to counter irrational and hostile approaches both towards refugees and migrants; and it has itself employed rhetoric that might be perceived as leaning in this direction. In a broadcast interview in November 2022, Starmer said that: '[w]e don't want open borders. Freedom of movement has gone and it's not coming back.' He called for 'fair rules, firm rules, a points-based system' and said that he what he would 'like to see is the numbers go down in some areas.' Starmer was supportive of the idea of 'high-skilled people' coming from outside the UK to work in 'in innovation in tech to set up factories etc'. But he suggested 'we're recruiting too many people from overseas into, for example, the health service.'[5]

From a practical perspective, such statements struggle to withstand scrutiny. It is clearly mistaken to imply – as Starmer could be interpreted as doing here – that a National Health Service suffering staff shortages could at any point in the foreseeable future function more effectively while recruiting less from overseas. Surely, indeed, the opposite must be the case. But the problems do not end here. Political nonsense, far from being a harmless diversion, can be deeply damaging: as the Brexit enterprise, which was founded to a significant extent in assertions not deserving of credence, demonstrates. Apologists for the present position of the Labour leadership claim that it is playing a long game. They hold that this stance is needed to win over voters in key 'Red Wall' seats, and that Labour can alter or reverse the course it appears to be laying out later. Those taking this view might also argue that gains in Labour popularity have been possible because voters alienated in 2019 have been won back by the change in policy, while those electors who dislike the stance will largely continue to support the party for want of a viable alternative.

Yet some at high levels in the party may have convinced themselves that their official policy is viable and correct, and find it hard to adjust later. Further-

---

4 Alan Wager and Sophie Stowers, 'A year in Brexit: five charts exploring how public opinion on the EU has changed in 2022', *UK in a Changing Europe*, 2 January 2023, accessed 4 May 2023, https://ukandeu.ac.uk/a-year-in-brexit-five-charts-exploring-how-public-opinion-on-the-eu-has-changed-in-2022/.

5 'Keir Starmer: Immigration not quick fix to NHS problems', *BBC News*, 6 November 2022, accessed 15 March 2023, https://www.bbc.co.uk/news/uk-scotland-63526167.

more, whatever actual Labour intentions may be, and should it come to power, perhaps assisted by these tactics, interventions such as the interview given by Starmer cited above will make it harder for the party, when in government, to correct tendencies of the sort assessed in this paper, even if it wishes to do so. Labour will, in fact, have endorsed and encouraged the malign instincts that underpin these patterns of development, and might find itself tied to a flawed, populist-inclined narrative. It will be harder for a Labour government to deliver reforms in areas such as social equality outside the EU than it would have been inside. By committing to Brexit and all that comes with it, including the rejection of freedom of movement, Labour might well suffer politically – perhaps including among those it hopes to appeal to through its populist stylings.

To assess how the many democratic weaknesses identified above have come about, and by extension how they might be corrected, it is necessary to identify some key motivating and enabling factors. The first, as discussion so far suggests, is Brexit. Without consideration of this prolonged political syndrome – which continues for the foreseeable future – present malaise is impossible to understand. The means by which it was realised, the forces, people, factions, and ideas it elevated to positions of prominence, and the further changes it has facilitated or encouraged, have all played a part in bringing about the current circumstances. Pursuing a full reversal of Brexit – that is, renewed UK membership of the EU – seems a direct means of beginning to undo the damage Brexit has, and will continue, to cause.

The task of securing UK re-entry into the EU is not to be taken lightly. It will involve overcoming considerable domestic resistance. Rejoining will also require the UK to address understandable and significant scepticism and reluctance on the EU side. The daunting nature of this project will deter some from embarking upon it; and others will seek to use the scale of the challenge as a means of supressing any discussion of the possibility of rejoining. They often hold that, even if the UK were to adopt a rejoin policy, the EU would simply not entertain such a proposition. But to fail to attempt to reverse Brexit is to accept ongoing and worsening deterioration for the UK, which might continue indefinitely. Conversely, rejoining is an act that might be completed, leading to benefits once achieved, rather than deepening problems. The UK should not simply accept as a permanent reality that its relations with some of its most vital allies have been harmed to the point that they would collectively block UK re-entry to the EU. Rather it should seek to revive its standing with them. An open recognition that Brexit was an error in need of correction could be a first step towards this goal.

What would follow is difficult precisely to predict. But it is reasonable to conceive of the EU being willing to enter into negotiations with a UK that had clearly changed in its posture. Another assertion made by those who seek to preclude re-entry as an option is that the UK would not be able to rejoin on the same terms it previously possessed. Various opt-outs – including from the single currency – would, they hold, not be on offer; nor would the budget rebate. While it seems likely that the UK would be denied the degree of flexibility it previously possessed, we cannot know for sure what the precise position would be in advance. Furthermore, it is important to challenge the assumption that having these exceptions was necessarily some kind of advantage. They were associated with a view of EU membership as a regrettable necessity, engagement with which should be kept to a minimum. That so many supposed advocates of the EU within the UK were willing to promote this outlook is a clue as to how the disaster of Brexit was allowed to befall the country. A successful campaign to rejoin should be founded instead in the principle that membership is a benefit with which the UK should aim to engage fully. Such a stance might serve to neutralise attempts to generate concern about the loss of opt-outs, and reconfigure it as a desirable outcome.

Some hold that there are more realistic means of addressing problems associated with Brexit than seeking full renewal of membership. They talk about prospects such as joining the Customs Union or Single Market (or perhaps both); or of more piecemeal, sector-specific arrangements (the obtaining of which appears to be current Labour policy). But such objectives are not necessarily a means of bypassing opposition within the UK. Supporters of Brexit will depict them as betrayal, and a first step towards rejoining. Moreover, arrangements such as Single Market membership are not clearly on offer from the EU, the agreement of which to them is no more guaranteed than it would be to UK re-entry. If the UK appeared to be seeking to combine the benefits of access in some areas while also exploiting the potential for divergence in others (which again appears to be the Labour stance), the EU might well be reluctant to cooperate.

Were the UK to achieve some kind of partial reversal of Brexit short of rejoining, moreover, it would surely entail the UK committing to some degree of compliance with EU regulations. The UK would thereby become subject to rules that it had no direct role in enacting. An important part of pro-Brexit narratives was that EU membership entailed subordination to an external power. Such accounts were misleading, overlooking the role that the UK played in EU decision-making. They would, however, be more accurate if applied to a post-exit UK: either one that voluntarily continued to follow EU rules (as is likely to happen in many instances even under the current arrangements); or one that engaged in more formal harmonisation. In any case, advocacy of measures such as sectoral deals, membership of the Customs Union, and entry into the Single Market, could be interpreted as an implicit admission that Brexit is a damaging enterprise. At the same time, they are all inferior to full EU membership, the explicit or implicit justification for which is that this ideal outcome presents political challenges that are too great to contemplate.

At present, both of the two main parties assert their absolute commitment to Brexit in perpetuity, ruling out also the Single Market and Customs Union. Significant numbers of MPs, in the Conservative Party as well as Labour, must privately be aware of the foolishness of such a stance, but feel politically obliged to accept it. When advocating adherence to Brexit, politicians tend to treat the 2016 referendum as yielding a definitive decision, the questioning of which amounts to some kind of democratic travesty. To present the outcome of an exercise in which no more than 37 percent of those who were allowed to take part supported a generally worded proposition as of such overriding force is not – despite what its proponents appear to believe – to advance an unanswerable democratic proposition. On the contrary, it is a means of restricting options and stifling dissent. (Even more curious are claims that the 2019 General Election, taken in combination with the 2016 vote, somehow permanently settled the matter. Problems with this position include the fact that a majority of voters in 2019 favoured parties either supporting a second referendum or opposing Brexit outright.)

This unsatisfactory position becomes all the more apparent as evidence grows of public opinion turning against Brexit. Populism does not necessarily equate with popularity; and has in its UK variant hardened a position, support for which seems to be dwindling. At leadership level within the Conservatives and Labour, purported adherence to the will of the people serves to deny the views of the public proper expression. Neither of the two main parties presently offers a home to the seemingly growing body of anti-Brexit opinion. This lacuna – rather than the desire to revisit a decision attributed to a referendum held seven years go – is the true affront to democratic principle. In a reversal of the standard populist depiction, Brexit is the project of an elite detached from a significant portion of the public.

A second source of present difficulties for UK democracy is the Single Member Plurality (or 'First-Past-the-Post') voting system employed for elections to the House of Commons. Among its distorting consequences for the political system are the tendency towards pre-eminence (though not total dominance) at UK level for two parties, the Conservatives and Labour. The Conservatives have tended to benefit the most, spending a significant proportion of the time since 1945 governing alone, having won more than half of the seats in the Commons while securing vote shares often well below 50 percent. The importance of divisions and minority viewpoints within the Conservatives thereby become magnified, taking on significance they would not otherwise attain. A related point is that Single Member Plurality also increases the likelihood of the two main parties including within them a wide range of positions, perhaps of contradictory nature. The chances of sharing in electoral success are far greater for those who remain within one of these two parties, rather than seeking to operate outside. This combination of qualities creates a motive for extremist, minority factions to seek ascendancy within Labour or the Conservatives, and thereby potentially achieve substantial influence over public policy and the conduct of government, or at least within the main Opposition.

The outcome can be – as we have seen in recent years in the UK – the pursuit of disruptive courses of action which run counter to large bodies of public opinion, are harmful to the country and its interests, and damaging to the democratic system itself. The Single Member Plurality system, then, enables parties to achieve majorities in the House of Commons out of proportion to their voter support; and within those parties it is possible for assertive sub-groupings, to achieve significant influence. Such factions may well be minorities, but attain impact through concerted effort, perhaps with assistance from party members and affiliates beyond Parliament.

These characteristics of Single Member Plurality were crucial to the 2016 EU referendum being held at all, and enabled the faction or factions that drove it to an extensive impact on and a presence within government thereafter. The Johnson premiership, detrimental as it was from the perspective of democratic stability, came about in the context of Brexit and was made possible in part because Johnson secured support from MPs associated with the radically pro-Brexit European Research Group (ERG), as well as from the wider party membership. Support from similar quarters ensured the ascendancy of Truss and her extreme, ideologically driven policy agenda, despite many Conservative MPs (and others) being opposed to it. Sunak was less clearly the favoured choice of the ERG and adjacent wings of the Conservative Party. But he had important support from sections of it, and seemed to feel a need to defer to it to some extent, confirming once again the potential for outlying groups to attain disproportionately large levels of influence within parties operating in the context of Single Member Plurality. For Labour, the Corbyn period was one in which a small, radical parliamentary group with support beyond Parliament captured the leadership. Under a proportional electoral system of some kind, tendencies of this type could be lessened, in that there would be an increased chance of more electorally viable parties. Groups and viewpoints that might otherwise engage in battles for control within the Conservatives and Labour could find their own dedicated space, alongside various others. The chances of any one party, within which an extremist faction might have become prominent, being able to govern alone, might be greatly reduced.

A further negative consequence of Single Member Plurality that has become more apparent during the ongoing political turbulence involves electoral calculations. At present, the relative importance of voters can vary immensely according to the constituency in which they are registered and whether parties judge they can be induced to change their voting behaviour (as between parties, or between voting at all or not) in ways that could be either helpful or detrimental. Parties are likely to place a premium on appealing to voters assessed as living in target constituencies and whose decisions about whether or how to vote remain in the balance. These considerations can encourage a party towards positions it might not otherwise adopt. At present, as noted above, the Labour stance on Brexit and related matters seems partly to derive from such pressures. Yielding to this tactical consideration makes it harder for the party to challenge and counteract the undermining of democratic norms experienced recently in the UK. Indeed, it may be adding to them.

To understand why the forces associated with Brexit and with the Single Member Plurality system have been able to act in a relatively unchecked fashion at governmental level, we need to appreciate certain aspects of the UK constitution. One is its tendency to confer substantial authority on majority groups within the House of Commons, the principle on which governments rest. They have the potential to drive through legislative measures that are disruptive or harmful to the UK democratic system without being subject to the kind of restrictions that another constitution, perhaps of a 'written' or 'codified' nature, might provide. Another significant factor is the extent to which the UK system relies heavily upon self-regulation by those in positions of power. Various departures from ethical and constitutional standards since 2016 have illustrated the weaknesses of such a model. Whether the UK is worse than other comparable countries in this regard is difficult to discern, but there is no doubt that it has problems.

Any attempt seriously to address the problems the UK has been experiencing needs to take into account the underlying factors set out above. The Conservative Party as currently configured is a central part of the problem and it is unrealistic to expect it to rectify it for the foreseeable future. But a change of government at the next General Election now seems plausible. Unfortunately, the Labour leadership – principally it seems for reasons of electoral calculation – is providing little cause for optimism. As discussed above, it has ruled out ever re-joining the EU, or even pursuing less good damage-limitation options. Furthermore, despite strong support within his own party for a move to proportional representation, Starmer has not adopted this policy.

In both respects, Labour is confirming regrettably myopic characteristics it has long displayed in both areas. It has a propensity to treat domestic political priorities as more important than and potentially in conflict with European commitments; and to be attached to Single Member Plurality, a system under which it can (sometimes) achieve power alone. In the current political environment, the Labour leadership has presumably judged that its Brexit stance has been exonerated. While following the 2019 General Election its chances of securing an outright majority in the House of Commons at the next contest seemed slight, the prospects subsequently improved significantly. In such circumstances, a proportional system is likely to seem even less attractive to the Labour leadership – and this tendency would probably intensify further still were Labour to achieve such an electoral victory.

Labour would do better to recognise that participation in the European integration project is essential to the fuller attainment of its objectives and values; and that the parliamentary electoral system has tended over time to work more in favour of the Conservative Party than of it. A proportional electoral system, moreover, would be a means of reducing the likelihood of a repetition of the circumstances in which Brexit came about (and unfortunate episodes that followed, such as the Truss experience). It would require consensus and cooperation across parties, reducing the possibility of small factions achieving magnified influence through operating within single parties. Such a safeguard might also help reassure the EU that to readmit the UK was not simply to invite further disruption. It might contribute to the development of a UK political culture characterised by greater acceptance of trade-offs and collaboration, and a movement away from a winner-takes-all model. Electoral reform might thereby make it easier for the UK to engage more fully with the EU once it had rejoined, founded in recognition of the benefits to be derived from the pooling of power.

It is possible, then, to construct a case for Labour taking a different way forward. But it must be recognised that adopting and pursuing policies of rejoining the EU and proportional representation (of some form) is not a politically easy proposition. Labour needs to win power if it is directly to affect change. Party concerns over the attitudes of some voters in the 'Red Wall' are understandable; so is the fear of jeopardising the progress it has made lately. The leadership might judge it is now too late to alter course again, even if it wanted to. Nor would the sequencing and implementation of these changes be simple to manage. However, polling that the author has worked on with the Constitution Society suggests that different approaches might be electorally viable.

First, there is evidence of willingness on the part of a substantial portion of voters to support any candidate from the Labour, Liberal Democrat or Green parties as a means of defeating the Conservatives. Were the three parties to enter a full pact in England and Wales, running only one candidate between them in every constituency there is evidence it would decisively remove the Conservatives from power at a General Election. Such an agreement might be formed around a pro-EU and electoral reform agenda. This scenario might seem far-fetched; and perhaps it could take another Conservative victory to make it even vaguely plausible. But there are other degrees of cross-party cooperation, falling short of a full deal, that might assist the defeat of the Conservative Party on the basis of a platform that more genuinely seeks to correct the objectionable aspects of the period since 2016.[6] Second, polling conducted in March 2023 suggested that were Labour to take the position that Brexit was a mistake, it could win more seats overall in a General Election, and would remain on course to victory in every 'Red Wall' constituency.[7] This finding does not measure what might be the reaction to Labour adopting a rejoin policy, or any other course of action it might recommend having pronounced Brexit an error. But it does suggest that Labour would be able to challenge the Brexit premise, and open up options that might otherwise be closed to it, without significant electoral harm arising.

A rejoin policy need not entail promising immediate re-entry into the EU, which is not obtainable anyway. However, it would require a clear statement that departure was regrettable, that the UK should make restored full membership its objective, and that it should start taking steps to facilitate this outcome immediately. In not taking on a programme including this stance and support for electoral reform, Labour fails meaningfully to address the worst features of the present Conservative government, and the period of pronounced disruption since 2016 with which it is associated. Were it able to secure, or at least take substantial steps towards the two key goals set out here, Labour could then consider a third objective: a 'written' or 'codified' constitution. Such an entity might be a means of restabilising the UK system in the context of renewed membership of the EU and the adoption of a new parliamentary electoral system. Rather than conceiving of such a document as a protracted and complicated list of regulations, it should be regarded as a means of entrenching the most important rules of a political community. The contents of the document would be protected from casual alteration by a heightened amendment procedure. It would be the ultimate source of legal authority within the UK system, upheld by the Supreme Court.

But what might it contain? Firmer protection for human rights and for the status of the judiciary in relation to the executive and legislature might be facilitated. Texts such as the *Ministerial Code* could be given a clearer legal grounding; as might the regulatory bodies charged with upholding them. The political adventuring lately experienced could, by such measures, be more effectively addressed. Repetition of such behaviour in the future might, furthermore, be held in check. Another potential objective might be to provide a firmer basis for the devolved systems, potentially integrating them into a fully federal system. Renewed membership

---

6 Andrew Blick, *Electoral Pacts and the Constitution: An update one year on* (London: Constitution Society, 2022), accessed 6 May 2023, https://consoc.org.uk/wp-content/uploads/2022/05/Electoral-pacts-and-the-constitution-an-update-one-year-on.pdf.
7 The Constitution Society, 'Labour could win increased majority by turning against Brexit, new poll finds', *Constitution Society*, 21 March 2023, accessed 6 May 2023, https://consoc.org.uk/publications/red-wall-polling-2023/.

of the EU would be a suitable context within which to establish state level governance covering the entirety of the UK, with an extensive set of powers available to all territories, subject to the UK constitution and European law. At present, the Labour Party seems to have an interest in this area (although it might not be its first priority). But to address it prior to the issues of electoral reform and rejoining the EU is to sequence incorrectly, and to seek to build a new system on insecure foundations. The most plausible means of introducing a more fully federal system for the UK would involve creating a set of regional units across England, alongside Wales, Scotland and Northern Ireland. The precise territorial demarcation for the English states within a putative federal UK has been a perennial subject of debate. But there can be no doubt that it would be possible to establish viable units, including parliaments with full legislative and tax-raising powers, based around cities and other areas in England. Greater London, for instance, could be a self-financing territory of substantial population and political and cultural significance.

Within such a federal model, a new constitutional text could re-establish the second chamber, presently the House of Lords, as a states' assembly. Such a measure could make good an omission within the devolution project to date. It has tended to emphasise the dispersal of powers from the centre; and less to address the way in which those authorities that remain reserved should be handled, and the part of the territorial institutions in this function. The newly-configured second chamber could provide the states with a firmer place in UK-level processes than they currently possess, contributing to a more inclusive, cohesive UK. It could also provide a more effective limitation on the House of Commons than currently offered by the House of Lords, which lacks the necessary degree of legitimacy for this essential task. Whether it would be directly elected or would be filled by the state governments and/or parliaments is a matter for discussion, though the latter option might be the simpler way to embed the territories within the federal system. A UK reconciled to full EU membership could provide a framework, via the new constitutional text, within which Northern Ireland could make decisions about its future constitutional status free from the added complicating factor created by Brexit. Furthermore, it might be possible to reach an arrangement whereby the remaining UK would agree to support applications for EU membership by other territories, should they choose to leave the UK, in particular but not only Scotland. Borders might come to lose the fraught implications they possess at present.

By what process might the programme envisaged here be legitimised? The prospect of any of the main three items – rejoining the EU, electoral change, and constitutional formalisation and reform – is likely to prompt demands that they be approved by referendum, in particular (but not exclusively) from those who are opposed to their coming about. Just as it is important to challenge populist axioms over particular issues, it is necessary to challenge the assumption that changes in this area can only properly be attained through such a mechanism. A critical means of meeting the international challenges discussed in this paper in the UK context is by asserting the principle of representative democracy. Governments formed out of Parliament, possessing the confidence of the House of Commons and securing parliamentary approval for legislative measures, should be regarded as able to operate with a degree of discretion across a range of areas, for so long as they hold office, subject to constitutional limitations and obligations (which the text discussed here could embody).

In seeking the authority to act in these areas without a specific popular vote, it would also be advisable to consider adapting a model used in advance of the 1997 General Election. Following talks led by Robin Cook and Robert Maclennan, their respective parties, Labour and the Liberal Democrats, issued a joint statement of intended reforms in areas including devolution, human rights protection and the House of Lords. A number of the components of this text were implemented, some without referendums being held. Labour might benefit from instigating talks on shared areas of interest with parties such as the Liberal Democrats and the Greens. Any agreement reached could be placed before voters at a General Election as a shared statement of intent, perhaps as part of some kind of pact or other electoral arrangement. Such an exercise might represent beneficial learning from a positive aspect of the relatively recent past. It could be turned to the vital task of stabilising UK democracy.

David Cameron's statement following EU referendum, 24 June 2016[8]
Excerpts with commentary

Excerpts

The country has just taken part in a giant democratic exercise – perhaps the biggest in our history. Over 33 million people – from England, Scotland, Wales, Northern Ireland and Gibraltar – have all had their say.
We should be proud of the fact that in these islands we trust the people with these big decisions.
We not only have a parliamentary democracy, but on questions about the arrangements for how we are governed, there are times when it is right to ask the people themselves, and that is what we have done.
The British people have voted to leave the European Union and their will must be respected.

---

8 David Cameron 'EU referendum outcome: PM statement, 24 June 2016', *gov.uk*, accessed 7 May 2023, https://www.gov.uk/government/speeches/eu-referendum-outcome-pm-statement-24-june-2016.

(continued)

I want to thank everyone who took part in the campaign on my side of the argument, including all those who put aside party differences to speak in what they believed was the national interest. And let me congratulate all those who took part in the Leave campaign – for the spirited and passionate case that they made.

The will of the British people is an instruction that must be delivered. It was not a decision that was taken lightly, not least because so many things were said by so many different organisations about the significance of this decision.

So there can be no doubt about the result.

. . .

And I would also reassure Brits living in European countries, and European citizens living here, that there will be no immediate changes in your circumstances. There will be no initial change in the way our people can travel, in the way our goods can move or the way our services can be sold.

We must now prepare for a negotiation with the European Union. This will need to involve the full engagement of the Scottish, Welsh and Northern Ireland governments to ensure that the interests of all parts of our United Kingdom are protected and advanced.

But above all this will require strong, determined and committed leadership . . . .

I have also always believed that we have to confront big decisions – not duck them . . .

I fought this campaign in the only way I know how – which is to say directly and passionately what I think and feel – head, heart and soul.

I held nothing back.

I was absolutely clear about my belief that Britain is stronger, safer and better off inside the European Union, and I made clear the referendum was about this and this alone – not the future of any single politician, including myself.

But the British people have made a very clear decision to take a different path, and as such I think the country requires fresh leadership to take it in this direction.

I will do everything I can as Prime Minister to steady the ship over the coming weeks and months, but I do not think it would be right for me to try to be the captain that steers our country to its next destination.

This is not a decision I have taken lightly, but I do believe it is in the national interest to have a period of stability and then the new leadership required.

. . .

Delivering stability will be important and I will continue in post as Prime Minister with my Cabinet for the next 3 months. The Cabinet will meet on Monday.

. . .

A negotiation with the European Union will need to begin under a new Prime Minister, and I think it is right that this new Prime Minister takes the decision about when to trigger Article 50 and start the formal and legal process of leaving the EU.

I will attend the European Council next week to explain the decision the British people have taken and my own decision.

The British people have made a choice. That not only needs to be respected – but those on the losing side of the argument, myself included, should help to make it work.

Britain is a special country.

We have so many great advantages.

(continued)

A parliamentary democracy where we resolve great issues about our future through peaceful debate.

. . .

Although leaving Europe was not the path I recommended, I am the first to praise our incredible strengths. I have said before that Britain can survive outside the European Union, and indeed that we could find a way.

Now the decision has been made to leave, we need to find the best way, and I will do everything I can to help.

Commentary

This statement discusses the relationship between direct and representative democracy that would become a key aspect of the tensions that would follow. That Cameron felt the need to stand down indicates the disruption to the political system that the 2016 result entailed. Cameron promotes the idea of exceptionalism, stating that 'Britain is a special country'.

Bibliography

All-Party Parliamentary Group on Democracy and the Constitution. *An Independent Judiciary – Challenges Since 2016*. London: Institute for Constitutional and Democratic Research, 8 June 2022, accessed 12 March 2023, https://static1.squarespace.com/static/6033d6547502c200670fd98c/t/62a05b38f1b9b809f61853ef/1654676281940/SOPI+Report+FINAL.pdf.

Applebaum, Anne. *Twilight of Democracy: the failure of politics and the parting of friends*. London: Penguin, 2021.

Bale, Tim. *The Conservative Party After Brexit: Turmoil and Transformation*. Cambridge: Polity, 2023.

Barber, Lionel. *The Powerful and the Damned: life behind the headlines in the financial times*. London: Penguin, 2020.

Barnier, Michael. *My Secret Brexit Diary: A Glorious Illusion*. Cambridge: Polity, 2021.

Barnard, Benjamin. *Government Reimagined: a handbook for reform*. London: Policy Exchange, 2021.

Barwell, Gavin. *Chief of Staff: An insider's account of Downing Street's most turbulent years*. London: Atlantic Books, 2022.

Bernhard, Michael and Daniel O'Neill 'Trump: causes and consequences'. *Perspectives on Politics* 17, no. 2 (2019): 317–324.

Bickerton, Chris. 'What happens after Brexit is up to us. Why not open our borders to non-EU workers?'. *LSE blog*, 25 May 2016. https://blogs.lse.ac.uk/brexit/2016/05/25/what-happens-after-brexit-is-up-to-us-why-not-open-our-borders-to-non-eu-workers/.

Blick, Andrew. *Taking Back Control? The EU referendum, Parliament and the 'May Doctrine'*. London: Federal Trust for Education and Research, 2016. https://fedtrust.co.uk/taking-back-control/.

Blick, Andrew. *Stretching the Constitution: the Brexit shock in historic perspective*. Oxford: Hart/Bloomsbury, 2019.

Blick, Andrew. *Electrified Democracy: The Internet and the United Kingdom Parliament in history*. Cambridge: Cambridge University Press, 2021.

Blick, Andrew. *Getting Brexit Undone*. London: Federal Trust, 2022. https://fedtrust.co.uk/wp-content/uploads/2022/07/Getting-Brexit-Undone-Andrew-Blick.pdf.

Blick, Andrew. *Electoral Pacts and the Constitution: An update one year on*. London: Constitution Society, 2022: accessed 6 May 2023. https://consoc.org.uk/wp-content/uploads/2022/05/Electoral-pacts-and-the-constitution-an-update-one-year-on.pdf.

Blick, Andrew and Peter Hennessy. *The Bonfire of the Decencies: Repairing and Restoring the British Constitution*. London: Haus, 2022.

Blick, Andrew and George Jones. *Premiership: the origins, nature and power of the office of the British Prime Minister*. Exeter: Imprint Academic, 2010.

Bogdanor, Vernon. *Beyond Brexit: towards a British constitution*. London: I. B. Tauris, 2019.

The Brexit Party. *Contract with the People*. London: The Brexit Party, 2019: accessed 19 March 2023. https://www.thebrexitparty.org/wp-content/uploads/2019/11/Contract-With-The-People.pdf.

Cabinet Office. *The Cabinet Manual: A guide to laws, conventions and rules on the operation of government*. London: Cabinet Office, October 2011: accessed 4 April 2023. https://assets.publishing.service.gov.uk/government/uploads/system/uploads/attachment_data/file/60641/cabinet-manual.pdf.

Cabinet Office. *Ministerial Code*. London: Cabinet Office, 22 December 2022, accessed 4 April 2023. https://www.gov.uk/government/publications/ministerial-code/ministerial-code.

Cardwell, Peter. *The Secret Life of Special Advisers*. London: Biteback, 2020.

Civil Service. *The Civil Service Code*. 16 March 2015: accessed 6 April 2023. https://www.gov.uk/govern
ment/publications/civil-service-code/the-civil-service-code.

Clarke, John and Janet Newman. '"People in this country have had enough of experts": Brexit and the
paradoxes of populism'. *Critical Policy Studies* 11, no. 1 (2017): 101–116.

Committee on Standards in Public Life. *Intimidation in Public Life*. London: Committee on Standards in
Public Life, December 2017: Cm 9543, 13, accessed 12 March 2023. https://assets.publishing.ser
vice.gov.uk/government/uploads/system/uploads/attachment_data/file/666927/6.3637_CO_v6_
061217_Web3.1__2_.pdf.

Conservative and Unionist Party. *Get Brexit Done: Unleash Britain's Potential*. Conservative and Unionist
Party, London, 2019: accessed 11 March 2023. https://assets-global.website-files.com/5da42e2
cae7ebd3f8bde353c/5dda924905da587992a064ba_Conservative%202019%20Manifesto.pdf.

*The Constitution in Review: Second Report from the United Kingdom Constitution Monitoring Group, For
period 1 July – 31 December 2021*, edited by Andrew Blick. London: Constitution Society,
February 2022. https://consoc.org.uk/wp-content/uploads/2022/02/UK-Constitution-Monitoring-
Group-Second-Report.pdf.

The Constitution Society. 'Labour could win increased majority by turning against Brexit, new poll
finds'. *Constitution Society*, 21 March 2023: accessed 6 May 2023. https://consoc.org.uk/publica
tions/red-wall-polling-2023/.

Curtice, John. *Legacy of Brexit: how Britain has become a country of 'remainers' and 'leavers'*. London:
National Centre for Social Research, 2018. https://whatukthinks.org/eu/wp-content/uploads/
2018/10/WUKT-EU-Briefing-Paper-15-Oct-18-Emotional-legacy-paper-final.pdf.

Curtice, John. 'Is the Brexit debate really over? Perhaps not'. *UK in a changing Europe*, 10 March 2023.
https://ukandeu.ac.uk/is-the-brexit-debate-really-over-perhaps-not/.

Curtice, John and Victoria Ratti. *Culture Wars: keeping the Brexit divide alive?* London: National Centre
for Social Research, 2022. https://www.bsa.natcen.ac.uk/media/39478/bsa39_culture-wars.pdf.

Curtice, John,Stephen Fisher and Patrick English. 'The Geography of a Brexit Election: How
Constituency Context and the Electoral System Shaped the Outcome', in *The British General
Election of 2019*, edited by Robert Ford, Tim Bale, Will Jennings and Paul Surridge. Basingstoke:
Palgrave Macmillan, 2021.

De Vries, Catherine E. and Erica E. Edwards. 'Taking Europe to its extremes: Extremist parties and
public Euroscepticism'. *Party Politics* 15, no. 1 (2009): 5–28.

Dicey, Albert Venn. *Introduction to the Study of the Law of the Constitution*. London: Macmillan, 1915.

Dorey, Peter and Andrew Denham. '"The longest suicide vote in history": the Labour Party leadership
election of 2015'. *British Politics* 11 (2016): 259–282.

Dorries, Nadine. *The Four Streets Saga*. London: Head of Zeus, 2017.

Duncan, Alan. *In The Thick Of It: the private diaries of a minister*. London: William Collins, 2021.

Dunin-Wasowicz, Roch. 'Knowing Me, Not Knowing EU: how misunderstanding the EU means
misunderstanding the UK (and makes it harder to leave)'. *LSE blog*, 8 October 2019.
https://blogs.lse.ac.uk/brexit/2019/10/08/knowing-me-not-knowing-eu-how-misunderstanding-
the-eu-means-misunderstanding-the-uk-and-makes-it-harder-to-leave/.

The Electoral Commission. *Digital campaigning: Increasing transparency for voters*. London: The
Electoral Commission, 2018. Accessed 3 April 2023. https://www.electoralcommission.org.uk/
sites/default/files/pdf_file/Digital-campaigning-improving-transparency-for-voters.pdf.

The Electoral Commission. 'Investigation: Vote Leave Ltd, Mr Darren Grimes, BeLeave, and Veterans
for Britain.'*electoralcommission.org.uk*, various dates. Accessed 2 April 2023. https://www.elector
alcommission.org.uk/who-we-are-and-what-we-do/our-enforcement-work/investigations/investi
gation-vote-leave-ltd-mr-darren-grimes-beleave-and-veterans-britain.

The Electoral Commission. 'Statement on the Metropolitan police's investigation into Vote Leave and Darren Grimes.' *electoralcommission*.org, 8 May 2020. Accessed 2 April 2023. https://www.elector alcommission.org.uk/media-centre/statement-metropolitan-polices-investigation-vote-leave-and -darren-grimes.

Engels, Friedrich. *The Condition of the Working Class in England*. London: Penguin, 2009.

Equality and Human Rights Commission. *Investigation into Anti-Semitism in the Labour Party*. London: Equality and Human Rights Commission, 2020: accessed 11 March 2023. https://www.equalityhu manrights.com/sites/default/files/investigation-into-antisemitism-in-the-labour-party.pdf.

Everett, Michael. *Collective responsibility*. London: House of Commons Library, 2016. https://researchbriefings.files.parliament.uk/documents/CBP-7755/CBP-7755.pdf.

Fall, Kate. *The Gatekeeper*. London: HQ, 2020.

Finnis, John. *The unconstitutionality of the Supreme Court's prorogation judgment* London: Policy Exchange, 2019.

Ford, Robert, Tim Bale, Will Jennings and Paul Surridge. *The British General Election of 2019*. Basingstoke: Palgrave Macmillan, 2021.

Ford, Robert and Matthew Goodwin. *Revolt on the Right: Explaining support for the radical right in Britain*. Abingdon: Routledge, 2014.

Francois, Mark. *Spartan Victory: the inside story of the battle for Brexit by The Rt Hon Mark Francois MP*. Privately published, 2021.

Freeden, Michael. 'After the Brexit referendum: revisiting populism as an ideology'. *Journal of Political Ideologies* 22, no. 1 (2017): 1–11.

Rt Hon Lord Frost of Allenton CMG. *Holy Illusions: Reality based politics and sustaining the Brexit revolt*. London: PolicyExchange, 2022.

Rt Hon Lord Frost of Allenton CMG. 'Statement after round 8 of the negotiations'. *No 10 media blog*. 10 September 2020, accessed 19 March 2023. https://no10media.blog.gov.uk/2020/09/10/lord-frost-statement-after-round-8-of-the-negotiations/.

Rt Hon Lord Frost of Allenton CMG. 'Lord Frost: Observations on the present state of the nation'. 12 October 2021, accessed 20 March 2023. https://www.gov.uk/government/speeches/lord-frost-speech-observations-on-the-present-state-of-the-nation-12-october-2021.

Glasman, Maurice. *Blue Labour: The Politics of the Common Good*. Cambridge: Polity, 2022.

Goodwin, Matthew. *Values, Voice and Virtue: The New British Politics*. London: Penguin, 2023.

Griffith, J.A.G. 'The political constitution'. *The Modern Law Review* 42, no. 1 (1979): 1–21.

Garry, John. *The EU Referendum Vote in Northern Ireland: Implications for our understanding of citizens' political views and behaviour*. Queens University, Belfast, 2017. https://www.qub.ac.uk/brexit/Brex itfilestore/Filetoupload.728121.en.pdf.

Grayling, A .C. *The Good State: On the Principles of Democracy*. London: Oneworld, 2020. e-book.

HM Government. *The Benefits of Brexit: How the UK is taking advantage of leaving the EU*. London: Stationery Office, January 2022: accessed 19 March 2023. https://assets.publishing.service.gov. uk/government/uploads/system/uploads/attachment_data/file/1054643/benefits-of-brexit.pdf.

HM Government. *Northern Ireland Protocol: the way forward*. CP 502. London: Cabinet Office, July 2021, accessed 20 March 2023. https://assets.publishing.service.gov.uk/government/uploads/system/ uploads/attachment_data/file/1008451/CCS207_CCS0721914902-005_Northern_Ireland_Protocol_ Web_Accessible__1_.pdf.

Haggard, Stephan and Robert Kaufman. *Backsliding: Democratic Regress in the Contemporary World*. Cambridge: Cambridge University Press, 2021.

Hancock, Matt with Isobel Oakeshott. *Pandemic Diaries: The inside story of Britain's battle against Covid*. London: Biteback, 2023.

Hansard Society. *Audit of Political Engagement 16: The 2019 Report.* London: Hansard Society, 2019.

Hale, Brenda. *Spider Woman: Lady Hale, a life.* London: Vintage, 2022.

Hardman, Isabel. *Why We Get the Wrong Politicians.* London: Atlantic, 2022.

Hayward, Katy. *What Do We Know and What Should We Do About the Irish Border.* London: Sage, 2021.

Heywood, Suzanne. *What Does Jeremy Think? Jeremy Heywood and the making of modern Britain.* London: William Collins, 2021.

History Matters Project Compendium, edited by Alexander Gray. 12th edition. London: Policy Exchange, 2022.

House of Commons Committee on Digital, Culture, Media and Sport. *Appointment of Richard Sharp as Chair of the BBC.* Eighth Report of Session 2022–2023. London: House of Commons, 12 February 2023: H.C. 1147, accessed 12 March 2023. https://committees.parliament.uk/publica tions/33962/documents/186346/default/.

House of Commons Committee on Digital, Culture, Media and Sport. *Rt Hon Nadine Dorries MP.* Fourth Special Report of Session 2022–2023. London: House of Commons, 20 October 2022: H.C. 801, 3, accessed 20 March 2023. https://committees.parliament.uk/publications/30386/docu ments/175488/default/.

House of Commons Committee on Digital, Culture, Media and Sport. *Disinformation and 'fake news': Interim Report.* Fifth Report of Session 2017–2019. London: House of Commons, 29 July 2019: H.C. 363, 40.

House of Commons Public Accounts Committee. *Selecting towns for the Towns Fund.* Twenty-Fourth Report of Session 2019–2021. London: House of Commons, 11 November 2020: H.C. 651, 3, accessed 12 March 2023. https://publications.parliament.uk/pa/cm5801/cmselect/cmpubacc/ 651/651.pdf.

House of Commons Public Accounts Committee. *Government's contracts with Randox Laboratories Ltd.* Seventeenth Report of Session 2022–2023. London: House of Commons, 27 July 2022: H.C. 28, 3, accessed 12 March 2023. https://committees.parliament.uk/publications/23257/documents/ 169721/default/.

House of Commons Public Administration Select Committee. *Leaks and Whistleblowing in Whitehall.* Tenth Report of Session 2008–2009, London: Stationery Office, 10 August 2009: H.C. 83, accessed 2 May 2023. https://publications.parliament.uk/pa/cm200809/cmselect/cmpubadm/ 83/83.pdf.

House of Commons Public Administration and Constitutional Affairs Committee. *Propriety of Governance in Light of Greensill.* Fourth Report of Session 2022–2023. London: House of Commons, 2 December 2022: H.C. 888, accessed 12 March 2023. https://committees.parliament. uk/publications/31830/documents/178915/default/.

House of Lords Delegated Powers and Regulatory Reform Committee. *Democracy Denied? The urgent need to rebalance power between Parliament and the Executive.* 12th Report of Session 2021–2022. London: House of Lords, 24 November 2021: H.L. 106, accessed 12 March 2023. https://committees.parliament.uk/publications/7960/documents/82286/default/.

House of Lords Secondary Legislation Scrutiny Committee. *Government by Diktat: A call to return power to Parliament.* 20th Report of Session 2021–2022. House of Lords, London, 24 November 2021: H.L. 105, accessed 12 March 2023. https://publications.parliament.uk/pa/ld5802/ldselect/ldsec leg/105/105.pdf.

House of Lords Select Committee on the Constitution. *COVID-19 and the use and scrutiny of emergency powers.* 3rd Report of Session 2021–2022. London: House of Lords, 10 June 2021: H.L. 15, 2, accessed 12 March 2023. https://committees.parliament.uk/publications/6212/documents/ 69015/default/.

House of Lords Select Committee on Democracy and Digital Technologies. *Digital Technology and the Resurrection of Trust*. Report of Session 2019–2021. London: House of Lords, 29 June 2020, accessed 15 March 2023. https://committees.parliament.uk/publications/1634/documents/17731/default/.

Hume, Mick. *Revolting! How the establishment are undermining democracy and what they're afraid of*. London: William Collins, 2017. e-book.

Institute for Public Policy Research. *Accountability and Responsiveness in the Senior Civil Service: Lessons from Overseas*. London: Cabinet Office, June 2013, accessed 2 May 2023. https://www.civilservant.org.uk/library/2013_ippr_Accountability_and_Responsiveness_in_the_SCS.pdf.

Intelligence and Security Committee of Parliament. *Russia*. HC 632. London: House of Commons, 21 July 2020.

Johnson, Boris. *Lend me your ears*. London: HarperCollins, 2004.

Kanagasooriam, James and Elizabeth Simon. 'Red Wall: The Definitive Description'. *Political Insight* 12, no. 3 (2021): 8–11.

Karcic, Harun. 'Democratic backsliding in Europe: Who is to blame?'. *RUSI*, 11 May 2021. https://rusi.org/explore-our-research/publications/commentary/democratic-backsliding-europe-who-blame.

Keter, Vincent. *Government policy on 'British jobs for British workers'*. London: House of Commons Library, 2009: 2, accessed 15 March 2023. https://researchbriefings.files.parliament.uk/documents/SN04501/SN04501.pdf.

Klemperer, David. *The Electoral System and British Politics*. London: Constitution Society, 2019, accessed 3 May 2023. https://consoc.org.uk/wp-content/uploads/2019/04/David-Klemperer-The-Electoral-System-and-British-Politics.pdf.

Labour Party. *For The Many Not The Few: the Labour Party manifesto 2017*. London: Labour Party, 2017: accessed 18 March 2023. https://labour.org.uk/wp-content/uploads/2017/10/labour-manifesto-2017.pdf.

Labour Party. *It's Time For Real Change: the Labour Party manifesto 2019*. London: Labour Party, 2019: accessed 18 March 2023. https://labour.org.uk/wp-content/uploads/2019/11/Real-Change-Labour-Manifesto-2019.pdf.

Larik, Joris, Juho Harkonen and Simon Hix. 'Will support for Brexit become extinct?'. *UK in a changing Europe*, 20 November 2022. https://ukandeu.ac.uk/will-support-for-brexit-become-extinct/.

Leadsom, Andrea. *Snakes and Ladders: navigating the ups and downs of politics*. London: Biteback, 2022.

Lenin, V. I. *The State and Revolution*. London: Penguin, 1992, first published 1918.

Levitsky, Steven and Daniel Ziblatt. *How Democracies Die: What History Reveals About Our Future*. London: Penguin, 2019.

Liberal Democrats. *Stop Brexit, Build a Brighter Future: Manifesto 2019*. London: Liberal Democrats, 2019: accessed 20 March 2023. https://www.libdems.org.uk/policy/2019-liberal-democrat-manifesto.

Lindstaedt, Natasha. *Democratic Decay and Authoritarian Resurgence*. Bristol: Bristol University Press, 2021.

McDonnell, Adam and Chris Curtis. 'How Britain voted in the 2019 General Election'. *YouGov*, 17 December 2019. https://yougov.co.uk/topics/politics/articles-reports/2019/12/17/how-britain-voted-2019-general-election.

Manners, Ian. 'Normative power Europe: a contradiction in terms?'. *Journal of Common Market Studies* 40, no. 2 (2002): 235–258.

Mattinson, Deborah. *Beyond the Red Wall: Why Labour lost, how the Conservatives won and what will happen next?* London: Biteback, 2020.

Menocal, Alina Rocha. 'The Elections Bill is about undermining democracy, not shoring it up'. *Open Democracy*, 18 April 2022, accessed 3 May 2023. https://www.opendemocracy.net/en/uk-elections-bill-tory-government-democracy/.

Miliband, Ed. *Go Big: How To Fix Our World*. London: The Bodley Head, 2021.

Milward, Alan. *The European Rescue of the Nation State*. Abingdon: Routledge, 1999.

Moore, Martin. *Democracy Hacked: Political Turmoil and Information Warfare in the Digital Age*. London: Oneworld, 2018.

Mordaunt, Penny and Chris Lewis. *Greater: Britain after the storm*. London: Biteback, 2021.

Mudde, Cass and Cristobal Kaltwasser. *Populism: A Very Short Introduction*. Oxford: Oxford University Press, 2017.

Muller, Jan-Werner. *What is Populism?* London: Penguin, 2017.

Nandy, Lisa. *All In: How We Build a Country That Works*. Manchester: HarperNorth, 2022.

Norris, Pippa and Ronald Inglehart. *Cultural Backlash: Trump, Brexit and Authoritarian Populism*. Cambridge: Cambridge University Press, 2019.

O'Neill, Brendan. *Anti Woke*. London: Connor Court, 2018.

Paun, Akash, Jess Sargeant, Elspeth Nicholson and Lucy Rycroft. 'Sewel convention'. *Institute for Government*, 16 January 2018. https://www.instituteforgovernment.org.uk/explainers/sewel-convention.

Payne, Sebastian. *The Fall of Boris Johnson*. London: Macmillan, 2022.

Phillips, Jess. *Everything You Really Need To Know About Politics: My Life as an MP*. London: Gallery Books, 2021.

Pomerantsev, Peter. *This Is Not Propaganda: Adventures in the War Against Reality*. London: Faber and Faber, 2019.

Raab, Dominic. *The Assault on Liberty: What Went Wrong with Rights*. London: Fourth Estate, 2009.

Raj, Kartik. 'The UK Government's Bill of Wrongs'. *Human Rights Watch*, 22 June 2022, accessed 3 May 2023. https://www.hrw.org/news/2022/06/22/uk-governments-bill-wrongs.

Raven, Peter. 'One in five who voted for Brexit now think it was the wrong decision'. *YouGov*, 14 November 2022, accessed 4 May 2023. https://yougov.co.uk/topics/politics/articles-reports/2022/11/17/one-five-who-voted-brexit-now-think-it-was-wrong-d.

Rees-Mogg, Jacob. *The Victorians: Twelve Titans Who Forged Britain*. London: Penguin, 2020.

Reland, Joel. 'Does Liz Truss want to build Singapore on Thames?'. *UK in a changing Europe*, 18 October 2022. https://ukandeu.ac.uk/does-liz-truss-want-to-build-singapore-on-thames/.

Renwick, Alan, Ben Lauderdale, Meg Russell and James Cleaver. *What Kind of Democracy Do People Want? Results of a Survey of the UK Population*. London: Constitution Unit, January 2022, accessed 12 March 2023. https://www.ucl.ac.uk/constitution-unit/sites/constitution_unit/files/report_1_final_digital.pdf.

Runciman, David. *How Democracy Ends*. London: Profile, 2018.

The Secret Barrister. *Fake Law: The Truth About Justice in an Age of Lies*. London: Picador, 2021.

Simon, Elizabeth. 'Educational attainment and referendum voting: questions and connections'. *UK in a changing Europe*, 16 March 2022. https://ukandeu.ac.uk/educational-attainment-referendum-voting/.

Sobolewska, Maria and Robert Ford. *Brexitland*. Cambridge: Cambridge University Press, 2020.

Sumption, Jonathan. *Trials of the State*. London: Profile, 2020.

Swire, Sasha. *Diary of an MP's Wife: Inside and outside power*. London: Abacus, 2021.

Torrance, David. 'EU powers after Brexit: "Power grab" or "power surge"?'. *House of Commons Library*, 29 July 2020. https://commonslibrary.parliament.uk/eu-powers-after-brexit-power-grab-or-power-surge/.

The UK in the World Values Survey. *Democracy in theory and practice: how UK attitudes compare internationally*. April 2023, 4, accessed 7 April 2023. https://www.kcl.ac.uk/policy-institute/assets/democracy-in-theory-and-practice.pdf.

'UK newspapers' positions on Brexit'. *University of Oxford*, 23 May 2016, accessed 3 May 2023. https://www.ox.ac.uk/news/2016-05-23-uk-newspapers-positions-brexit.

UKIP. *Believe in Britain*. London: UKIP, 2015: 71, 35, accessed 20 March 2023. https://d3n8a8pro7vhmx.cloudfront.net/ukipdev/pages/1103/attachments/original/1429295050/UKIPManifesto2015.pdf.

Wager, Alan and Sophie Stowers. 'A year in Brexit: five charts exploring how public opinion on the EU has changed in 2022'. *UK in a Changing Europe*, 2 January 2023, accessed 4 May 2023. https://ukandeu.ac.uk/a-year-in-brexit-five-charts-exploring-how-public-opinion-on-the-eu-has-changed-in-2022/.

'What was the People's Vote Campaign?'. *UK in a changing Europe*, 24 September 2020. https://ukandeu.ac.uk/the-facts/what-is-the-peoples-vote-campaign/.

White, Isobel and Neil Johnston. *Referendum campaign literature*. London: House of Commons Library, 2016. https://researchbriefings.files.parliament.uk/documents/CBP-7678/CBP-7678.pdf.

'Who Governs Britain?'. Accessed 19 March 2023. https://digital.library.lse.ac.uk/objects/lse:nij973dof/read/single#page/1/mode/1up.

The Wit and Wisdom of Boris Johnson. edited by Harry Mount. London: Bloomsbury, 2019.

Young, Alison L. 'Populism and the UK Constitution'. *Current Legal Problems* 71, no. 1 (2018): 17–52.

Young, Alison L. 'Four Reasons for Retaining the Charter Post Brexit: Part 1 – A Broader Protection of Rights'. *Oxford Human Rights Hub*. 2 February 2018, accessed 18 March 2023. https://ohrh.law.ox.ac.uk/four-reasons-for-retaining-the-charter-post-brexit-part-1-a-broader-protection-of-rights.

Young, Alison L. 'What impact has Brexit had upon devolution?'. *Constitutional Law Matters*, 5 May 2022. https://constitutionallawmatters.org/2022/05/devolution-what-impact-has-brexit-had-on-devolution/.

News and Magazine Articles

Allen-Kinross, Pippa. 'Vaccine approval isn't quicker because of Brexit.' *Full Fact*, 4 December 2020. Accessed 2 April 2023. https://fullfact.org/health/coronavirus-vaccine-brexit/.

'Article 50 petition to cancel Brexit passes 6m signatures.' *Guardian*, 31 March 2019. Accessed 30 March 2023. https://www.theguardian.com/politics/2019/mar/31/article-50-petition-to-cancel-brexit-passes-6m-signatures.

'Articles by Munira Mirza.' *Spiked*, accessed 1 May 2023. https://www.spiked-online.com/author/munira-mirza/.

'Boosterism blinds us to the possible benefits of Brexit.' *Nuffield Trust*, 3 March 2022. Accessed 2 April 2023. https://www.nuffieldtrust.org.uk/news-item/boosterism-blinds-us-to-the-possible-benefits-of-brexit.

'Boris Johnson: British public "don't give a monkey's" about Downing Street leaks.' *LBC*, 24 April 2021. Accessed 10 March 2023. https://www.lbc.co.uk/news/boris-johnson-denies-blocking-inquiry-carrie-symonds-dominic-cummings/.

Bowcott, Owen and Sam Jones, 'Johnson's "picaninnies" apology.' *Guardian*, 23 January 2008. Accessed 30 April 2023. https://www.theguardian.com/politics/2008/jan/23/london.race.

'Brexit: Lord Frost accuses EU of "ill will" over UK exit.' *BBC News*, 8 March 2021. Accessed 2 April 2023. https://www.bbc.co.uk/news/uk-politics-56311605.

'"Brexit changed everything": revisiting the case for Scottish independence.' *Guardian*, 3 July 2021. Accessed 29 April 2023. https://www.theguardian.com/books/2021/jul/03/brexit-changed-everything-revisiting-the-case-for-scottish-independence.

'British government delays import checks for the fourth time since Brexit.' *Speciality Food Magazine*, 13 May 2022. Accessed 20 March 2023. https://www.specialityfoodmagazine.com/news/british-government-delays-import-checks-for-the-fourth-time-since-brexit.

Buchan, Lizzy. 'We have to make the case for freedom of movement.' *Independent*, 31 January 2020. Accessed 27 April 2023. https://www.independent.co.uk/news/uk/politics/labour-leadership-keir-starmer-brexit-freedom-movement-a9310996.html.

Bychawski, Adam. 'US climate deniers pump millions into Tory-linked think tanks.' *Open Democracy*, 16 June 2022. Accessed 1 May 2023. https://www.opendemocracy.net/en/dark-money-investigations/think-tanks-adam-smith-policy-exchange-legatum-iea-taxpayers-alliance-climate-denial/.

Cohen, Nick. 'The far-left origins of No 10s desperate attack on all things "woke".' *Guardian*, 20 June 2020. Accessed 1 May 2023. https://www.theguardian.com/commentisfree/2020/jun/20/the-far-left-origins-of-no-10s-desperate-attack-on-all-things-woke-.

Coman, Julian. 'Maurice Glasman, architect of "Blue Labour": "Labour needs to be itself again".' *Guardian*, 25 September 2022. Accessed 1 May 2023. https://www.theguardian.com/books/2022/sep/25/maurice-glasman-blue-labour-book-interview.

Crerar, Pippa. 'Jacob Rees-Mogg and his family harassed by activists.' *Guardian*, 12 September 2018. Accessed 29 April 2023. https://www.theguardian.com/politics/2018/sep/12/jacob-rees-mogg-and-his-family-harassed-by-activists.

Crerar, Pippa and Libby Brooks. 'Rishi Sunak blocks Scotland's gender recognition legislation.' *Guardian*, 16 January 2023. Accessed 19 March 2023. https://www.theguardian.com/world/2023/jan/16/rishi-sunak-blocks-scotlands-gender-recognition-legislation.

Cross, Michael and Monidipa Fouzder. 'Raab unveils his "modern bill of rights" plan.' *The Law Society Gazette*, 14 December 2021. Accessed 1 May 2023. https://www.lawgazette.co.uk/law/raab-unveils-his-modern-bill-of-rights-plan/5110944.article.

Cummings, Dominic. '"Two hands are a lot" – we're hiring data scientists, project managers, policy experts, assorted weirdos . . . .' *Dominic Cummings's Blog*, 2 January 2020. Accessed 15 March 2023. https://dominiccummings.com/2020/01/02/two-hands-are-a-lot-were-hiring-data-scientists-project-managers-policy-experts-assorted-weirdos/.

Daly, Patrick. 'Sunak used incorrect asylum backlog figures in Parliament, stats tsar finds.' *Independent*, 25 March 2023. Accessed 4 May 2023. https://www.independent.co.uk/news/uk/robert-chote-prime-minister-labour-home-office-uk-statistics-authority-b2307958.html.

Dando, Melissa. 'Northern Ireland Still Doesn't Have An Executive, What Happens Now?' *PoliticsHome*, 5 August 2022. Accessed 29 April 2023. https://www.politicshome.com/news/article/northern-ireland-still-doesnt-have-an-executive-what-happens-now.

Dathan, Mat. 'Now he's going for the domino effect: Nigel Farage pledges to use his time to help other EU nations win their own independence after quitting as UKIP leader.' *Mail Online*, 6 July 2016. Accessed 2 April 2023. https://www.dailymail.co.uk/news/article-3676746/Now-s-going-domino-effect-Nigel-Farage-pledges-use-time-help-EU-nations-win-independence-quitting-Ukip-leader.html.

Dearden, Lizzie. 'Every misleading statement Boris Johnson has made to parliament since the general election', *Independent*, 19 April 2022. Accessed 5 April 2023 https://www.independent.co.uk/news/uk/politics/boris-johnson-false-statements-list-parliament-b2060797.html.

Dearden, Lizzie. 'Suella Braverman say it is her "dream" and "obsession" to see a flight take asylum seekers to Rwanda.' *Independent*, 5 October 2022. Accessed 12 March 2023. https://www.independent.co.uk/news/uk/politics/suella-braverman-rwanda-dream-obsession-b2195296.html.

'Dominic Raab: Resignation letter and Rishi Sunak's response in full.' *BBC News*, 31 April 2023. Accessed 6 May 2023. https://www.bbc.co.uk/news/uk-politics-65333734.

Edwards, Jim. 'This is the size of the majority in the House of Commons against Brexit.' *Business Insider*, 3 November 2016. Accessed 18 March 2023. https://www.businessinsider.com/majority-house-of-commons-against-brexit-2016-11?r=US&IR=T.

'Equality watchdog concludes monitoring of Labour Party action plan.' *Equality and Human Rights Commission*, 15 February 2023. Accessed 11 March 2023. https://www.equalityhumanrights.com/en/our-work/news/equality-watchdog-concludes-monitoring-labour-party-action-plan.

Este, Jonathan. 'Boris Johnson's claim of a "mandate" from the people isn't accurate – here's how prime ministers really get power.' *The Conversation*, 8 July 2022. Accessed 3 April 2023. https://www.reuters.com/article/britain-eu-leader-johnson-europe-idINKCN1UI1AE.

Este, Jonathan. 'Labour's Brexit policy explained'. *The Conversation*, 19 November 2019. https://theconversation.com/labours-brexit-policy-explained-127380.

Este, Jonathan. 'Theresa May loses another Brexit vote.' *The Conversation*, 29 March 2019. Accessed 21 March 2023. https://theconversation.com/theresa-may-loses-another-brexit-vote-heres-why-april-12-is-now-the-key-date-to-watch-114543.

'EU vote: Where the cabinet and other MPs stand.' *BBC News*, 22 June 2016. Accessed 20 March 2023. https://www.bbc.co.uk/news/uk-politics-eu-referendum-35616946.

Forrest, Adam. 'Jacob Rees-Mogg says general election needed if Boris Johnson ousted.' *Independent*, 26 January 2022. Accessed 30 April 2023. https://www.independent.co.uk/news/uk/politics/boris-johnson-general-election-mogg-b2000833.html.

Forrest, Adam. 'Lee Anderson says Tories should fight election on "culture wars and trans debate".' *Independent*, 14 February 2023. Accessed 19 March 2023. https://www.independent.co.uk/news/uk/politics/lee-anderson-tories-election-trans-b2282185.html.

Francis, Sam. 'Jeremy Corbyn banned from standing as candidate for Labour party.' *BBC News*, 28 March 2023. Accessed 30 April 2023. https://www.bbc.co.uk/news/uk-politics-65102128.

Gauke, David. 'Northern Ireland protocol shows how Brexit is still destroying the Tory Party.' *New Statesman*, 16 June 2022. Accessed 20 March 2023. https://www.newstatesman.com/comment/2022/06/northern-ireland-protocol-shows-how-brexit-is-still-destroying-tory-party.

Guinan, Joe. 'Lexit: the EU is a neoliberal project, so let's do something different when we leave it.' *New Statesman*, 20 July 2017. Accessed 20 March 2023. https://www.newstatesman.com/politics/brexit/2017/07/lexit-eu-neoliberal-project-so-lets-do-something-different-when-we-leave-it.

Hayes, Andy. 'Attack ad "not racist": Starmer defends claim Sunak does not want child abusers jailed.' *Sky News*, 30 April 2023. Accessed 30 April 2023. https://news.sky.com/story/attack-ad-not-racist-starmer-defends-claim-sunak-does-not-want-child-abusers-jailed-12869340.

Helmore, Edward and Martin Pengelly. 'Nigel Farage discusses "freedom and winning" in meeting with Trump.' *Guardian*, 13 November 2016. Accessed 3 April 2023. https://www.theguardian.com/politics/2016/nov/12/nigel-farage-arrives-in-new-york-to-meet-president-elect.

Henley, John. 'Support for Eurosceptic parties doubles in two decades across EU.' *Guardian*, 2 March 2020. Accessed 2 April 2023. https://www.theguardian.com/world/2020/mar/02/support-for-eurosceptic-parties-doubles-two-decades-across-eu.

'In full: the letters between Nadhim Zahawi, Rishi Sunak and his ethics adviser.' *Guardian*, 29 January 2023. Accessed 8 May 2023. https://www.theguardian.com/uk-news/2023/jan/29/in-full-the-letters-between-nadhim-zahawi-rishi-sunak-and-his-ethics-adviser.

'Johnson accused of being Putin apologist.' *Sky News*, 9 May 2016. Accessed 2 April 2023. https://news.sky.com/story/johnson-accused-of-being-putin-apologist-10275259.

Jones, Morgan. 'Boris Johnson's readiness to mention deep state conspiracy theories will have a dangerous ripple effect.' *I*, 20 July 2022. Accessed 3 April 2023. https://inews.co.uk/opinion/boris-johnson-deep-state-conspiracy-theories-ripple-effect-1752148.

'Keir Starmer: Immigration not quick fix to NHS problems.' *BBC News*, 6 November 2022. Accessed 15 March 2023. https://www.bbc.co.uk/news/uk-scotland-63526167.

Kirby, Jen. 'Boris Johnson just suspended Parliament over Brexit.' *Vox*, 28 August 2019. Accessed 20 March 2023. https://www.vox.com/2019/8/28/20836579/boris-johnson-brexit-parliament-prorogue.

'Labour has changed on immigration, says Ed Miliband', *Guardian*, 28 April 2015, accessed 15 March 2023, https://www.theguardian.com/uk-news/2015/apr/28/labour-changed-immigration-ed-miliband-promise.

Lord Ashcroft. 'How the United Kingdom voted on Thursday . . . and why', *Lord Ashcroft Polls*, 24 June 2016. Accessed 19 March 2023. https://lordashcroftpolls.com/2016/06/how-the-united-kingdom-voted-and-why/.

Lord Frost. 'Statement after round 8 of the negotiations.' *No 10 media blog*, 10 September 2020. Accessed 19 March 2023. https://no10media.blog.gov.uk/2020/09/10/lord-frost-statement-after-round-8-of-the-negotiations/.

MacAskill, Ewen. 'Donald Trump arrives in UK and hails Brexit vote as "great victory".' *Guardian*, 24 June 2016. Accessed 2 April 2023. https://www.theguardian.com/us-news/2016/jun/24/donald-trump-hails-eu-referendum-result-as-he-arrives-in-uk.

MacAskill, Andrew. 'Factbox: Die-hard eurosceptic or opportunist? Johnson's views on the EU.' *Reuters*, 23 July 2019. Accessed 3 April 2023. https://www.reuters.com/article/britain-eu-leader-johnson-europe-idINKCN1UI1AE.

Mance, Henry. 'Britain has had enough of experts, says Gove.' *Financial Times*, 3 June 2016. Accessed 10 May 2023. https://www.ft.com/content/3be49734-29cb-11e6-83e4-abc22d5d108c.

Marshall, Joe and Dan Goss. 'What "benefits of Brexit" does the government claim?' *Institute for Government*, 1 April 2022. Accessed 2 April 2023. https://www.instituteforgovernment.org.uk/article/explainer/what-benefits-brexit-does-government-claim.

Mason, Rowena. 'Flagship post-Brexit Australia trade deal "not actually very good", MPs hear.' *Guardian*, 14 November 2022. Accessed 20 March 2023. https://www.theguardian.com/politics/2022/nov/14/flagship-post-brexit-australia-trade-deal-not-actually-very-good-george-eustice.

Mason, Rowena. 'Local election observers say 1.2% of voters turned way for lacking ID.' *Guardian*, 13 May 2023. Accessed 18 June 2023. https://www.theguardian.com/politics/2023/may/13/local-election-observers-say-12-of-voters-turned-away-for-lacking-id.

Massie, Graeme. 'Nigel Farage praises Trump at rally after being introduced as one of Europe's "most powerful men".' *Independent*, 29 October 2020. Accessed 2 April 2023. https://www.independent.co.uk/news/world/americas/us-election-2020/trump-farage-rally-arizona-election-brexit-b1405731.html.

Mead, Walter Russell. 'Liz Truss's Big Gamble on the U.K. Economy.' *Wall Street Journal*, 26 September 2022. Accessed 20 March 2023. https://www.wsj.com/articles/liz-trusss-big-gamble-on-the-u-k-economy-british-eu-reform-prime-minister-brexit-protocol-good-friday-agreement-11664220025.

Menocal, Alina Rocha. 'The Elections Bill is about undermining democracy, not shoring it up.' Open Democracy, 18 April 2022. Accessed 3 May 2023. https://www.opendemocracy.net/en/uk-elections-bill-tory-government-democracy/.

Monbiot, George. 'Right wing think tanks run this government. But first, they had to capture the BBC.' *Guardian*, 5 October 2022. Accessed 1 May 2023. https://www.theguardian.com/commentis free/2022/oct/05/rightwing-thinktanks-government-bbc-news-programmes.

Neate, Rupert. 'Does Rishi Sunak's £730m fortune make him too rich to be PM?', *Guardian*, 22 October 2022. Accessed 30 April 2023. https://www.theguardian.com/politics/2022/oct/22/rishi-sunak-rich-730m-fortune-prime-minister#:~:text=Sunak%20and%20his%20wife%2C%20Ak shata,III%20and%20Camilla%2C%20Queen%20Consort.

Neate, Rupert and Rowena Mason. 'Five key questions Rishi Sunak and Akshata Murty have yet to answer.' *Guardian*, 9 April 2022. Accessed 18 June 2023. https://www.theguardian.com/politics/2022/apr/09/five-key-questions-rishi-sunak-and-akshata-murty-have-yet-to-answer.

'Partygate: A timeline of lockdown parties.' *BBC News*, 21 March 2022. Accessed 6 April 2023. https://www.bbc.co.uk/news/uk-politics-59952395.

Rankin, Jennifer. 'Brexit party MEPs turn backs on Ode to Joy at European parliament.' *Guardian*, 2 July 2019. Accessed 3 April 2023. https://www.theguardian.com/politics/2019/jul/02/brexit-party-meps-turn-their-backs-european-anthem-ode-to-joy.

Rawnsley, Andrew. 'After the fall of Richard Sharp, the next BBC chair must not be a political appointment.' *Observer*, 30 April 2023. Accessed 3 May 2023. https://www.theguardian.com/com mentisfree/2023/apr/30/bbc-chair-role-independence-cronyism-richard-sharp-exit.

'Resignation statement in full as Boris Johnson steps down'. *BBC News*, 8 June 2023. Accessed 15 June 2023. https://www.bbc.co.uk/news/uk-politics-65863336.

Reuben, Anthony and Peter Barnes. 'Reality Check: Checking the Vote Leave leaflet.' *BBC News*, 11 April 2016. Accessed 3 April 2023. https://www.bbc.co.uk/news/uk-politics-eu-referendum-36014941.

Richards, Andy. 'Enoch Powell: What was the "Rivers of Blood" speech? Full text here.' *BirminghamLive*, 30 March 2015. Accessed 18 June 2023. https://www.birminghammail.co.uk/news/midlands-news/enoch-powell-what-rivers-blood-8945556.

'Rishi Sunak fined for not wearing seatbelt in back of car.' *BBC News*, 21 January 2023. Accessed 30 April 2023. https://www.bbc.co.uk/news/uk-politics-64353054.

Robertson, Adam. 'Keir Starmer panned for saying UK recruits too many overseas workers into NHS.' *The National*, 6 November 2022. Accessed 3 April 2023. https://www.thenational.scot/news/23104735.keir-starmer-panned-saying-uk-recruits-many-overseas-workers-nhs/.

Rogers, Alexandra. 'Labour tweets second attack ad against Rishi Sunak despite "gutter politics" row.' *Sky News*, 7 April 2023. Accessed 30 April 2023. https://news.sky.com/story/labour-tweets-second-attack-ad-against-rishi-sunak-despite-gutter-politics-row-12851979.

Rosenberg, David. 'Ukip is nothing new: the British Brothers' League immigration fears in 1901.' *Guardian*, 4 March 2015. Accessed 16 April 2023. https://www.theguardian.com/uk-news/2015/mar/04/ukip-nigel-farage-immigrants-british-brothers-league.

Roth, Andrew. 'Putin tells May to "fulfil will of people" on Brexit.' *Guardian*, 20 December 2018. Accessed 2 April 2023. https://www.theguardian.com/politics/2018/dec/20/vladimir-putin-theresa-may-brexit-fulfil-will-of-the-people.

Scholli, Sam. 'Ed Miliband: "The argument is over, I've got to embrace Brexit".' *LBC*, 3 June 2021. Accessed 20 March 2023. https://www.lbc.co.uk/radio/presenters/matt-frei/ed-miliband-the-argument-is-over-ive-got-to-embrace-brexit/.

Slack, James. 'Enemies of the People: Fury over "out of touch" judges who have "declared war on democracy" by defying 17.4m Brexit voters and who could trigger constitutional crisis.', *Mail Online*, 3 November 2016. Accessed 3 May 2023. https://www.dailymail.co.uk/news/article-3903436/Enemies-people-Fury-touch-judges-defied-17-4m-Brexit-voters-trigger-constitutional-crisis.html.

Smith, Beckie. 'Attorney General's "Remain bias" jibe "damaging to civil service morale".' *Civil Service World*, 4 July 2022. Accessed 20 March 2023. https://www.civilserviceworld.com/professions/arti cle/unsubstantiated-criticism-damaging-civil-service-morale-after-attorney-general-slams-remain-bias.

Smith, Evan. 'How a fringe sect from the 1980s influenced No 10's attitude to racism.' *Guardian*, 23 June 2020. Accessed 1 May 2023. https://www.theguardian.com/commentisfree/2020/jun/23/fringe-1980s-communist-faction-no-10-attitude-racism-munira-mirza.

Smith, Hannah. '"New" UK trade deals don't account for "over £800 billion worth of new global trade".', *Full Fact*, 3 November 2022. Accessed 14 January 2023. https://fullfact.org/economy/post-Brexit-trade-deals-Gove/#actions.

Sommerlad, Joe. 'What controversies has Rishi Sunak been involved in?' *Independent*, 25 October 2022. Accessed 30 April 2023. https://www.independent.co.uk/news/uk/politics/rishi-sunak-controversies-partygate-tax-b2209390.html.

Stewart, Dan. 'This Is the Fateful Decision That Led to Theresa May's Downfall.' *Time*, 24 May 2019. Accessed 29 April 2023. https://time.com/5595424/theresa-may-brexit-downfall/.

Stewart, Heather. 'Theresa May announces she will resign on 7 June.' *Guardian*, 24 May 2019. Accessed 9 May 2023. https://www.theguardian.com/politics/2019/may/24/theresa-may-steps-down-resigns-tory-leader-conservative-brexit.

Stone, Jon. 'Brexit lies: The demonstrably false claims of the EU referendum campaign.' *Independent*, 17 December 2017. Accessed 20 March 2023. https://www.independent.co.uk/infact/brexit-second-referendum-false-claims-eu-referendum-campaign-lies-fake-news-a8113381.html.

Syal, Rajeev. 'Dominic Cummings found in contempt of parliament.', *Guardian*, 27 March 2023. Accessed 2 May 2023. https://www.theguardian.com/politics/2019/mar/27/commons-report-rules-dominic-cummings-in-contempt-of-parliament#:~:text=The%20report%20concluded%20that%20Cummings,house%27s%20order%20of%207%20June".

Syal, Rajeev. 'Number of UK civil servants leaving Whitehall rises by 9% in a year.' *Guardian*, 28 August 2020. Accessed 2 May 2023. https://www.theguardian.com/politics/2020/aug/28/num ber-of-uk-civil-servants-leaving-whitehall-rises-by-9-in-a-year.

Syal, Rajeev. 'Outcry over Suella Braverman's return as home secretary.' *Guardian*, 25 October 2022. Accessed 30 April 2023. https://www.theguardian.com/politics/2022/oct/25/outcry-suella-braverman-return-home-secretary.

'The Socialist case against the EU: TUSC tour continues.' *Socialist Party*, 8 June 2016. Accessed 19 March 2023. https://www.socialistparty.org.uk/articles/22984/08-06-2016/the-socialist-case-against-the-eu-tusc-tour-continues/.

'Theresa May vows to put Conservatives "at service" of working people.' *BBC News*, 11 July 2016. Accessed 18 March 2023. https://www.bbc.co.uk/news/uk-36760953.

'Tory leadership: Truss criticised for Macron "jury is out" remark.' *BBC News*, 26 August 2022. Accessed 2 April 2023. https://www.bbc.co.uk/news/uk-politics-62682448.

'UK plunges to lowest ever position in Corruption Perceptions Index.' *Transparency International UK*, 31 January 2023. Accessed 12 March 2023. https://www.transparency.org.uk/uk-corruption-perceptions-index-2022-score-CPI.

van Deurzen, Emmy. 'The Brexit vote unleashed a nasty tide of xenophobia, racism and bigotry in the UK – I no longer felt welcome.' *Independent*, 22 June 2021. Accessed 3 April 2023. https://www. independent.co.uk/voices/brexit-xenophobia-racism-nazi-uk-b1869927.html.

Walker, Natasha. '"They've taken away my freedom": the truth about the UK state's crackdown on protestors.' *Guardian*, 5 February 2023. Accessed 3 May 2023. https://www.theguardian.com/ world/2023/feb/05/protest-laws-state-police-crackdown-uk-activists-prison.

Walker, Peter. 'PM's former aide apologises for Downing Street party held in his honour.' *Guardian*, 14 January 2022. Accessed 3 May 2023. https://www.theguardian.com/politics/2022/jan/14/pms-ex-press-official-james-slack-apologises-for-downing-street-party-held-in-his-honour.

Waterson, Jim. 'BBC funding "up for discussion", says Nadine Dorries, as licence fee frozen.', *Guardian*, 17 January 2022. Accessed 3 May 2023. https://www.theguardian.com/media/2022/ jan/17/no-final-decision-made-on-bbc-licence-fee-says-nadine-dorries.

Waterson, Jim. 'James Slack: the Sun deputy editor in latest No 10 party scandal.' *Guardian*, 14 January 2022. Accessed 3 May 2023. https://www.theguardian.com/media/2022/jan/14/james-slack-the-sun-deputy-editor-in-latest-no-10-party-scandal.

Waterson, Jim. 'Rightwing papers backpedal after helping Liz Truss reach No 10.' *Guardian*, 20 October 2022. Accessed 30 April 2023. https://www.theguardian.com/media/2022/oct/20/ rightwing-papers-backpedal-after-helping-liz-truss-reach-no-10.

Weaver, Matthew. 'Starmer blames PM's Savile slur for inciting mob that accosted him.' *Guardian*, 10 February 2022. Accessed 30 April 2023. https://www.theguardian.com/uk-news/2022/feb/10/ keir-starmer-blames-pm-boris-johnson-savile-slur-inciting-mob.

Woodcock, Andrew. 'Boris Johnson speech factchecked: How do the former PM's claims about his legacy stack up?' *Independent*, 6 September 2022. Accessed 9 May 2023. https://www.indepen dent.co.uk/news/uk/politics/boris-johnson-legacy-fact-check-b2160660.html.

Woodcock, Andrew. 'Churchill's grandson among 10 Tories to have whip restored after rebelling against no-deal Brexit.' *Independent*, 29 October 2019. Accessed 18 March 2023. https://www.in dependent.co.uk/news/uk/politics/boris-johnson-tory-whip-brexit-no-deal-conservative-mps-churchill-general-election-a9176741.html.

Worrall, Patrick. 'Vote Leave's "dark" Brexit ads.' *Channel Four FactCheck*, 27 July 2018. Accessed 2 April 2023. https://www.channel4.com/news/factcheck/factcheck-vote-leaves-dark-brexit-ads.

Speeches

Braverman, Suella. '2022 speech to Conference Party conference.' *ukpol.co.uk*, 4 October 2022. Accessed 12 March 2023. https://www.ukpol.co.uk/suella-braverman-2022-speech-to-conservative-party-conference/.

Cameron, David. 'EU referendum outcome: PM statement, 24 June 2016.' *gov.uk*, 24 June 2016. Accessed 7 May 2023. https://www.gov.uk/government/speeches/eu-referendum-outcome-pm-statement-24-june-2016.

Johnson, Boris. 'Boris Johnson's final speech as Prime Minister: 6 September 2022', *gov.uk*, 6 September 2022. Accessed 7 May 2023. https://www.gov.uk/government/speeches/boris-johnsons-final-speech-as-prime-minister-6-september-2022.

Johnson, Boris. 'Boris Johnson's first speech as Prime Minister: 24 July 2019.' *gov.uk*, 24 July 2019. Accessed 7 May 2023. https://www.gov.uk/government/speeches/boris-johnsons-first-speech-as-prime-minister-24-july-2019.

Johnson, Boris. 'PM statement in Downing Street: 13 December 2019.' *gov.uk*, 13 December 2019.
    Accessed 7 May 2023. https://www.gov.uk/government/speeches/pm-statement-in-downing-
    street-13-december-2019.

Johnson, Boris. 'Prime Minister Boris Johnson's statement in Downing Street: 7 July 2022.' *gov.uk*,
    7 July 2022. Accessed 7 May 2023. https://www.gov.uk/government/speeches/prime-minister-
    boris-johnsons-statement-in-downing-street-7-july-2022.

Johnson, Boris. 'Uniting for a Great Brexit: Foreign Secretary's speech.' *gov.uk*, 14 February 2018.
    Accessed 2 April 2023. https://www.gov.uk/government/speeches/foreign-secretary-speech-
    uniting-for-a-great-brexit.

Lord Frost. 'Lord Frost: Observations on the present state of the nation.' *gov*.uk, 12 October 2021.
    Accessed 20 March 2023. https://www.gov.uk/government/speeches/lord-frost-speech-
    observations-on-the-present-state-of-the-nation-12-october-2021.

May, Theresa. 'PM statement: General election 2017.' *gov.uk*, 9 June 2017. Accessed 7 May 2023,
    https://www.gov.uk/government/speeches/pm-statement-general-election-2017.

May, Theresa. 'Prime Minister's statement in Downing Street: 24 May 2019.' *gov.uk*, 24 May 2022.
    Accessed 7 May 2023. https://www.gov.uk/government/speeches/prime-ministers-statement-in-
    downing-street-24-may-2019.

May, Theresa. 'Statement from the new Prime Minister Theresa May.' *gov.uk*, 13 July 2016. Accessed
    7 May 2023. https://www.gov.uk/government/speeches/statement-from-the-new-prime-minister
    -theresa-may.

May, Theresa. 'Theresa May's keynote speech at Tory conference in full.' *Independent*,
    5 October 2016. Accessed 20 March 2023. https://www.independent.co.uk/news/uk/politics/
    theresa-may-speech-tory-conference-2016-in-full-transcript-a7346171.html.

Starmer, Keir. 'Keir Starmer's New Year's speech.' *labour.org.uk*, 25 January 2023. Accessed
    15 March 2023. https://labour.org.uk/press/keir-starmer-new-years-speech/.

Starmer, Keir. 'Keir Starmer speech to the Confederation of British Industry Conference 2022.' *labour.
    org.uk* 22 November 2022. Accessed 15 March 2023. https://labour.org.uk/press/keir-starmer-
    speech-to-the-confederation-of-british-industry-conference-2022/.

Sunak, Rishi. 'Rishi Sunak's first speech as Prime Minister: 25 October 2022.' *gov.uk*, 25 October 2022.
    Accessed 7 May 2023. https://www.gov.uk/government/speeches/prime-minister-rishi-sunaks-
    statement-25-october-2022.

Truss, Liz. 'Liz Truss's final speech as Prime Minister: 25 October 2022.' *gov.uk*, 25 October 2022.
    Accessed 7 May 2023. https://www.gov.uk/government/speeches/liz-trusss-final-speech-as-
    prime-minister-25-october-2022.

Truss, Liz. 'Prime Minister's Speech to Conservative Party Conference 2022', *conservatives.com*,
    5 October 2022. Accessed 10 March 2023. https://www.conservatives.com/news/2022/prime-
    minister-liz-truss-s-speech-to-conservative-party-conference-2022.

Truss, Liz. 'Prime Minister Liz Truss's statement: 6 September 2022.' *gov.uk*, 6 September 2022.
    Accessed 7 May 2023. https://www.gov.uk/government/speeches/prime-minister-liz-trusss-
    statement-6-september-2022.

Truss, Liz. 'Prime Minister Liz Truss's statement in Downing Street: 20 October 2022.' *gov.uk*,
    20 October 2022. Accessed 7 May 2023. https://www.gov.uk/government/speeches/prime-
    minister-liz-trusss-statement-in-downing-street-20-october-2022.

Index

https://doi.org/10.1515/9783110735925-009